Aspects of
Anglican Identity

Aspects of
Anglican Identity

Colin Podmore

CHURCH HOUSE
PUBLISHING

Church House Publishing
Church House
Great Smith Street
London SW1P 3NZ

Tel: 020 7898 1451
Fax: 020 7898 1449

ISBN 0 7151 4074 4

Published 2005 by Church House Publishing

The opinions expressed in this book are those of the author and do not necessarily reflect the official policy of the General Synod or The Archbishops' Council of the Church of England.

Printed in England by The Cromwell Press, Trowbridge, Wiltshire

Contents

Foreword

For some years, the Church of England and the Anglican Communion (in common with much of the rest of the Church, at least in Europe and North America) have been preoccupied to a greater or lesser extent with debates about the place of women in the Church's ministry (at a time when their role in society at large has changed very considerably) and about the ordination of those living in sexually consummated same-sex partnerships (at a time when in society at large such relationships have come to receive widespread public acknowledgement and acceptance).

At one level, these debates (which are similar and interrelated in some respects, though distinct and different in others) are about the Church's response to changes in society and about the interpretation of Scripture in the light of tradition and reason. At another, arguably deeper, level, however, the issues they raise are issues of ecclesiology – issues about our theology of the Church. When the General Synod debated the final approval of the Priests (Ordination of Women) Measure on 11 November 1992, it often seemed as if the two sides in the debate were arguing not with but past each other – passing as ships in the night. Some were arguing that it was right to ordain women to the priesthood, others that (whether or not that was so) the General Synod, representing as it does only two provinces of the Church catholic, was not competent – ecclesiologically speaking – to decide the question.[1] Similarly, the Archbishop of Canterbury's comment on the withdrawal of the then Canon Jeffrey John (now Dean of St Albans) from his appointment as Bishop of Reading in July 2003 was an ecclesiological one: 'There is an obvious problem in the consecration of a bishop whose ministry will not be readily received by a significant proportion of Christians in England and elsewhere.'[2] Objections to the action of bishops of the Episcopal Church in the United States of America in confirming the election of Canon Gene Robinson as Bishop of New Hampshire and consecrating him to the episcopate in November 2003 were also, at least in part, ecclesiological: how could someone whose ministry was clearly not going to be accepted by much of the Communion to which his diocese belongs fulfil the task, central to a catholic understanding of the episcopate, of representing his local church to the wider Church and the wider Church to the local?[3]

Not only do these debates have ecclesiological content, but the actions taken also have consequences for our understanding of the Church and indeed for the very structures of relationship within the Church, involving as they do the impairment or even breaking of communion. Furthermore, the steps taken to mitigate those consequences, such as the conferring on parishes of rights to refuse the ministry of canonically ordained priests and the provision of 'extended episcopal care', themselves have ecclesiological implications. It is not surprising that aspects of Anglican ecclesiology have come to be the subject both of comment in the columns of the secular press and of discussion in church circles well beyond those usually concerned with such matters.

The issues raised in these debates concern in particular how parts of the Church in different countries should relate to each other and to the Church as a whole; the role of bishops in the Church and how they are chosen; and the role of diocesan, provincial and national synods in taking decisions – in these instances, decisions which affect not just their own part of the Church but the Church throughout the world. Discussion of these issues in turn prompts more fundamental questions about how the Church of England and the other Anglican churches understand their identity and their place within the one holy, catholic and apostolic Church, in which we profess our belief Sunday by Sunday in the Nicene Creed. These issues and questions are the themes of this book, and I hope that in looking at the origins and identity of the Church of England and the Anglican Communion, at the roles within them of primates, bishops and synods, and at questions of communion between the Church of England and other churches, the book will offer members of synods and other interested church members resources which will help them to engage with and participate in current debates.

None the less, it must be stressed that most of the chapters were originally written before recent events gave them a heightened relevance. My hope is, therefore, that they will not only illuminate those events and the discussions which they have provoked but also continue to be of interest in the longer term. Events have drawn attention to the importance of ecclesiology – not in the abstract, but applied to real situations in the life of the Church – but that importance will continue even after events have moved on.

✠

This book draws together studies of various aspects of Anglican ecclesiology written over the past 15 years, several of which were originally published as separate articles. All have been revised and updated, and some have been expanded with significant new material. The chapters are intended to remain complete in themselves, and to that end occasional overlaps have been retained.

The scene is set in Chapter 1 with an overview of the history of the Church of England. This survey makes no pretence to originality and is necessarily highly selective, but when it was first published and circulated to members of the General Synod in 1996 a number of Synod members said how helpful they had found it – one priest had even serialized it in his parish magazine. In this revised form it aims to provide a framework for what follows. Chapter 2 continues the scene-setting by focusing on the period from 1801 to 1838. This period is highlighted because of its importance for Anglican ecclesiology. As we shall see in Chapter 3, it was in the early years of the nineteenth century that the idea of the Anglican Communion was conceived and nurtured in the high-church circles on which Chapter 2 concentrates. It was also in the 1830s, in response to a revolution in the relations between church and state, that the Oxford Movement highlighted the Church of England's distinctive identity. The Church of England, the Movement's leaders pointed out, was not just part of the apparatus of the state or an aspect of English national life: it had a separate identity and legitimacy of its own. In the words of the Nicene Creed, it was catholic (part of the one holy, catholic Church throughout the world) and it was apostolic (standing in continuity with Christ's first apostles and sharing in their mission and calling). Its apostolic continuity was signified and effected by the apostolic succession of its bishops, the successors of the apostles. This greater identity and legitimacy beyond anything conferred by the Church of England's position as the established church meant that, theologically speaking, it was ultimately and essentially independent of the state.

Chapters 3 and 4 are essentially about this identity. Chapter 3 examines the origins of the idea, and later the name, of 'the Anglican Communion'. It offers some reflections on the identity and self-understanding of the Church of England and the Anglican Communion within the one holy, catholic and apostolic Church. The theme of Anglican identity is pursued in Chapter 4, which details how the Declaration of Assent – now the classic statement of the Church of England's identity, made by every deacon, priest and bishop when they are ordained and again every time they take up a new ministry – came to be formulated between 1967 and 1975, and points to some of its key themes.

Chapters 5 and 6 study topical aspects of the ecclesiology of the Church of England and the Anglican Communion. Chapter 5 looks at primacy (the primates of the Anglican Communion and, indeed, the primacy of the Archbishop of Canterbury are much talked about, but what are primates and what is primacy?). Chapter 6 investigates the related subjects of territoriality (the territorial nature of the Church), communion (the relationship between the Church in different territories) and parallel episcopates (more than one bishop exercising an espiscopal ministry within the same territory).

Chapters 7–9 complete the circle with further historical surveys. The history and principles of synodical government in the Church of England are presented in Chapter 7, and the workings of the present-day system of synodical government are illustrated in Chapter 8 through an account of the process which led to the ordination of women to the priesthood in 1994 – a process which legislation for the ordination of women to the episcopate would also have to follow. Finally, Chapter 9 looks at the history of how diocesan bishops have been chosen in the early Church and in the Church of England.

✠

A brief comment on the term 'Anglican ecclesiology' is needed at the outset. Much of this book is concerned specifically with aspects of the ecclesiology of the Church of England. Those are, of course, in turn, aspects of wider Anglican ecclesiology, since the Church of England is an Anglican church (and, indeed, the original Anglican Church). It should not be supposed, however, that these features of the Church of England's ecclesiology are necessarily typical of the Anglican Communion more generally. Some of the chapters examine aspects of the ecclesiology of the Communion as a whole, but they do not attempt to look in detail at the ecclesiology of other individual Anglican churches.

As will be pointed out, there are (albeit to varying degrees) significant differences between the ecclesiology of the Church of England and that of other Anglican churches – so much so, that it is more appropriate to speak of 'Anglican ecclesiologies' than 'an Anglican ecclesiology'. It is important to be conscious of this, since the differences between the ecclesiology of the Episcopal Church in the USA (ECUSA) and that of the Church of England have played a significant part in creating recent tensions within the Anglican Communion. The Presiding Bishop of ECUSA is not a primate in the traditional sense – he is not the occupant of a primatial see, or indeed of any see. He is not a metropolitan (and hence has no jurisdiction over the bishops of his church), nor is he the bishop of a diocese (though he does have oversight, through an assistant bishop, of the eight 'parishes' and four 'missions' which make up the Convocation of American Episcopal Churches in Europe). Indeed, though the Episcopal Church in the USA has groups of dioceses called 'provinces', they too are not provinces in the traditional sense, in that they have no metropolitans, and hence the diocesan bishops of the province owe canonical obedience to no one. These factors may well not have been without significance for the course that recent events have taken.

✠

In concluding this Foreword, I should like to express my gratitude to those from whom I have learned – in particular Dr Geoffrey Rowell, at whose feet I sat for six years when he was my college chaplain in Oxford from 1978 to 1981 and again from 1985 to 1988, and Dr Mary Tanner, with and for whom I worked for ten years from 1988 to 1998. I am also grateful to my colleague Prebendary Dr Paul Avis for encouraging me to present this material in book form, and to my editor at Church House Publishing, the Revd Kathryn Pritchard, for her wise advice on the presentation of the work. Other debts are acknowledged in notes to the individual chapters.

Since I am not just an observer of the ecclesiological scene but also a practitioner of ecclesiology – formerly as an ecumenist and latterly as a member of the General Synod's secretariat – it is important to stress that any opinions expressed are not necessarily those of the General Synod or of its subordinate bodies.

Colin Podmore

Westminster

25 April 2005

1

The origins and development
of the Church of England[1]

This brief (and necessarily highly selective) overview of the history of the Church in England provides the context for what follows. While it will offer some readers new information, for others it may simply serve to highlight some of the most significant moments in a history stretching over around eighteen hundred years – from the origins of Christianity in Roman Britain to the most significant event of recent years, the admission of women to the priesthood in 1994.

When Christianity came to Britain is not known, although some evidence suggests a Christian presence by about 200. In 314 a church was sufficiently well established to be represented by the Bishops of London, York and a third British see at the Council of Arles. In the fifth century, however, southern and eastern Britain was invaded by pagan Angles, Saxons and Jutes. The Church continued in Wales, and in the sixth century Cornwall was evangelized from there and from Ireland. It was from Ireland, too, that St Columba (c.521–97) travelled to found Iona, from whence St Aidan (d. 651) led the mission which was to re-establish the Church in Northumbria. He was consecrated bishop in 635 and established his see on Lindisfarne. Meanwhile, in 597 St Augustine (d. c.604) had landed in Kent at the head of a mission sent by the pope, St Gregory the Great, to re-evangelize England.

Although St Augustine's mission was thus by no means the only source of English Christianity, the *Ecclesia Anglicana* (Anglican or English Church) can be said to stem chiefly from it. Seventy years after Augustine's arrival, however, the English Church was in a state of some disorder. Theodore of Tarsus (c.602–90) was sent from Rome to become Archbishop of Canterbury, arriving in 669. Having supplied bishops for the many vacant sees, he called a council which met at Hertford in 672. This council involved the whole English Church, and agreed a set of canons which could be described as its founding charter.[2] Bede described Theodore as 'the first of the archbishops whom the whole English Church consented to obey'. Perhaps Theodore's most lasting achievement was the creation of the English diocesan system. Dividing the existing large dioceses, most of which covered the area of one of the English kingdoms, he established diocesan boundaries which are still recognizable on

1

the map of English dioceses today. It is not too much to claim that Theodore was the English Church's second founder.

The division of the English Church into two provinces dates from 735, when Pope Gregory III approved the raising of the Bishopric of York to an archbishopric. Lanfranc (c.1010–89), who was Archbishop of Canterbury from 1070, asserted the supremacy of Canterbury over York, but this was not finally settled until 1353, when it was accepted that the Archbishop of Canterbury should be styled Primate of All England and the Archbishop of York Primate of England. By the beginning of the fifteenth century the Convocations of Canterbury and York, provincial synods each consisting of an upper house of bishops and a lower house of clergy, had taken shape.

The English Reformation

The series of events which are collectively described as 'the English Reformation' took place over 30 years, in several distinct phases, beginning with the meeting of the Reformation Parliament in 1529 and culminating in the 'Elizabethan Settlement' of 1559. What came (anachronistically) to be termed 'Anglicanism' was to reach maturity only in the following century, however.

The first phase, under Henry VIII, was essentially political. On 15 May 1532 the Convocation of Canterbury agreed the Submission of the Clergy, whereby the Convocations could meet only if summoned by royal writ and could make no canons without royal licence. Canon law was subordinated to the common and statute law of England. Acts of Parliament abolished payments and appeals from England to Rome, and the pope's legal rights in England were divided between the Crown and the archbishops. The 1534 Act of Supremacy declared that the king was 'the only supreme head in earth of the Church of England'. Between 1536 and 1540 the monastic houses of England were dissolved, a development which arguably owed more to the Crown's need for money and the financial aspirations of its supporters than to any strictly theological or ecclesiastical motives. Thus, in the reign of Henry VIII the English Church was effectively nationalized and then, to a significant extent, privatized. The king replaced the pope and seized a considerable proportion of the church's wealth, but with the notable exception of the monastic life its internal system remained intact. An English Bible was ordered to be placed in every parish church (1538) and an English Litany introduced (1544), but otherwise little official doctrinal or liturgical change occurred. Indeed, the Ecclesiastical Licences Act 1533 (25 Hen 8, c 20), which is still on the statute book, contains the following proviso (s. 13):

> Provided always that this Acte nor any thyng or thynges therin
> conteyned shalbe herafter interpreted or expounded that your
> Grace your nobles and subjects intende by the same to declyne
> or vary from the congregacion of Christis Churche in any
> thynges concnyng the veray articles of the Catholyke feith of
> Christendome.[3]

Henry VIII died in 1547, more than 17 years after the meeting of the
Reformation Parliament, never having heard the Mass other than in Latin.

The second phase of the English Reformation occurred in the brief but turbulent
reign of Edward VI (1547–53). Now there was doctrinal change; significantly, it
was expressed first and foremost in liturgical change, centrally in the Prayer
Books of 1549 and 1552, of which the Archbishop of Canterbury, Thomas
Cranmer, was the chief author. The Church of England would continue to
express its beliefs chiefly in its liturgy. Cranmer's liturgies built on the medieval
liturgical tradition, echoing its prayers. In this they resembled those of German
Lutheranism and differed from the essentially non-liturgical worship of the
Swiss Reformed churches. Doctrinally, however, the 1552 Prayer Book showed
Reformed influence, as did the Forty-two Articles which followed in 1553. One
important difference was that the English Ordinal consciously retained the term
'priest' and provided for the continuation of the three orders of bishop, priest
and deacon inherited from the early Church. In this second phase of the
Reformation, liturgy and doctrine had been changed, but again the historic
structure and order of the Church remained intact.

In the even briefer reign of Mary (1553–8), most of the changes made by her
father and brother were undone. Reginald Pole, as papal legate, was invited to
reconcile England to the Holy See, and on 30 November 1554, 500 Members of
Parliament knelt to receive his absolution, as did the Convocation of Canterbury
six days later. Papal supremacy and the Latin Mass were restored. In 1556
Cardinal Pole succeeded Cranmer as Archbishop of Canterbury, but he was to
be the last archbishop who was in communion with the See of Rome. He and
his queen both died on 17 November 1558.

By the 1559 Act of Supremacy, Elizabeth I accepted the amended title 'Supreme
Governor of the Church of England'. The 1559 Act of Uniformity reintroduced
the 1552 Book of Common Prayer, slightly amended in a conservative direction.
Of the bishops, only those of Llandaff and Sodor and Man remained in office.
Matthew Parker was appointed Archbishop of Canterbury and consecrated in
Lambeth Palace Chapel on 17 December 1559. None of Mary's bishops being
willing to act, the consecration was performed by three former diocesan
bishops and a suffragan. Again, liturgy preceded doctrinal definition. In 1562–3
the Forty-two Articles were amended and reduced in number, and as the

Thirty-nine Articles they reached their final form in 1570. The articles can be characterized as moderately Reformed, but they were so framed as to comprehend as many as possible within the Church of England. The 1604 canons of the Church of England furnished the church with a code of canon law, but they did not repeal the medieval canon law in areas that they did not address.

The English Reformation was marked not by innovation but by rejection of the innovations of Rome. Its intention was to get back to the pure faith and order of the early or 'primitive' Church. This position was defended against Roman Catholic criticism on the one hand by Bishop John Jewel (1522–71) in his *Apology* (1562) and against Puritan insistence that the Church of England was not fully reformed by Richard Hooker (c.1554–1600). In the seventeenth century this concern led to a flowering of patristic scholarship on the part of Anglican divines which was unrivalled in any other church, and devotion to the ideal of the primitive Church was to persist into the middle years of the eighteenth century and beyond.[4]

Abolition and restoration

First, however, this developing Anglican tradition was driven underground or into exile by the victory of Parliament over Charles I in the Civil War (1642–6). In 1645 Archbishop William Laud and then in 1649 the king himself were executed. During this radical break in the Church of England's history, its structure, episcopal ministry and liturgy were abolished. Only its buildings remained, and they were despoiled. From as early as 1651 concern grew amongst loyal churchmen that the Church of England's episcopal succession might die out, and indeed by the end of 1659 all but nine of its 27 sees were vacant. The exiled King Charles II repeatedly attempted to persuade the survivors to consecrate new bishops, but they were too fearful to act on his orders within England, while age and infirmity held them back from travelling to the Continent. Had the interregnum lasted even just ten years longer, the Anglican episcopal succession would probably have been extinguished.

In fact, after the restoration of the monarchy in 1660 the episcopally ordered Church of England was restored also. Under the 1662 Act of Uniformity some 1,900 clergy who were not episcopally ordained or who refused to use the revised *Book of Common Prayer* were ejected. After the 'Glorious Revolution' of 1689 toleration was preferred to comprehension, and it was tacitly accepted that there would continue to be substantial bodies of Christians who dissented from the Church of England and maintained a separate religious life. The Church of England was now settled in its identity. In the eighteenth century the

Church of England's failure to retain John Wesley's Methodism within its structures increased the proportion of English Christians who did not belong to it, as did large-scale (Roman Catholic) Irish immigration in the following century.

The nineteenth and twentieth centuries

During the nineteenth century a number of developments and movements greatly affected the Church of England's character. From the 1830s, ecclesiastical reforms began to modernize the church's organization and redistribute its revenues, while evangelicals, liberals and catholics occupied increasingly distinctive positions. Each of these streams has its successors today, and in addition to this, practices and insights that were originally distinctive to each of them can now be found much more widely within the Church of England. Visually (in the conduct of worship, liturgical dress, church furnishings, etc.) and in terms of its understanding of its own identity, the image that the Church of England overall has presented for the last half-century owes more to the Anglo-Catholic Oxford Movement and its successors than to either of the other streams. In these respects, the Church of England as a whole would have been very different had it not been for the Oxford Movement. *The Tracts for the Times* (1833–41), whose main authors were John Henry Newman, John Keble and Edward Bouverie Pusey, stressed the Church of England's identity as part of the catholic Church and the apostolic authority of its bishops – derived from the historic apostolic succession. The Tractarians also published a *Library of the Fathers* (translations of the major patristic writings) and an 83-volume *Library of Anglo-Catholic Theology* (1841–63), an edition of the works of the most notable seventeenth-century Anglican divines – the heritage the Tractarians revived and on which they built. As time went on, the Oxford Movement's emphasis on sacramental worship combined with other Victorian influences to revive catholic ritual, architecture and church furnishing and enrich the Church of England's worship liturgically and musically. It also resulted in the revival of religious orders in the Church of England.

The twentieth century saw a gradual increase in the practical independence of the church from the state. In 1919 the Church Assembly, consisting of the Convocations and a House of Laity, was established to process church legislation, which Parliament would approve or reject but not amend. In 1970 a new General Synod, inheriting most of the powers of the Convocations (which continued to exist) and all those of the Church Assembly, was inaugurated. By the Worship and Doctrine Measure 1974 the General Synod received powers to authorize new and alternative services without parliamentary approval. Under a protocol of 1977 a church body, the Crown Appointments Commission (renamed the Crown Nominations Commission in 2003), was given a decisive role in the choice of diocesan bishops. A new code of canon law was promulged by the Convocations between 1964 and 1969, replacing the canons of 1604, and in *Common Worship* (the successor of *The Alternative Service Book 1980*) the Church has gained a definitive modern liturgy to complement the historic liturgy of *The Book of Common Prayer.*

In February 1994 the General Synod promulged a canon providing for the ordination of women to the priesthood. This was seen by the majority as a legitimate development of the ordained ministry, but by a substantial minority as effecting a major change in the Church of England's identity and self-understanding as part of the catholic Church, and provision was made (by the Episcopal Ministry Act of Synod 1993) for continuing diversity of opinion in the Church of England in this matter.

2

High churchmen, church and state, 1801–38[1]

This chapter focuses on the first half of the nineteenth century, because in a number of respects that period was crucial for the shaping of Anglican identity. As we shall see in Chapter 3, it was in those years that the idea of what came to be called the Anglican Communion was conceived and nurtured in high-church circles. One of the period's notable features was the growth of the church 'parties' which have played a major part in the life of the Church of England ever since. The first part of this chapter concentrates on the high-church 'Hackney Phalanx', whose members dominated the Church of England in the quarter-century before 1833.

This group is now probably unknown to most members of the Church of England, but the themes with which they were concerned are still surprisingly topical 200 years later. Contrary to their dessicated, 'high and dry' image, these high churchmen were vigorous reformers who founded or reinvigorated many of the Anglican voluntary societies that remain prominent today. They also raised prodigious amounts of money which not only made an immediate impact on the church's mission but also effectively created central endowments for church activities from which the Church of England and the church overseas still benefit. In all of this they held firm to the principle that in an episcopal church lay initiatives should always be carried out under episcopal oversight and leadership. They also breathed new life into the structures of the church at the diocesan level, thereby helping to shape the modern Anglican understanding of episcopacy and paving the way for the later revival of synodical government.

The men of Hackney worked in close cooperation with the governments of the day, but from 1828 to 1833 the Church of England was rocked by a revolution in relations between church and state. One response was the Oxford or Tractarian Movement, which was to have an unparalleled impact on the Church of England's self-understanding: arguably it was only when the church was viewed as having an identity essentially independent of the state that Anglican ecclesiology could fully flower.

Much has been written in the last quarter-century about the history of the Church of England in this period, and our understanding of it has grown and changed as a result. Drawing on that published research, this chapter will survey some of the key developments – focusing, because of their significance for the development of the Church of England's self-understanding, on the Hackney Phalanx and their Oxford successors.

Evangelicals: The Clapham Sect

Though there have been different schools or traditions of 'churchmanship' in the Church of England since the sixteenth century, it was only in the nineteenth that these grew into more closely defined parties. It was the evangelicals who led the way in this development; at the beginning of the century they, more than other groupings, 'were perceived as having some of the attributes of a church party'.[2] In the first decade of the nineteenth century they were arguably the most dynamic movement within the Church of England. The evangelicals' London centre was the fashionable suburb of Clapham, of which John Venn (1759–1813) was rector from 1792. The circle of wealthy evangelical merchants, barristers and politicians that developed there came to be known as the 'Clapham Sect'. Chief among these men was William Wilberforce (1759–1833), a friend of William Pitt the Younger. In the House of Commons he led a group of nearly 30 MPs known as the 'Saints', who voted together on religious and moral issues and whose chief achievement was the abolition of the slave trade in 1807. A second centre of the evangelical party was in Cambridge, where Magdalene and Queens' colleges were for a time evangelical strongholds. Macaulay believed that the impact of Charles Simeon (1759–1836), Vicar of Holy Trinity, Cambridge, from 1783, on generations of ordinands was such that his influence on the Church of England at large extended to the remote corners of the country and 'was far greater than that of any primate'.[3]

Evangelical clergy formed a network of local clerical societies, of which the most celebrated was the London Eclectic Society, established in 1783. It was at a meeting of the Eclectic Society in 1799 that what became known as the Church Missionary Society (CMS) was founded. CMS was a product of these evangelical networks, but Elizabeth Elbourne has argued that its founders 'did not have a well-defined national "Evangelical party" behind them in 1799'. Rather, the CMS 'helped to *create* a network of self-defining "Evangelicals"'.[4]

Evangelicals did not scruple to cooperate with dissenters in societies such as the British and Foreign Bible Society and the Religious Tract Society. Although these were interdenominational, their leaderships were dominated by evangelical members of the established church. Indeed, the Bible Society, founded in 1804, should probably be accounted the most successful of all the

Clapham Sect's initiatives: in its first ten years it distributed no fewer than 950,000 copies of the Bible.[5] Through CMS, the Bible Society and the other voluntary societies they established, through the network of clerical societies and through the impact of Simeon and others on future clergy, the evangelicals became an influential force in the Church of England at large, as Wilberforce and his colleagues were in Parliament and London society. Within the episcopate and such established structures as the Church of England had at national level, however, evangelical influence was very limited. Not until the appointment of Henry Ryder as Bishop of Gloucester in 1815 was there an evangelical on the bench, and not until the later 1820s was he joined by the brothers C. R. Sumner (Bishop of Llandaff, 1826–7; Bishop of Winchester, 1827–69) and J. B. Sumner (Bishop of Chester, 1828–48; Archbishop of Canterbury, 1848–62). Geoffrey Best commented that the evangelicals were 'kept disdainfully at a distance' by the established church's ruling powers.[6]

High churchmen: The Hackney Phalanx

Much more influential in church circles, at least from around 1810, were the high churchmen (or 'Orthodox', as they preferred to call themselves). Peter Nockles has defined high churchmen in this period as those who upheld the doctrine of apostolical succession, looked to the creeds, *The Book of Common Prayer* and the early fathers (especially when enjoying 'catholic consent') for authoritative interpretation of Scripture, emphasized the doctrine of sacramental grace and stressed the importance of a religious establishment, viewing the state as divinely ordained.[7]

Nineteenth-century high churchmanship had its antecedents in a group of high-church 'Tories', born for the most part in the 1730s. Their most prominent figure was George Horne (1730–92), who became Bishop of Norwich in 1790. Among his protégés were his cousin and school contemporary William Stevens (1732–1807), Treasurer of Queen Anne's Bounty from 1782, and Jonathan Boucher (1738–1804), for whom Stevens obtained an assistant secretaryship to the Society for the Propagation of the Gospel (SPG) after he was forced to return from revolutionary America in 1775.[8] Boucher became Vicar of Epsom in 1785. It was the plight of the Scottish Episcopal Church that helped to mould high churchmen into a movement.[9] The London committee constituted in 1790 to press for the repeal of the earlier legislation banning clergy ordained by the Scottish bishops from ministering even in Scotland consisted of three noted high churchmen – Stevens and his younger friends Dr George Gaskin (1751–1824; Secretary of the Society for Promoting Christian Knowledge (SPCK) and later Rector of Stoke Newington) and James (later Sir James) Allan

Park (1763–1838; a barrister and future judge).[10] Their campaign was successful, resulting in the 1792 Relief Act.[11]

The Relief Act's leading advocate in the House of Lords was the high-church Bishop of St Davids, Samuel Horsley (1733–1806; later Bishop of Rochester and of St Asaph). He was a patron of the writer William Jones (1726–1800), Perpetual Curate of Nayland in Suffolk (as was Horne, who had been at University College, Oxford, with Jones).[12] Jones was instrumental in the founding in 1792 of the Society for the Reformation of Principles, which was designed to counteract the influence of the French Revolution, and the establishment in 1793 of the *British Critic*, at the time London's only 'Church and King' periodical, seems to have been his idea.[13] The most important high-church publication of the period, however, was not a periodical but the *Guide to the Church* published by Charles Daubeny (1745–1827; Archdeacon of Salisbury from 1804) in 1798.

William Jones died in 1800, and within a few years the remaining members of this first generation of high churchmen followed – Jonathan Boucher in 1804, Samuel Horsley in 1806 and William Stevens in 1807. 'Nobody's Friends', a high-church dining club founded by Stevens in 1800, survived his death,[14] but at this point, as F. C. Mather commented, 'except as a loose bond of sentiment, no High Church party was to be found.'[15] (Charles Daubeny, for example, was only tenuously connected with Stevens's circle, chiefly through his friendship with Jonathan Boucher.[16]) In this respect, high churchmen lagged behind the evangelicals of the Clapham Sect.

Things soon changed under a new generation of leaders. Foremost among these was the wine merchant Joshua Watson (1771–1855), on whom Stevens's mantle fell. Watson and his brother John James (1767–1839) were connected by ties of friendship to several of the earlier high-church leaders. Boucher, a school friend of their father, took John James Watson as his curate at Epsom.[17] The young Joshua Watson became a friend of Horne, Jones and Stevens as well as Boucher. In 1797 he married Mary Sikes, niece of Charles Daubeny and sister of another high churchman, Thomas Sikes (1766–1834).[18] Watson had met Henry Handley Norris (1771–1850), the son of a Hackney merchant, in 1794,[18] and in 1800 the Watson brothers and Norris were among the 13 men present at the inaugural dinner of Nobody's Friends;[20] after Stevens's death they became the movement's leading triumvirate. John James Watson was Vicar and subsequently Rector of Hackney from 1799, remaining as rector after his appointment as Archdeacon of St Albans in 1816; Norris was Perpetual Curate and subsequently Rector of South Hackney from 1809. Because of this, the group came to be known as the Hackney Phalanx. The members of the phalanx intermarried, so that familial ties were added to those of friendship and shared opinion as bonds between them.[21]

An early recruit to Nobody's Friends, in 1802, was William Van Mildert (1765–1836), who had become a close friend of Joshua Watson soon after being appointed Rector of St Mary-le-Bow in 1796.[22] After Charles Manners-Sutton (1755–1828) became Archbishop of Canterbury in 1805, Van Mildert met Manners-Sutton's first domestic chaplain, Christopher Wordsworth (1774–1846), and introduced him to Watson; by 1807 Wordsworth was a key member of the phalanx, and persuaded Manners-Sutton to treat Watson as his principal lay adviser.[23] Manners-Sutton became a staunch supporter and patron of the phalanx; all of his domestic chaplains were high churchmen.[24] The phalanx's influence reached its zenith in 1812, when the Earl of Liverpool, John James Watson's contemporary at Charterhouse and University College, Oxford, became prime minister, a position he retained until 1827. Norris was generally thought to be Liverpool's chief adviser on ecclesiastical patronage and was popularly known as 'the Bishop maker'.[25] Not surprisingly, high-church dominance of the Church of England increased, so that it is not too much to claim that in the first third of the century the Church of England was in fact led and run by high churchmen and their sympathizers. By 1832 only four of the 27 bishops (Ryder, the Sumner brothers and the liberal Edward Maltby) were not high churchmen of some variety,[26] and this preponderance of high churchmen in the episcopate was mirrored among archdeacons by the 1820s.[27]

Despite the importance of Simeon in Cambridge, both Cambridge and Oxford were dominated by high churchmen in the period from 1790 to 1830.[28] The leading high-church figure in Oxford throughout this period was Martin Routh (1755–1854), President of Magdalen College from 1791 until his death over 60 years later. In 1813 Lord Liverpool appointed William Howley (1766–1848), the high-church Regius Professor of Divinity, as Bishop of London, and Van Mildert to succeed him in Oxford. (Van Mildert went on to become Bishop of Llandaff in 1819 and Bishop of Durham in 1826.) Howley came into contact with the phalanx when he became Bishop of London, and during his episcopate his involvement with it became increasingly close. All his domestic chaplains were also high churchmen.[29] In 1828 Howley succeeded Manners-Sutton as Archbishop of Canterbury and was replaced as Bishop of London by his protégé Charles James Blomfield (1786–1857). In 1822 the Regius Professorship of Divinity went to another member of the phalanx, Charles Lloyd (1784–1828). Lloyd had been introduced to Watson and Norris by Van Mildert and had served as Manners-Sutton's domestic chaplain.[30] He became Bishop of Oxford in 1827 but died the following year.

The Watsons and Norris used their influence not only to gain preferment for their supporters but also to secure government and episcopal support for a remarkable series of successful initiatives. Key positions were sought not just for their own sake, but also because they bestowed power and influence which could be used to further the phalanx's aim of strengthening the church. Patronage, for example, was used quite deliberately in order to promote high-church reform in the early and mid-nineteenth century.[31]

The need for such strengthening seemed urgent. The period from 1790 to 1815 saw an unprecedented growth in dissent. It has been estimated that before 1790, 90 per cent of the British population were at least nominal adherents of the established churches, whereas by 1815 one-third were dissenters, with the numbers of active members of dissenting bodies approaching those of active members of the established churches.[32] Against this background, high churchmen bitterly opposed the creation of the British and Foreign Bible Society in 1804, and the evangelicals' involvement in it, for a number of reasons. They saw cooperation with dissenters as blurring the distinctions between the episcopal church and non-episcopal dissent. In 1805 a tract attributed to Van Mildert warned every honest churchman against associating with 'those who, he knows, can never be conciliated without a desertion of principle on his part, and who probably only court his alliance for the purpose of more successfully compassing his degradation and destruction'.[33] Furthermore, distributing the Bible to the poor without the Prayer Book to interpret it was, according to the Lady Margaret Professor of Divinity at Cambridge, Herbert Marsh (1757–1839; Bishop of Peterborough from 1819), in 1812, to 'neglect the means of preventing their seduction from the Established Church'. The creation from 1809 of a national network of local Bible Society branches with lay leadership gave rise to further objections; to high churchmen this amounted to a rival structure to that of the dioceses and parishes over which bishops and their clergy presided.[34]

The Bible Society had been established because of evangelicals' frustration with the inefficiency of the high-church dominated Society for Promoting Christian Knowledge. The best answer to the creation of the Bible Society was therefore to revitalize the SPCK, which Marsh described as 'the appropriate authoritative Bible Society for Churchmen',[35] and create a rival network of local committees. In 1810 this was done, on the initiative of Watson, Norris, Wordsworth, Van Mildert and others.[36] Resistance to change from the secretary, William Stevens's friend George Gaskin, and his supporters was overcome in January 1811, when Watson, Norris and their allies effectively seized control of the society in a 'boardroom coup'. Van Mildert became treasurer in 1812 and was succeeded in 1814 by Watson himself, who retired from business at the age of 43 to devote himself to religious and philanthropic work. The society's headquarters became the phalanx's administrative focus and meeting place.[37]

The crucial difference between the SPCK's new district committees and the Bible Society's local branches was that the SPCK committees were established 'with the sanction' of the diocesan bishop and worked under his direction. It was to be a fundamental principle of all the phalanx's work that it should be undertaken by committees established under episcopal oversight and leadership. In 1825 Walter Farquhar Hook (1798–1875), a young high churchman of the generation below that of the phalanx's leaders, expressed this shibboleth as follows:

> The great objection to what is fallaciously termed 'the Church Missionary Society' is, that those who have never received any commission for the purpose – inferior Clergy and even laymen – presume to send forth preachers of the Gospel. The same objection also holds with respect to the Bible Society. By the laws of the Church from the days of the Apostles down to the present hour, all societies for the promotion of Christian knowledge ought to be under the direction and control of the Bishops.[38]

If the CMS was misnamed, then so was the Church of England's official missionary society, the Society for the Propagation of the Gospel, the SPCK's sister foundation; it was doing little to propagate the gospel. As Alan Webster commented, 'In 1814 . . . the S.P.G. was neither an instrument of the Church nor a missionary society, but had degenerated into a board for holding various trust funds . . . The Society was moribund and in urgent need of reform.'[39] Watson, Wordsworth and Norris duly set about reinvigorating the SPG, for which diocesan and district committees were established from 1818 to 1819 – subject, of course, to the approval of the diocesan bishop, who was to be invited to be president. Subscription income quickly rose from less than £500 per annum to £1,300 in 1820. Two missionaries were sent to India in 1823, and in 1825 the SPG took over the management of the SPCK's East India Mission (a rationalization which Watson had first proposed in 1817). Whereas the SPCK had employed non-episcopally ordained Lutheran missionaries, in 1829 the SPG resolved, in keeping with the views of the Hackney Phalanx, that all future missionaries should be clergy in Church of England orders.[40]

A third institution which the phalanx took over was the *British Critic*. Though founded as a high-church periodical, it had become somewhat distanced from the movement, and sided against the phalanx in the controversy over the Bible Society. In 1811 Watson and Norris bought it back and removed the editor. He was replaced initially by Van Mildert and then by Thomas Middleton (1769–1822; later Bishop of Calcutta).[41] In the *British Critic* the phalanx now had a platform for its views. A second Hackney periodical, the *Christian Remembrancer*, commenced in 1819.

The phalanx's activities were by no means limited to reinvigorating existing societies and promoting high-church principles. They were also responsible for a remarkable number of completely new initiatives. Perhaps the most important of these was the first – the National Society for Promoting the Education of the Poor in the Principles of the Established Church, which was founded in 1811 with the Archbishop of Canterbury as president and the other bishops as vice-presidents (in accordance with the Hackney principle), the Prince Regent as patron, Watson as treasurer and Norris as temporary acting secretary. Within 20 years its schools were educating a million children.[42]

The next initiative was in response to the devastation of Germany by the Napoleonic wars. At Watson's suggestion the Westminster Association for German Relief was formed in 1814, at a meeting chaired by the Duke of York. The speakers included not only the Archbishop of Canterbury but also William Wilberforce, and members of the Clapham Sect joined those of the Hackney Phalanx in the audience. Watson served as secretary of the association. At his suggestion the archbishop persuaded the Government to grant £100,000 for distribution by the association, which was wound up in 1816 when its work was done.[43]

Watson now turned his attention to the provision of additional church accommodation, by both the building of new churches and the extension of existing ones. For him, this was a necessary consequence of the National Society's work: 'it matters comparatively little how much, or even how well, we teach our children in the week-day, if we do not carry them to church on the Sunday',[44] and this could only be done if there was room in church to accommodate them. A prime mover in this initiative was the layman John Bowdler (1746–1823), a founder member of Nobody's Friends (and brother of the man who 'bowdlerized' Shakespeare). Convinced that it was the Government's responsibility to provide sufficient churches for the populace, he and Watson had already approached in vain first Spencer Perceval and then his successor as prime minister, Lord Liverpool (who was sympathetic but unable to offer immediate help). A Church Building Society was therefore launched in 1818, with the aim of promoting government action as well as raising funds by subscription. Typically, the organizing committee assured themselves before proceeding that the initiative enjoyed the support of the prime minister, the Archbishop of Canterbury and the Bishop of London. The archbishop chaired the inaugural meeting and (as an indication that this was another 'cross-party' initiative) Wilberforce was chosen as a vice-president along with (in true Hackney fashion) all the bishops. Watson, who had been the organizing committee's link with the archbishop, was, of course, a member of the society's committee, as were other members of the phalanx.

The Government was spurred into action, and granted £1 million for the building of new churches. The grant was to be distributed by a Church Building Commission, the membership of which naturally included Watson and other members of the phalanx, as well as bishops (including the archbishops), senior church dignitaries, politicians and evangelical leaders. A further grant of £500,000 followed in 1824. The commission was responsible for building 612 churches, while the society concentrated in its early years on the complementary work of the repair and extension of existing churches. Watson was the driving force of both bodies.[45]

The next initiative in which the Hackney Phalanx was heavily involved was, like many of the others, a response to a development with which high churchmen disagreed – on this occasion, a secular liberal initiative rather than an evangelical or dissenting one. The establishment in 1825 of University College, London (dubbed 'godless Gower Street' by a younger member of the phalanx, Hugh James Rose (1795–1838), writing in the *British Critic*), prompted a meeting on 21 June 1828 at which the prime minister (the Duke of Wellington) was joined on the platform by three archbishops, seven bishops and senior members of the nobility, which resulted in the foundation of King's College, London. The prime mover was George D'Oyly (1778–1846), a member of the phalanx and one of Manners-Sutton's former chaplains.[46] King's College was soon followed by the University of Durham, founded by Van Mildert, who had become Bishop of Durham in 1826. It opened in 1833, with Hugh James Rose as professor of divinity.[47]

The last Hackney-founded society was again a response to an initiative from another quarter. In 1836 evangelicals founded the Church Pastoral Aid Society (CPAS) to provide for assistant clergy. Several of its features prevented high churchmen from cooperating in it: it laid down doctrinal tests, it was unwilling to leave the licensing of a curate to the bishop, and it employed lay workers. When negotiations failed to persuade the new society to modify its rules, Watson, the MP for Oxford Sir Robert Inglis (a staunch churchman, though identified with evangelicalism) and a young member of the phalanx, Benjamin Harrison (1808–87), formed the Additional Curates Society in 1837. One of its rules was that 'no application for aid can be received by the Committee but through the Bishop of the Diocese; or taken into consideration without his previous sanction'. By 1851 the society was aiding 323 curates.[48]

The members of the Hackney Phalanx were not just defenders of high-church principles; they were engaged in innovative initiatives to strengthen the church. They ensured that the societies and institutions they founded were led by the bishops both nationally and at diocesan level, and acted under their direction or at least with their approval. Where it was possible to work together with evangelicals without compromising these and other church principles, they did so – for example in the National Society and the Church Building Society. Where evangelicals cooperated with dissenters or set up structures without episcopal oversight, however, the Hackney Phalanx responded by either revitalizing existing societies (the SPCK and the SPG) or founding a new one (the Additional Curates Society). The episcopate was central not only to their ecclesiology but also to the life and mission of the Church as they conceived it. The phalanx was a reforming and innovating movement, but a conservative one; it worked by breathing new life into existing structures or supplementing them, not by weakening or overturning them. Its achievements were remarkable and long-lasting.

It was not just at the national level that high churchmen promoted initiatives to strengthen the church and increase its influence and efficiency. By the 1820s a movement of reform and renewal was under way within the dioceses of the Church of England which Arthur Burns, its historian, has described as a 'diocesan revival'.[49] Clergy discipline and diligence were improved, the number of services on a Sunday and the frequency of celebrations of Holy Communion increased. The revival involved purposeful use of visitations, charges and the office of archdeacon, and the revival of that of rural dean. Diocesan societies were founded – in some cases in relationship with national societies such as the SPCK, the National Society and the Church Building Society. One consequence of this diocesan revival was growing consciousness of the diocese as a community – as a local church rather than just a collection of individual priests and parishes or an area in which a bishop performed his episcopal ministrations.[50] Churchmen of all traditions were involved in this revival, but the high-church dominance of diocesan hierarchies in the 1820s and 1830s, when, in some respects at least, the revival was at its height, meant that the high churchmen were crucially important to its success and their influence in shaping it strong. Moreover, it was high-church ecclesiology, with its high regard for the episcopal office and for the contemporary Church of England's historic continuity with the medieval Church, that underlay the revival.[51] Like the national initiatives of the Hackney Phalanx, this reform movement was essentially conservative, reviving or reinvigorating ancient offices, structures and traditions and complementing them with new ones, rather than demolishing in order to rebuild.

Church and state: The cataclysm of 1828–33

For high churchmen of this era, religion and politics were 'two aspects of the same thing'. High churchmanship and what came to be called 'Toryism' were intertwined, and enjoyed a revival from the early 1790s onwards in response to the French Revolution and Jacobinism. High churchmen rejected theories of the origin of government which stressed rights derived from 'natural law' and instead reasserted the patriarchal theory of the origin of government which they derived from Scripture; to them, political insubordination and theological heterodoxy were inseparably connected.[52] Dissent was a threat to the integrity of the state, not just to the position of the church within it.

It was on the basis of such shared views that the ecclesiastical and political heirs of the Tory high-church revival of the 1790s – the Hackney Phalanx and the Governments of Spencer Perceval and Lord Liverpool – cooperated in the defence and strengthening of the church against the rise of dissent. When Perceval became prime minister in 1809 he began a series of annual government grants of £100,000 to Queen Anne's Bounty for the augmentation of poor livings which were continued by his successor, Lord Liverpool. Between 1809 and 1821 eleven such grants, totalling £1.1 million, were paid.[53] In addition to this, as we have seen, government grants of £1 million and £500,000 for the building of new churches were paid in 1818 and 1824. These grants of £2.6 million to the Church of England were paralleled by grants of almost £1 million to the Church of Ireland and over £350,000 to the Church of Scotland. The state was investing unprecedented amounts of public money in strengthening the established churches.[54] Representatives of church and state cooperated in distributing the grants through the Church Building Commission. As Peter Nockles has pointed out, 'the union of Church and State appeared to be working more in the Church's interests . . . than at any time since the reign of Charles II'.[55]

This harmonious union came to a sudden end. In February 1828 an unexpected motion, moved by the Whig MP Lord John Russell, for examination of the Test and Corporation Acts was passed by the House of Commons despite government opposition; two days later a resolution in favour of their repeal was similarly passed. The Duke of Wellington's Government became convinced that if it opposed a repeal bill it would be defeated in the House of Commons, and persuaded the bishops not to oppose repeal in the House of Lords.[56] Once the repeal act was passed in April, English dissenters could sit in the House of Commons. The Whig peer Lord Holland was clear as to the cataclysmic effect of the repeal for the existing constitution of church and state:

> Practically, . . . the Catholick Emancipation when it comes will be a far more important measure, more immediate & more extensive in its effects – but *in principle* this is the greatest of them all as it explodes the real Tory doctrine *that Church & State are indivisible*.[57]

Once the principle of the union of church and state had been breached, Roman Catholic emancipation was inevitable. Fearing civil war in Ireland, the Government decided to bring forward a bill which would be steered through the House of Commons by the Home Secretary, Sir Robert Peel. Because it represented the complete abandonment of the principles on which he had stood for election as MP for Oxford University, Peel resigned his seat and fought a by-election. Opposition to Peel's re-election was organized by John Keble (1792–1866) and a group of younger Fellows, including John Henry Newman (1801–90) and Richard Hurrell Froude (1803–36) – both, like Keble, Fellows of Oriel College – and Peel was defeated by Sir Robert Inglis.[58] This campaign against Peel, the first in which the future Tractarians Keble, Newman and Froude cooperated, was the real origin of the Oxford Movement, which burst forth four years later, in 1833.[59] Peel quickly obtained another seat, and the bill became law the following month, the majority of the bishops having voted against it.[60]

A sudden growth in pressure for parliamentary reform followed. In 1831 a new Whig government introduced a Reform Bill, which was defeated in the House of Commons. In October 1831, after a general election, the Commons passed a second bill. Archbishop Howley spoke against it in the House of Lords, and 20 bishops joined him in voting against. It was pointed out that had they voted in favour, the bill would have passed.[61] Popular fury erupted against the bishops, and this produced calls for disestablishment and attacks on abuses within the church. There were numerous examples of bishops being threatened, abused and burned in effigy, sometimes by large mobs; in Bristol the Bishop's Palace was burned down.[62] A third bill passed its second reading in the House of Lords in April 1832. Sixteen bishops still voted against, the Bishop of Rochester arguing that the bill involved 'the total subversion and annihilation of law and justice', but this time twelve voted in favour, led by Blomfield, who persuaded them that if the bill were rejected 'a great political convulsion' would follow.[63] The bill eventually became law in June.

The 1832 Reform Act, passed as it was in the teeth of episcopal opposition and on a tide of agitation for church reform, significantly weakened the position of the Church of England and strengthened the political influence of dissent. But it was the Church of Ireland, a reformed church in a country whose population largely remained loyal to Roman Catholicism, that suffered the most immediate consequences. Lord Liverpool's Government had attempted to bolster the Irish church establishment as it had those of England and Scotland, but Roman Catholic emancipation and a poor harvest in 1829 were followed, from late 1830, by widespread refusal to pay tithes. The Government prepared a new bill, which it hoped would end conflict over the Church of Ireland. In the event, the measures were insufficient to do that, but the Irish Church Temporalities Act of

1833 nevertheless signalled the effective end of the Church of Ireland as a national church establishment. Church cess, a local property tax for the maintenance of church buildings and parsonages, was to be replaced by a graduated income tax on church livings worth over £200, cathedral sinecures were to be abolished, and parishes in which no services had been held for three years were suspended indefinitely. Furthermore, 10 of the 22 Irish bishoprics were to be suppressed, and the incomes of the two richest sees reduced significantly. The income from these measures would be redistributed within the church by an Ecclesiastical Commission with a majority of lay members.[64]

Oxford's response to revolution: The Tractarians

The events of 1828–32 constituted a revolution in relations between church and state to which responses varied. It is important to be clear that the high-church tradition did not assume the *identity* of church and state – that they were one and the same. Archdeacon Daubeny had written 30 years earlier that 'the union [of Church and State], being an accidental circumstance, did not affect the original independent rights of either party'; should a separation take place, 'the state will leave the church, so far as respects its government, just in the same condition in which it was, previous to their original connexion'.[65]

In 1829 John Keble still believed that the advantages of union outweighed its disadvantages: 'I am now, and have been for some time convinced that the spiritual advantages enjoyed by ourselves and our charges at present are much greater than we have reason to expect, humanly speaking, if we were separated from the State.'[66] As the crisis in church and state developed, however, Keble came to expect separation and even to approve of it: 'I do not think the privileges of the establishment can possibly out-last another Parliament', he wrote in March 1831.[67] By May 1832 his radicalism had developed further:

> I am more and more inclined to think, that the sooner we come to an open separation from these people [Roman Catholics and 'shopkeeping orators'], the better for ourselves and our flocks: and this is some comfort as one watches the progress of Revolution, in w[hi]ch the said separation will, I expect, be a very early step.[68]

Writing in Hugh James Rose's new *British Magazine* (founded the previous year) in March 1833, Keble asserted that the Irish Church Temporalities Bill signalled that the 'persecution of the church has begun'; he could now envisage a time when the church would be well advised 'to throw from her those state privileges, which in such a case would prove only snares and manacles; and to excommunicate, as it were, the civil government'. 'It is not affirmed, that things are, as yet, come to such a pass in this church and realm. But he must be blind, who looks that way, and cannot see ominous symptoms.' The clergy should brace themselves 'for a time when it may be necessary for them to chuse between separation and virtual apostasy'.[69] Privately he went further, believing that 'anything, humanly speaking, will be better, than for the Church to go on in union with such a state'. The dilemma was 'how to conduct a separation without producing a schism in the Church?' – though 'even that I am not sure that I should so very much deprecate, if I were sure of getting rid of the right persons'.[70] Keble had come to the conclusion that 'the Union of Church and State as it is now understood' was 'actually sinful'.[71] On 14 July Keble preached his Assize Sermon, which was published under the title 'National Apostasy'. For John Henry Newman, who had returned to England earlier that week, this sermon marked the start of what came to be known as the Oxford Movement.[72]

There was a widespread fear that the clamour for reform of abuses in the Church of England would result in measures comparable to those embodied in the Irish Church Temporalities Act. In September, the first of a series of 'Tracts for the Times' (after which the movement's adherents came to be known as 'Tractarians') was published. In it Newman asked the clergy:

> Should the Government and the Country so far forget their God
> as to cast off the Church, to deprive it of its temporal honours
> and substance, on what will you rest the claim of respect and
> attention which you make upon your flocks? . . . on what are we
> to rest our authority when the state deserts us? . . . I fear we
> have neglected the real ground on which our authority is built
> – OUR APOSTOLICAL DESCENT.[73]

For the Oxford Movement, it was the Church of England's apostolic succession from the primitive Church, rather than its position as the established church, that was the bedrock of its identity and its claim to allegiance. Like Keble, Newman had come to the conclusion that separation from the state was now desirable, but as yet he was unwilling to say so publicly. Writing to one correspondent, he said: 'I agree with you in wishing the Church loose from the tyranny of the state, but should not yet like to say so in print'.[74] In a letter to Keble he spoke of the possibility that future state actions might make it necessary to call on the laity 'to follow us *from* the Establishment'.[75] Replying, Keble argued that supporters of church principles 'ought to be prepared to sacrifice any or all of our endowments' if the state did not 'undo what has been done' and thereby retract 'Anti Church principles': '"Take every pound, shilling and penny . . . only let us make our own Bishops and be governed by our own laws."'[76] It is important to be clear that Keble and his fellow Tractarians continued to believe in the principle of establishment. What they were now beginning to resist was establishment on its current terms, whereby a Parliament which now included non-members of the established church could legislate, for example, to alter the church's provincial and diocesan structure.[77] 'Theoretically and historically', Newman explained to another correspondent, he remained a 'Tory', but the changed circumstances had forced him to 'begin to be a Radical practically'.[78] As J. H. L. Rowlands pointed out in his study of the Tractarians' attitudes, 'every true conservative is also a radical'.[79]

It was Hurrell Froude, the youngest and most radical of the three Tractarian leaders, who first voiced such thoughts openly. In a paper written in 1833, parts of which were published in the *British Magazine*, he observed that 'many considerate and right-minded persons . . . have judged it, humanly speaking, impossible for the church of England to recover her lost ascendancy in the councils of this nation'.[80] He went on to argue that it was only because Parliament could be said to constitute a 'lay Synod of the Church of England' that Richard Hooker had 'justified himself in consenting to its *interference in matters spiritual*'.[81] Now, however,

> The joint effect of three recent and important Acts, (1.) the Repeal of the Test and Corporation Acts, (2.) the Concessions to the Roman Catholics, (3.) the late Act for Parliamentary Reform, has most certainly been to efface in at least one branch of our Civil Legislature, that character which, according to our great Authorities, qualified it to be at the same time our Ecclesiastical Legislature.[82]

A House of Commons which included among its members dissenters and Roman Catholics could hardly be described as a 'lay Synod' of the Church of England. Therefore, 'the conditions on which Parliament has been allowed to interfere in matters spiritual are cancelled'.[83] He called on members of the church to 'open your eyes to the fearful change which has been so noiselessly effected; and acknowledge that by standing still you become a party to revolution'.[84] The following year Froude contemplated the church giving up its established status, arguing that if a desire to keep up the appearance of being a national church resulted in an unwillingness to exclude people and hence the abandonment of church discipline, it would be better not to be a national church at all:

> The body of the English nation either are sincere Christians or they are not: if they are, they will submit to Discipline as readily as the primitive Christians did. If not, let us tell the truth and shame the devil: let us give up a *national* church, and have a *real* one.[85]

21

Led by Newman, the Tractarians eventually concluded (in Froude's case reluctantly) that while disestablishment was to be expected and welcomed, it should be the work of the state alone; the clergy should stay out of politics and not campaign actively for separation.[86] From 1834, when he accepted the living of Hursley, Keble became more conservative, and in 1835 he preached on the sacredness of the alliance between church and state and expressed criticism of Froude's 'young ideas'.[87] By 1836, Newman had noticed that 'his *tone* is changed'.[88]

Keble, Newman and Froude were joined in their Oxford Movement by a number of Oxford friends and pupils. At the end of 1833 the movement was strengthened by the accession to it of the Regius Professor of Hebrew, Edward Bouverie Pusey (1800–82), whose Tract 18 – 'Thoughts on the Benefits of the System of Fasting, Enjoined by our Church' (a title indicative of his primary interest in the Christian life) – was published in 1834. Hurrell Froude died in 1836, and two years later Keble and Newman published his *Remains*, the extremism of which shocked the Hackney leaders. The story of the movement engendered by the tracts has been told too often to need repeating here. Unlike the high-church initiatives enumerated above, it was more an intellectual than a practical movement; its events were publications and responses to them, rather than meetings. The Tractarians did not work through committees (Newman observed that 'living movements do not come of committees'[89]) and they did not create societies; their legacy consisted not of institutions but of a way of thinking; but their impact on the Church of England could hardly have been more profound.

The Establishment response: Cooperation with reform

Watson and Norris had spent the last quarter of a century cooperating closely with governments in church extension – doing what was possible in the situation in which the Church of England found itself, rather than just arguing from first principles about what its situation should be. Furthermore, in 1833 they were both 62; dismayed as they were by developments, they were too old, and too enmeshed in the establishment, to think radically and contemplate the separation of church and state. Their instinct was pragmatic: to make the best of the situation.

In early 1831 Watson had sought to pre-empt expected radical suggestions of a commission of enquiry by suggesting such a royal commission (but one with an entirely clerical membership) himself. As Newman commented of the high-church leaders in another context, 'of course their *beau idéal* in ecclesiastical action was a board of safe, sound, sensible men'.[90] Such a royal commission was eventually appointed in June 1832, with the task of reporting on the facts about the church's finances.[91] Its 24 members included 6 bishops (both English archbishops, Blomfield, Van Mildert, Kaye of Lincoln and Bethell of Bangor) and 6 senior clergy. Five of the six bishops, and at least one of the clergy (Wordsworth), were associates of the phalanx.[92] (Initially, however, Watson distrusted those who agreed to serve on a commission which included laymen rather than leaving matters of church governance to the bishops and clergy.[93]) After the passing of the Irish Church Temporalities Act, which he bitterly opposed, Van Mildert withdrew from the commission's work. In his speech on the second reading of the bill, his last major speech in the House of Lords, Van Mildert argued that the spiritual reality of establishment, as he understood it, was at an end. His biographer Elizabeth Varley concludes that the argument of the speech suggests that he was now 'making a radical shift in directions that were, in the last analysis, disestablishmentarian'.[94] In the autumn Van Mildert's wife suffered a stroke, and thereafter he was reluctant to leave her. He withdrew from active involvement in the work of the Commission of Enquiry and did not sign its June 1835 report. In Elizabeth Varley's words, he was 'quietly but ruthlessly sidelined from central Church policy-making'. Increasingly physically infirm, he died in 1836.[95]

As early as December 1832 Blomfield suggested to Howley that a further commission should be established to make recommendations about reform. When the Conservatives returned to power in 1834, one of Peel's first acts was to establish such a commission. It consisted of five bishops (the archbishops, Blomfield, Kaye and Monk of Gloucester), and six laymen (including Peel himself) chosen for their support for the establishment. When Peel's government fell, Melbourne replaced most of the lay members with Whigs (including himself and Russell).[96] The commission recommended three bills, which became law as the Ecclesiastical Commissioners Act 1836, the Pluralities Act 1838 and the Ecclesiastical Commissioners Act 1840. The first of these established a permanent reforming body, the Ecclesiastical Commissioners for England; the 1840 act expanded this to include (in an echo of the Hackney principle) all the bishops of England and Wales. (This principle persisted in the Ecclesiastical Commissioners and its successor, the Church Commissioners, until 1998, when the National Institutions Measure reduced the number of episcopal Church Commissioners to six: the two archbishops plus four bishops – not necessarily diocesans – elected by the House of Bishops.) The Deans of Canterbury, St Paul's and Westminster, as well as six judges and eight lay commissioners (six appointed by the Crown and two by the Archbishop of Canterbury), were also included among the Ecclesiastical Commissioners by the same act.

Younger high churchmen

The Hackney Phalanx's younger members and their associates were much more sympathetic to the Tractarians than its leaders. The leading younger figure was Hugh James Rose, now 38. He convened a conference at his rectory in Hadleigh, Essex, in July 1833, which was attended by William Palmer (1803–85; a Fellow of Worcester College, Oxford), Arthur Perceval (1799–1853) and Froude, to discuss how to respond to the crisis. In 1832 Rose had preached a sermon more conservative in tone than Keble's Assize Sermon, and as editor of the *British Magazine* from 1832 to 1836 he allowed Froude and Newman to use it as a vehicle for their views. Rose was ready to admit the 'mischiefs' which resulted from union with the state, but he nonetheless continued to insist that these were outweighed by the advantages.[97] In 1836 he became the second principal of King's College, London, but in 1838 death removed him from the scene. Perceval wrote three of the earlier 'Tracts for the Times', but eventually distanced himself from the movement, as did Palmer, the most cautious of the three, who was nonetheless concerned, as late as 1843, to shield and defend the Tractarian leaders.[98]

Another of this group was W. F. Hook, who was 35 in 1833. He was Vicar of Holy Trinity, Coventry, from 1828 and then Vicar of Leeds from 1837. Like Rose, he had initially taken an even more serious view of the 1828–9 legislation than Keble. By 1831 he had concluded that 'as a Church, the Reformed Catholic Church in England will be benefited by its disunion from the State'. For him, it was the admission of dissenters to Parliament in 1828 that marked the decisive turning point:

> I refer our calamities to the repeal of the Test Act; for then the State virtually renounced every connexion with religion. It pronounced religion to be, so far as the State is concerned, a thing indifferent. England is now in the position of a man who has excommunicated himself.

Hook nonetheless continued to support establishment, weakened as it was, as 'one of the means appointed to lead men gradually to a serious sense of the faith'.[99] Like the others in this group of younger adherents of the Hackney Phalanx, Hook was reluctant to criticize the Tractarians publicly,[100] and it was not until the later 1840s that he ended his friendship with Pusey (by then the Oxford Movement's acknowledged leader).

These younger pre-Tractarian high churchmen remained separate from the Tractarians, but they were the last of their line. By the early 1830s the phalanx had run out of steam. Its leaders were losing control of the SPCK, and in July 1833 Joshua Watson resigned as treasurer (officially for health reasons).[101] In

Peter Nockles's judgement, the phalanx 'lacked the power to move or inspire a new generation', leaving a vacuum which the Oxford men filled.[102] The publication of Hurrell Froude's *Remains* in 1838 may have dismayed the Hackney leaders, but, Nockles has suggested, Newman calculated that 'the mixture of romantic historicism, youthful zest and ascetic holiness . . . would exert an almost hypnotic appeal on his own younger followers'.[103] The Tractarians were now the dynamic, radical party of principle, and the future belonged to them. In 1838 the Tractarians won exclusive control of the *British Critic* and installed Newman as editor; he excluded all but one of the phalanx high churchmen from further contribution to the journal.

Gladstone, Manning and Hope

Also in 1838, the young MP William Ewart Gladstone (1809–98) published *The State in its Relations with the Church*. Gladstone had left Oxford at the end of 1831 and taken his seat in Parliament in February 1833. Influenced at most only indirectly by the Oxford Movement, during the mid-1830s he moved from the evangelicalism of his upbringing (without rejecting most of its positive tenets) to an independent high-church position, and became a close friend of Henry Edward Manning (1808–92) and James Robert Hope (later Hope-Scott, 1812–73), both of whom had similarly moved from evangelicalism to high churchmanship.[104] Manning, who became Rector of Lavington, Sussex, in 1833, joined the Tractarians in 1835; his Tract 78 on catholic Tradition was published in February 1837.[105] He became Archdeacon of Chichester in 1841, but died as Cardinal Archbishop of Westminster. Hope, a barrister, was received into the Roman Catholic Church together with Manning in 1851.[106] Gladstone's response to the revolution of 1828–32, as documented in his book, was opposite to that of the Tractarians. They had come to believe that the church was disadvantaged by its relationship with the state (a view shared to some extent, as we have seen, by some of the younger associates of the Hackney Phalanx). Gladstone, by contrast, believed that the real interests of the church – those of its members (i.e. all the baptized) – were best met by union such as that which had obtained before 1828.[107] The Tractarians had come to believe in the separation of church and state, but Gladstone called for the reversal of the changes of 1828–9. It was, as J. C. D. Clark has pointed out, a counter-revolutionary doctrine: Gladstone's views, commonplace only ten years earlier, now belonged to a lost world. As he later admitted, 'Scarcely had my work issued from the press, when I became aware that there was no party, no section of a party, no individual person, probably, in the House of Commons, who was prepared to act upon it. I found myself the last man on a sinking ship.'[108] Even in Oxford University, which Matthew Arnold dubbed the 'home of lost causes', it had been recognized that this cause was lost.

3

The Anglican Communion: Idea, name and identity[1]

This book is published at a time of crisis in the Anglican Communion. In its Windsor Report, the Lambeth Commission on Communion has spoken of 'a very real danger that we will not choose to walk together', and observed that 'Should the call to . . . find ways of continuing in our present communion not be heeded, then we shall have to begin to learn to walk apart'.[2] But where does the belief that the churches of 'the Anglican Communion' should form a single communion come from, how did that communion get its name, and why are the terms 'Anglican' and 'Anglican Communion' completely absent from the Church of England's formal expressions of its own identity?

Historical accounts of the development of the Anglican Communion tend to begin with the expansion of the Church of England into the overseas colonies from the sixteenth century onwards.[3] This approach is obviously legitimate and necessary, but it may sometimes give rise to an impression (at least on the part of those who do not get as far as the middle of the books concerned!) that the concept of what came to be called 'the Anglican Communion' similarly existed from the sixteenth century, whereas in fact it dates only from the earlier part of the nineteenth. In the early nineteenth century the idea that the United Church of England and Ireland (with the 'Colonial Church'), the Scottish Episcopal Church and the Protestant Episcopal Church in the USA belonged to each other was (in England at least) a belief advocated by high churchmen, not an established fact. Their ministries were not interchangeable. This chapter will trace the origins and development of the idea (which today is taken for granted) that what we now call the 'Anglican' churches in different countries were or should be branches of one communion (or even form one church). It will go on to survey the variety of names used for this communion in the earlier nineteenth century. It records use of the name 'Anglican Communion' in the modern sense in 1847 – more than three years earlier than previously known. Finally, it will offer some related reflections on the identity and self-understanding of the Church of England and the Anglican Communion. One reason for the absence of the terms 'Anglican' and 'Anglican Communion' from the Church of England's formal expressions of identity is its reluctance to view itself as a denomination with a particular ('Anglican') identity. In the third part of the chapter, mid-twentieth-century statements to this effect are recorded and defended against more recent criticism. Indeed, as we shall see, Michael Ramsey placed a question mark against the very concept of 'Anglicanism'. References to the provisionality of the Anglican Communion – most recently by Archbishop Runcie – are cited with approval.

Related episcopal churches

The Church of England's separation from Rome in the sixteenth century did not leave it standing alone. It had a counterpart in the Church of Ireland (though that church differed from it in some respects, not least in having been unable to retain the loyalty of the majority of the Irish people). In Scotland the picture was much more complex; the Church of Scotland, though influenced at various times and to differing extents by developments in England, had its own distinctive identity and characteristics, and a much more complicated history. After episcopacy was finally abolished in the established church in 1690, those who remained loyal to the bishops became a separate free church, known today as the Scottish Episcopal Church. By 1792 its clergy numbered just 4 bishops and 40 priests, and its people about 5 per cent of the Scottish population.[4]

To these three churches in Britain and Ireland (the Welsh dioceses formed an integral part of the Church of England until 1920) a fourth was added in the 1780s, following American independence. A bishop for the former Church of England congregations in Connecticut was consecrated by the Scottish bishops in 1784, and bishops for Pennsylvania and New York by the English bishops in 1787 (under the Foreigners Consecration Act 1786,[5] which empowered the Archbishops of Canterbury and York to consecrate candidates who were not British subjects to foreign sees without a royal mandate). In 1789 a General Convention then agreed a constitution and canons for the Protestant Episcopal Church in the United States of America (known today as the Episcopal Church in the USA). This church was unusual in that its congregations pre-dated its episcopal sees; in terms of church order (though not, of course, of ordination) episcopacy was 'bolted on' to a system which was in practice essentially congregational. Even after its constitution as a separate episcopal church, the polity of the Episcopal Church in the USA differed in important respects not only from that of the Church of England and the Church of Ireland but also from that of the Scottish Episcopal Church (itself already different from that of the English and Irish churches). The fact that its constitution was drawn up in the same place (Philadelphia) as the United States' constitution two years earlier, and by some of the same people, was not insignificant. (As a result, it is arguably a misleading oversimplification to speak of 'Anglican ecclesiology': there are significant differences in the ecclesiology of the churches of the Anglican Communion – especially between that of the Church of England and the churches derived from it on the one hand and that of the Episcopal Church in the USA and the churches derived from it on the other. These differences are to some extent masked by the use of the same terminology.[6])

At the beginning of the nineteenth century the number of churches in this family was reduced back to three when the United Church of England and Ireland came into existence as a result of the Union with Ireland Act 1800.[7]

The Colonial Church

When it was formed, the United Church of England and Ireland consisted not only of the Provinces of Canterbury and York and the four Irish provinces (Armagh, Dublin, Cashel and Tuam – Cashel and Tuam not being downgraded to ordinary bishoprics until the Irish Church Temporalities Act of 1833), but also of two colonial dioceses in British North America – Nova Scotia (1787) and Quebec (1793). To these, further colonial dioceses overseas were added: three in the first quarter of the nineteenth century – Calcutta (1814), Barbados (1824) and Jamaica (1824) – and then a further five in the later 1830s – Madras (1835), Australia (1836), Bombay (1837), Newfoundland (1839) and Toronto (1839). By 1840 the United Church thus had an overseas branch, 'the Colonial Church', consisting of ten dioceses.

A communion of churches?

In the first quarter of the nineteenth century, the idea that these three churches – the United Church of England and Ireland with its colonial appendages, the Scottish Episcopal Church and the Protestant Episcopal Church in the USA – belonged to each other was, in England at least, a belief advocated by high churchmen rather than an accepted fact. Indeed, if being in communion is understood as necessarily involving a mutual interchangeability of ministries, the three churches were not even in communion with one another. The Foreigners Consecration Act 1786, which permitted the consecration of bishops for America, contained the following proviso:

> Provided also, and be it hereby declared, That no person or persons consecrated to the office of a bishop in the manner aforesaid, nor any person or persons deriving their consecration from or under any bishops so consecrated, nor any person or persons admitted to the order of deacon or priest by any bishop or bishops so consecrated or by the successor or successors of any bishop or bishops so consecrated, shall be thereby enabled

to exercise his or their respective office or offices within his Majesty's dominions.[8]

The 1792 Relief Act (for granting relief to pastors, ministers and lay persons of the Episcopal Communion of Scotland) contained a similar proviso:

> Provided also, and be it further enacted, that no person exercising the function, or assuming the office or character of a pastor or minister of any order in the Episcopal Communion in Scotland, as aforesaid, shall be capable of taking any benefice, curacy or other spiritual promotion within that part of Great Britain called England, the dominion of Wales, or town of Berwick-on-Tweed, or of officiating in any church or chapel within the same, where the liturgy of the Church of England, as now by law established, is used, unless he shall have been lawfully ordained by some Bishop of the Church of England or of Ireland.[9]

Ironically, American and Scottish clergy were in a less favourable position than Roman Catholic clergy, who, if received into the Church of England, could minister in it as priests without re-ordination. The principle of inter-changeability of ministries between the English, Scottish and American churches was not established until 1840, and even then the relevant act merely allowed Scottish and American clergy to officiate for one or two days, the consent of the diocesan bishop being required.[10] An Act of Parliament was still needed in 1843 to enable Henry Caswall, a British subject ordained in America, to hold a benefice or preferment in the United Church of England and Ireland.[11] (Scottish clergy were finally permitted to hold benefices within the United Church by the Episcopal Church (Scotland) Act 1864,[12] and other episcopally ordained clergy by the Colonial Clergy Act 1874.[13])

All of this does not necessarily mean that Scottish and American ordinations were not recognized as valid. It is difficult to imagine that an English or Irish bishop would have been willing to re-ordain someone ordained in Scotland or America, even if the person concerned had been willing to submit to re-ordination. A leading advocate of the 1792 Relief Act explained:

> It does not follow, that because the same regard is not paid to the letters of orders of a Protestant Bishop in Scotland as to those of a Popish Bishop abroad, therefore the validity of the former, in a spiritual or ecclesiastical sense, is in the least degree a doubtful point.[14]

Indeed, it was *because* the English bishops recognized the validity of Scottish orders that the proviso was inserted into the Relief Act;[15] had Scottish orders not been recognized as valid, it would have been unnecessary. But recognition of validity of orders does not necessarily imply that churches are in communion: the Church of England's recognition of the orders of the Roman Catholic Church does not alter the fact that the two churches are not in communion.

The barriers to communion were not solely those imposed by statute law. In the 1780s, Jacobite sympathies remained alive among at least some of the Scottish clergy and bishops, who believed that by accepting William III and his successors, the Church of England had placed itself in schism. Thus in 1784 George Gleig (later Bishop of Brechin), who had invited a Church of England priest, Dr George Berkeley, to officiate in his church, received notice that 'the Primus expects that . . . you will write to him . . . and let him know upon what principles you justify a procedure which seems to imply our being in full communion with that church to which Dr Berkeley belongs'.[16] When Jacobite loyalties declined, they were replaced not so much by loyalty to the Hanoverians as by an anti-erastianism which similarly reduced sympathy for the Church of England, albeit for different reasons.[17]

Support for the persecuted Episcopal Church in Scotland and identification of it, rather than the established (but non-episcopal) Church of Scotland, as the Church of England's natural counterpart, were among the distinguishing marks of English high churchmen in the late eighteenth and early nineteenth centuries. The London committee constituted in 1790 to press for the repeal of the earlier legislation banning clergy ordained by the Scottish bishops from ministering even in Scotland consisted of three noted high churchmen: William Stevens (1732–1807; Treasurer of Queen Anne's Bounty, who was later to found the high-church club of Nobody's Friends[18]), his barrister friend James Allan Park (1763–1838; later a judge and knight) and Dr George Gaskin (1751–1824; Secretary of the SPCK and later Rector of Stoke Newington). A leading advocate of the 1792 Relief Act in the House of Lords was the high-church Bishop of St Davids, Samuel Horsley (1733–1806; later Bishop of Rochester and of St Asaph). Support for the Scottish Episcopal Church was more than simply characteristic of the English high churchmen. Its plight helped to galvanize them into a movement, of which the campaign which resulted in the 1792 act was the first corporate venture, and support for the Scottish bishops was to become an institutionalized component of English high churchmanship in the early decades of the nineteenth century.[19] It also continued to mark avant-garde high churchmen out from other members of the Church of England: in 1807 even the moderate high-church Bishop of Bangor, John Randolph, criticized John Bowdler's view of the Scottish Episcopal Church as the Church of England's Scottish counterpart as having 'not a little of the spice of the nonjuror in it'.[20]

Interest in the American Church and relations between it and the Church of England came to be similarly characteristic of English high churchmen. Indeed, it was through the Scottish bishops' consecration of Samuel Seabury to be Bishop of Connecticut in 1784 that the Scottish Episcopal Church had first come to the notice of both Horsley and Stevens.[21] As already mentioned, the English bishops consecrated bishops for Pennsylvania and New York in 1787. They consecrated a further bishop, for Virginia, in 1790, but for over 30 years thereafter there was little contact between the Episcopal Church in the USA and the Church of England. The American church now had sufficient bishops to consecrate its own bishops without recourse to Britain, so one reason for continuing contact was removed. During the war years British–American relations deteriorated, and from 1812 to 1814 Britain and the United States were themselves again at war. By 1822 the American presiding bishop was not in contact with anyone in England.[22] Contacts were restored by a visit of the leader of the high-church party in America, Bishop Henry Hobart of New York, to England in 1823–4.[23] Hobart stayed with Henry Handley Norris (1771–1850; Perpetual Curate and then Rector of South Hackney), one of the leaders of the high-church grouping known as the Hackney Phalanx. A young high churchman of the next generation, Walter Farquhar Hook (1798–1875), who had been making a study of the American Episcopal Church, sought an introduction to Norris from his father (whose assistant curate he was), and through Norris was able to meet Hobart.[24]

Hook first came to public attention in 1825, when he preached the sermon at the consecration by Scottish bishops of Matthew Luscombe as a bishop for members of the three churches resident in continental Europe. It was Hook who had suggested to Luscombe (his former headmaster, who had also served as his father's honorary assistant curate) that he should apply to the Scottish bishops for episcopal consecration. In his sermon, published as *An Attempt to Demonstrate the Catholicism of the Church of England and the other Branches of the Episcopal Church*, Hook stressed the essential unity of the three branches of what he called 'the reformed Catholic Church':

> There is, accordingly, among all true members of the reformed Catholic Church, a bond of union which no time, no distance, no disagreement even, on certain points in themselves indifferent, can ever dissolve. In its welfare, wherever it may exist, in England, in Ireland, in presbyterian Scotland or republican America, in regions of the East, or the islands of the West, a true Episcopalian will take an interest, not less fervent, not less

sincere, not less devoted than that which he experiences for the particular branch of it to which he may himself belong, 'whether one member suffer, all the members suffer with it, or one member be honoured, all the members rejoice with it'.[25]

Given Hook's stress on the unity of the three churches, it was appropriate that Bishop Hobart visited Bishop Luscombe in Paris in the summer of the same year.[26]

In 1841 Hook, by now Vicar of Leeds, used the consecration of the new Leeds parish church as an opportunity to demonstrate this unity publicly. For the reading and signing of the deed of consecration the Bishop of Ripon (the future Archbishop of Canterbury Charles Longley) and the Archbishop of York stood on the north side of the altar; opposite them, on the south side, stood the Bishop of New Jersey, George Washington Doane, who preached the sermon, and the Bishop of Ross and Argyll.[27]

In 1852 the unity of the three churches was manifested more officially when, at the invitation of the Archbishop of Canterbury, J. B. Sumner, American and Scottish bishops participated in the 150th anniversary celebration of the Society for the Propagation of the Gospel (SPG), held in Westminster Abbey. The archbishop's invitation to the American episcopate to send a delegation said that this was in order to 'manifest the essential unity of the sister Churches of England and America'.[28] Henry Caswall described the procession as follows:

> And what a procession! Such a procession as the Anglican Church has never before witnessed. Seventeen Bishops approach in the order of their consecration, the eldest closing the apostolic line . . . Four of these Bishops belong to the Church of Scotland – a Church once persecuted under the same authority which legalized the Church in England. Two of them are citizens of the United States, republicans by education and allegiance, yet in close communion with their English brethren who rejoice in the Royal Supremacy and the union of Church and State. Some of them are Colonial Bishops, who experience the combined disadvantages of the voluntary system and of an establishment. And the remainder are Bishops of the Church at present happily established in the southern portion of our island; but which may again be called to endure suffering as in the times of old. While that procession of Bishops advances towards the sacrarium, let us inwardly pray for them, and for the 108 Bishops of the Anglican communion, whom they may be considered to represent.[29]

(The reference to the 'Church of Scotland' is of course to the Scottish Episcopal Church, not to the Presbyterian established church.)

It was no accident that this demonstration of unity between the three churches took place at a celebration of the high-church SPG. Evangelicals were much more cautious in their attitude to the Scottish and American episcopal churches. They tended to identify the established Church of Scotland as the Church of England's Scottish counterpart, and were critical of the Scottish Episcopal Church's Communion rite, with its more high-church features. When in Scotland, a leading evangelical such as Charles Simeon would worship and preach in the Church of Scotland.[30] The evangelical Church Missionary Society (CMS) also enjoyed strong support from independent congregations in Scotland which used the English *Book of Common Prayer*, and this was a cause of tension between CMS and the Scottish bishops, especially between 1843 and 1845. Henry Venn (1796–1873), the secretary of CMS from 1841 to 1872, was similarly cautious about relations with the American church. Writing to Bishop Trower of Glasgow and Galloway in 1848–9, he commented that the 1840 act making it possible for Scottish and American clergy to minister in England 'makes no allusion to "communion" between the churches nor as far as we know [does] any other law or ecclesiastical authority'. For Venn, the difference between the Holy Communion rites of the two churches cast doubt on the existence of full communion.[31] In 1852, the year of the SPG anniversary celebrations, a CMS circular described the Church of England and the American church as 'separate and independent branches of the Church of Christ'.[32]

Names

Just as the idea that the three churches belonged together grew up only gradually (principally in the second quarter of the nineteenth century), so as yet there was no agreed collective name for them. In the eighteenth century and the earliest years of the nineteenth, the Church of England was perhaps most frequently referred to simply as 'The Establishment' – a term, of course, which by definition could not be used of the Scottish and American churches.[33]

In the first half of the nineteenth century the designation 'episcopal chapel' was very commonly used to differentiate Church of England chapels from what in earlier years would have been called dissenting meeting houses. As long as the Church of England's principal rivals were non-episcopal protestant churches, 'Episcopal' was an obvious term to use in distinguishing it from them. For similar reasons, 'Episcopal' was and remained the designation of the Scottish Church.

'Episcopal' was, however, not a sufficient term of distinction in the context of overseas territories in which the Roman Catholic Church was prominent. Writing to Bishop Luscombe in 1829, Bishop Blomfield of London spoke of 'the Protestant episcopal Clergy resident in France',[34] and in 1841 Archbishop Howley of Canterbury similarly spoke of 'the Protestant Episcopal Churches in the British dominions'.[35] As already indicated, 'Protestant Episcopal' was the name of the American church ('Protestant' being eventually dropped in 1979).

Some high churchmen, at least, were not enamoured of the label 'Protestant', however. Henry Handley Norris wrote in 1812:

> If names had any weight, I much more highly prize the title of a Catholic than that of a Protestant which later appellation I am by no means proud of, as it confounds one with those from whom Christianity I verily believe has suffered more outrages than from the Papists themselves. The distinguishing title of a member of the Church of England is a Reformed Catholic – and this places him in a central position from which the Papist and the larger portion of that mixed multitude known by the name of Protestant diverge, in opposite directions indeed but to equal distances.[36]

As we have seen, 'the reformed Catholic Church' was the term that Hook used for the three churches in his 1825 sermon (with 'Episcopalian' to describe their members). Use of this name persisted: in July 1847, for example, the first article in the first issue of the new *Colonial Church Chronicle* was entitled 'The Extension of the Reformed Catholic Church'.[37] An example of its use as late as 1867 is given below.[38]

'The Reformed Episcopal Church', avoiding both 'Protestant' and 'Catholic', was another solution that was tried, as for example by the Irish high churchman Alexander Knox (1757–1831) in a letter to his friend John Jebb in 1813:

> What perverse influence the nickname of Protestant has had upon our Church! . . . It will, perhaps, be at length discovered, that there is a medium between the two extremes, which combines the advantages, and shuts out the evils of both; which Vincentius Lirinensis clearly marked out, in the fifth century; and which at this day exists no where, but in the genuine central essence of our own reformed episcopal church.[39]

(The reference is to St Vincent of Lérins's threefold test of catholicity known as the Vincentian Canon: 'quod ubique, quod semper, quod ab omnibus creditum est' – what has been believed everywhere, always and by all.) The phrase 'the reformed episcopal church of England' had already appeared in 1790 in a tract attributed to Samuel Horsley.[40] In 1840 Bishop Blomfield of London argued that if the Church of England founded more overseas bishoprics, 'she will in due time cause the reformed episcopal Church to be recognised, by all the nations of the earth, as the stronghold of pure religion',[41] while in 1841 Bishop Kaye of Lincoln, another moderate high churchman, wrote: 'I consider the Reformed Episcopal Church to be the true representatives of the Primitive Church: the Roman and Greek churches to be branches, but erring branches, of the Catholic Church.'[42]

The term which won through in the end – 'Anglican' – was in one sense the oldest, resting as it did on the English Church's Latin name. The Supremacy of the Crown Act 1534 declared the king 'the only supreme head in earth of the Church of England called *Anglicana Ecclesia*'.[43] (Elizabeth I's Act of Supremacy 1559 (1 Eliz. 1 c. 1) replaced this with the statement that the queen was 'the only supreme governor of this realm and of all other her Highness's dominions and countries, as well in all spiritual or ecclesiastical things or causes as temporal'.[44]) The expression '*Ecclesia Anglicana*' had been in common use from the mid-twelfth century and famously occurred in Magna Carta (1215).[45] 'Anglican' appeared as an adjective from 1650,[46] but like the name 'Church of England' it simply distinguished the English Church and its members from other national churches and theirs, as well as from the Roman Catholic Church; these were not denominational labels. Within England the usefulness of the term 'Anglican' was severely limited, as it simply meant 'English'; it could not mark the Church of England out from protestant churches that were equally English.

There are isolated examples from the 1820s of the use of the term 'Anglican' (rather than the more common 'Episcopal', for example) to describe congregations and churches on the Continent,[47] and references to 'the Anglican Church' and 'Anglican Bishops' seem to become more common from about 1840, at least in high-church circles. This may, at least in part, have resulted from Newman's coining of the term 'Anglicanism' in 1837 to describe the religion of the seventeenth- and eighteenth-century Anglican fathers, which he saw as a *via media* between 'Romanism' and 'Popular Protestantism'.[48] (As late as 1846 Edward Churton referred to 'what is now called Anglicanism' when describing the tradition bequeathed by Richard Hooker and the Caroline Divines.[49]) In each case where 'the Anglican Church' or 'Anglican Bishops' are referred to at this time, however, 'English' could be substituted for 'Anglican' without altering the meaning.[50] 'Anglican' was still an ecclesiastical synonym for 'English', and as such it was not the most obvious term to use of churches in Scotland and America which remained proudly independent of the English Church.

It is therefore remarkable that it seems to have been American Episcopalians who first used the terms 'Anglican Church' and 'Anglican Communion' to denote not just the Church of England but all three churches. By contrast, it is not at all surprising that the first use of the terms of which the present author is aware should have been by a bishop sent to Constantinople to represent the American church to the Eastern churches; those who represent their church to others are forced to reflect on its identity. In a letter dated 12 November 1847, Horatio Southgate, 'Missionary Bishop in the Dominions and Dependencies of the Sultan of Turkey', summarized a treatise which he intended to publish in Armenian, Greek and Arabic in order to present 'the Anglican Church' to the Eastern churches:

> I next spoke of each of the three branches of the Anglican Communion separately, namely, the English, the Scotch, and the American . . . I then combined the three under the title, 'The Anglican Branch of the Church of Christ' . . . Next, I have given the main points of difference between us and Rome . . . Finally, I have spoken of the differences between us and the various Protestant denominations. I have spoken plainly, but not harshly . . . But . . . I cannot consent . . . that the Anglican Church should be confounded with the multifarious sects which abound in our own country.[51]

This use of the term 'Anglican Communion' pre-dates by more than three years those identified by Robert Bosher in his 1962 monograph *The American Church and the Formation of the Anglican Communion, 1823–1853* (John McVickar, preaching in Trinity Church, New York in July 1851; W. E. Gladstone, writing in December 1851; and Henry Caswall, in his description of the SPG anniversary celebration quoted above).[52]

It was to be some time before the new usage became universal. For the author of an article in the *Quebec Mercury*, reprinted in the *Colonial Church Chronicle* at the request of the Bishop of Quebec in August 1854, the term 'Anglican' still distinguished the United Church of England and Ireland from its Scottish and American sister churches: 'The Bishops of the Protestant Episcopal Communion in Scotland and foreign America, who have no such title as that conferred upon the Anglican Bishops, hold precisely the same office and authority in the Church of Christ, and exercise the same spiritual functions.'[53] In 1867, on the eve of the first Lambeth Conference, Walter John Trower, the former Bishop of Glasgow and Galloway who was now Bishop of Gibraltar, used 'the Reformed Catholic Church' rather than 'the Anglican Communion' as the designation for the churches in communion with the See of Canterbury. He wrote to the Archbishop of Canterbury of his hope that the conference's main object (next to the worship of God) would be 'the perpetuation for ever of full Visible communion among all Branches of the Reformed Catholic Church, – whether of those branches which are in Canonical obedience to the See of Canterbury, or of those which are now or may become hereafter, independent of that spiritual authority'.[54] The persistence even in 1867 of the term 'the Reformed Catholic Church' helps to explain calls, for example in the *Colonial Church Chronicle*, for the Swedish bishops to be invited to the Lambeth Conference – calls which were sufficiently serious for Archbishop Longley to consult his fellow English bishops before rejecting them.[55]

As late as 1878, after the second Lambeth Conference, the Bishop of Meath, Lord Plunket (later Archbishop of Dublin), wrote of 'the desirability of finding, if possible, some more appropriate term than "Anglican" whereby to describe the great communion from which the Conference at Lambeth has taken, hitherto, its name'. He pointed out that this name played into the hands of Roman Catholic controversialists who argued that the Church of Ireland was 'the church of the Anglo-Saxon invaders', and suggested that many in the Scottish and American Episcopal churches were 'not quite satisfied' with the name either.[56] None the less, since 1867 not only the terms 'Anglican' and 'Anglican Communion' but also the concepts which they now designate have achieved widespread acceptance.

Church of England identity and Anglican provisionality

It is interesting to note, however, that the terms 'Anglican' and 'Anglican Communion' have yet to figure in the Church of England's formal expressions of its identity and self-understanding. Chief among these is the Preface to the Declaration of Assent, contained in Canon C 15, which will form the subject of Chapter 4:

> The Church of England is part of the One, Holy, Catholic and Apostolic Church, worshipping the one true God, Father, Son and Holy Spirit. It professes the faith uniquely revealed in the Holy Scriptures and set forth in the catholic creeds, which faith the Church is called upon to proclaim afresh in each generation. Led by the Holy Spirit, it has borne witness to Christian truth in its historic formularies, the Thirty-nine Articles of Religion, *The Book of Common Prayer* and the Ordering of Bishops, Priests and Deacons.

There is no mention here of the Anglican Communion or of the name 'Anglican'; nor, indeed, do they appear in any of the other canons of the Church of England. Not the least significant of the differences between the Church of England and the other churches of the Anglican Communion is that it is possible to explain the existence, and hence the identity, of the Church of England without making reference to the Anglican Communion, but very difficult to explain the existence of most of the other Anglican churches without referring to the Church of England. This may be one reason for the lack of reference to the Anglican Communion in this statement of the Church of England's identity and self-understanding. It is also true that the 157 years that have passed since the first known use of the name 'Anglican Communion' form only a very small proportion of the Church of England's history – only a third of the period since the separation from Rome, and not much more than a tenth of that since St Augustine was sent to Canterbury.

A further reason why the Anglican Communion, and more particularly the term 'Anglican', are not mentioned may be the Church of England's reluctance to view itself as a denomination with a particular ('Anglican') denominational identity, preferring instead to see itself as – historically at least – simply the English Church or the English way of being Christian. This 'non-denominational' understanding of Anglican identity is bolstered by the fact that the name 'Anglican' merely makes a geographical reference, rather than alluding to a belief or practice (like 'Baptist') or to the doctrines promoted by an individual (like 'Lutheran'), and it is an understanding that has been shared by some non-English Anglicans at least. Archbishop Geoffrey Fisher expressed it thus: 'We have no doctrine of our own – we only possess the Catholic doctrine of the Catholic Church enshrined in the Catholic creeds, and those creeds we hold without addition or diminution.'[57] Bishop Stephen Neill made the same point:

> There are no special Anglican doctrines, there is no particular
> Anglican theology. The Church of England is the Catholic Church
> in England. It teaches all the doctrines of the Catholic Faith, as
> these are found in Holy Scripture, as they are summarized in the
> Apostles', the Nicene, and the Athanasian Creeds, and set forth
> in the dogmatic decisions of the first four General Councils of
> the undivided Church.[58]

Similar statements may be found in the writings of Bishop Wand of London and Professor John Macquarrie.[59]

On this understanding there is in fact no such thing as 'Anglicanism', if the ending '-ism' implies (as it otherwise generally does) a distinctive system of beliefs. Michael Ramsey commented:

> The Anglican will not suppose that he has a system or a
> Confession that can be defined and commended side by side
> with those of others; indeed, the use of the word 'Anglicanism'

can be very misleading. Rather will he claim that his tasks look beyond 'isms' to the Gospel of God and to the Catholic Church.[60]

Ramsey argued that 'there *is* such a thing as Anglican theology', but that 'it is neither a system nor a confession (the idea of an Anglican "confessionalism" suggests something that never has been and never can be) but a method, a use and a direction'.[61] Bishop (later Archbishop) H. R. McAdoo echoed this assessment: 'There is a distinctively Anglican theological ethos, and that distinctiveness lies in method rather than in content', but 'There is no specifically Anglican corpus of doctrine'.[62]

More recently, however, Stephen Sykes has argued in favour of a concept of 'Anglicanism' – indeed, 'Unashamed Anglicanism' – and accordingly rejected the claim that Anglicans have 'no special doctrines'.[63] Paul Avis has engaged sympathetically with Sykes's argument.[64] While accepting that Anglicanism 'does not wish to be different in fundamental doctrine and basic practice', Avis argues that there are nonetheless 'distinctive Anglican tenets in ecclesiology with regard to both faith and order'. Because 'faith is concerned with beliefs, with doctrine, and Anglicanism believes and teaches certain distinctive things about the Church', he concludes that it is incorrect to say that Anglicanism has 'no special doctrines'.[65]

As Avis accepts, those against whom Sykes is arguing 'would probably not have denied that Anglicanism exhibits certain distinctive traits in order'.[66] Clearly, Anglican ecclesiology, or Anglican ecclesiologies,[67] has/have indeed acquired some distinctive features. How far this distinctiveness amounts to divergence from 'the Catholic doctrine of the Catholic Church' might be questioned, however. Does distinctive ecclesiology amount to the 'specifically Anglican *corpus* of doctrine', the existence of which Archbishop McAdoo denied? Or, if the claim that Anglicans have 'no special doctrines' is wrong only because they have distinctive ecclesiology and ecclesiology is the doctrine of the Church, does this recognition not in fact mean that in general terms Michael Ramsey's assertion that there is no Anglican '*system* or confession' is broadly true? In other words, even if the distinctiveness of Anglican ecclesiology is admitted, might this not be regarded as the exception that proves the rule, which the Anglican consensus represented by Fisher and Ramsey, McAdoo and Macquarrie was at pains to uphold?

A final reason for the lack of reference to the Anglican Communion in the Church of England's formularies may be that while there are those in other churches of the Anglican Communion who still look to the Church of England (maybe with mixed emotions) as their 'mother church', for many in the Church of England the comparable feeling has been directed not towards the Anglican Communion but towards the Western Church in general and its centre, Rome, in particular. For the Church of England, the breach with Rome is immediate, whereas for most other Anglican churches, which formerly belonged to the Church of England but then became independent of it, the breach with Rome is at one remove. The ancient parishes of England were in communion with the See of Rome for the greater part of their history; by contrast, all of the congregations of the Episcopal Church in the USA were founded after the Church of England's separation from Rome. Looking to Rome as the 'mother church' of the Church of England, the church that sent St Augustine to Canterbury, leads to the Church of England being defined not primarily as a church of the Anglican Communion but as two provinces of the Western Church, to which they were linked for almost 950 years – twice as long as the subsequent period of separation. (It is perhaps not without significance that the resolution passed by the General Synod in 1984 which resulted in the ordination of women to the priesthood ten years later was 'That this Synod asks the Standing Committee to bring forward legislation to permit the ordination of Women to the Priesthood *in the Provinces of Canterbury and York*' [my italics].[68]) At best, this perspective places the Church of England on the widest canvas, stressing not its allegiance to a particular family of churches but its being 'part of the One, Holy, Catholic and Apostolic Church' and, as a mere part, its incompleteness in itself.

Such longing for the recovery of the visible unity of the whole Church, combined with the fact that the Anglican Communion does not exist to promote any particular doctrine or way of being the Church, but is simply a family of churches with common or related origins and history and hence similar identity, leads to the structures of the Anglican Communion being seen as provisional and hence of secondary importance. This understanding of the Anglican Communion (or 'Anglicanism') as provisional was well expressed by the American bishop Stephen Bayne (later the first Executive Officer of the Anglican Communion) in 1954:

> In the familiar phrase, . . . the 'vocation of Anglicanism is, ultimately, to disappear.' That is its vocation precisely because Anglicanism does not believe in itself but believes only in the Catholic Church of Christ; therefore it is forever restless until it finds its place in that one Body.[69]

David Paton, Secretary of the (English) Church Assembly's Council for Ecumenical Co-operation, pithily summed up both the 'non-denominational' identity and the provisionality of Anglicanism, and hinted at the causal link between them, as follows: 'Anglicanism is not a confession: and it is not permanently interested in Anglicanism.'[70]

One of the most recent and authoritative expressions of the provisionality of the Anglican Communion was that given by Archbishop Robert Runcie in his opening address to the 1988 Lambeth Conference, entitled 'The Nature of the Unity We Seek':

> We must never make the survival of the Anglican Communion an end in itself. The Churches of the Anglican Communion have never claimed to be more than a part of the One Holy Catholic and Apostolic Church. Anglicanism has a radically provisional character which we must never allow to be obscured.[71]

It was, however, his predecessor, Michael Ramsey, writing long before his elevation to the throne of St Augustine, in *The Gospel and the Catholic Church* (1936), who perhaps best expressed the Anglican sense of brokenness, incompleteness and provisionality, of a church which looks beyond itself to the greater whole of which it is part:

> While the Anglican Church is vindicated by its place in history, with a strikingly balanced witness to Gospel and Church and sound learning, its greater vindication lies in its pointing through its own history to something of which it is a fragment. Its credentials are its incompleteness, with the tension and the travail in its soul. It is clumsy and untidy, it baffles neatness and logic. For it is sent not to commend itself as 'the best type of Christianity', but by its very brokenness to point to the universal Church wherein all have died.[72]

PREFACE

The Church of England is part of the One, Holy, Catholic and Apostolic Church, worshipping the one true God, Father, Son and Holy Spirit. It professes the faith uniquely revealed in the Holy Scriptures and set forth in the catholic creeds, which faith the Church is called upon to proclaim afresh in each generation. Led by the Holy Spirit, it has borne witness to Christian truth in its historic formularies, the Thirty-nine Articles of Religion, The Book of Common Prayer *and the Ordering of Bishops, Priests and Deacons. In the declaration you are about to make, will you affirm your loyalty to this inheritance of faith as your inspiration and guidance under God in bringing the grace and truth of Christ to this generation and making him known to those in your care?*

DECLARATION OF ASSENT

I, A B, do so affirm, and accordingly declare my belief in the faith which is revealed in the Holy Scriptures and set forth in the catholic creeds and to which the historic formularies of the Church of England bear witness; and in public prayer and administration of the sacraments, I will use only the forms of service which are authorized or allowed by Canon.

4

The Church of England's Declaration of Assent[1]

When they are ordained, all deacons, priests and bishops have to make the Declaration of Assent printed opposite. They make it again every time they take up a new appointment. Readers too make the declaration (minus the reference to 'administration of the sacraments') when they are admitted and licensed. But where does the Declaration of Assent come from? This chapter answers that question, and in doing so illuminates something of what this important statement says about the Church of England and its identity.

Canon C 15 of the Church of England, which requires all those about to be ordained, admitted to any benefice or preferment, or licensed, to make the Declaration of Assent after its preface has been spoken, came into force on 1 September 1975. Since then, the Declaration of Assent and its Preface have become a fixed part of the Church of England's title deeds, and as such, in 2000 it was placed at the front of the main volume of *Common Worship*. When representatives of the Church of England are asked in ecumenical discussions for a definition of the Church of England's position, it is to the Declaration of Assent and its Preface that they increasingly turn. To cite only one example, the response of the English House of Bishops (published in 1997) to the papal encyclical *Ut Unum Sint* refers to this document no fewer than three times. In paragraph 58 it highlights the Church of England's description of itself in the Preface as 'part of the One, Holy, Catholic and Apostolic Church', while in earlier paragraphs it describes the Christian faith as being 'uniquely revealed in the Holy Scriptures and set forth in the catholic creeds', and speaks of the Church proclaiming that faith 'afresh in each generation'.[2]

More than a quarter of a century having now passed since Canon C 15 went through its synodical process, the events are sufficiently distant for memories as to the precise origins of the Declaration of Assent and its Preface to have become hazy, but they are not yet remote enough for reference books to make up the deficiency. This chapter seeks to fill that gap by outlining how the Church of England got its Declaration of Assent, and in doing so to give the document its due honour as a defining text for the Church of England's identity.

Subscription and assent, 1571–1968

The requirement of assent to the Church of England's doctrinal position dates from 1571, the year in which the Thirty-nine Articles of Religion reached their final form.[3] The Convocation of Canterbury stipulated that those about to be ordained or presented to a benefice should subscribe to all 39 articles, even though Parliament, out of concern for Puritan sensibilities, had ordered subscription only to those articles 'which . . . concern the confession of the true Christian faith and the doctrine of the Sacraments'.

No form of subscription was laid down in 1571, but this was done by Canon 36 of the canons of 1604, which required subscription to three articles composed by Archbishop Whitgift in 1583 and set out (after slight alteration) in the canon.[4] The first of these affirmed the royal supremacy. The second asserted that *The Book of Common Prayer* and the Ordinal contained nothing contrary to the word of God and that in public prayer and administration of the sacraments the person subscribing the article would use the form prescribed in the Prayer Book 'et non aliam'. The third gave assent to the Thirty-nine Articles and acknowledged them to be agreeable to the word of God. The form of subscription was 'Ego N. N. tribus his praefixis articulis, omnibusque in eisdem contentis, lubens et ex animo subscribo'. Eventually this became: 'I . . . do willingly and from my heart subscribe to the 39 Articles of Religion of the United Church of England and Ireland, and to the three articles in the 36th Canon, and to all things therein contained'. It is significant that from 1604 onwards Anglican clergy were thus required not only to declare their assent to the Thirty-nine Articles, but also to acknowledge that *The Book of Common Prayer* and the Ordinal, with its threefold ministry, contained nothing contrary to the word of God, and to promise to use the Prayer Book exclusively in public worship. The Prayer Book and the Ordinal thereby became associated, to an extent at least, with the Articles as part of what continental Protestants would call the 'confessional basis' of the Church of England. *Lex orandi, lex credendi* was to remain the classical Anglican approach.

In 1865, section 1 of the Clerical Subscription Act replaced this form of subscription with the following declaration:

> I, *A.B.*, do solemnly make the following declaration: I assent to the Thirty-nine Articles of Religion, and to *The Book of Common Prayer* and of the ordering of bishops, priests, and deacons. I believe the doctrine of the [United] Church of England [and Ireland] as therein set forth, to be agreeable to the Word of God; and in public prayer and administration of the sacraments I will use the form in the said book prescribed, and none other, except so far as shall be ordered by lawful authority.

New incumbents were also required to read the Thirty-nine Articles and repeat the declaration before the congregation on their first Sunday in office.

At the time, it was thought by some (including speakers in the parliamentary debates) that the replacement of subscription 'willingly and from the heart' with 'assent' somehow made the assent required only 'general'. However, against this view it was held, both in 1865 and subsequently, that 'in law, "assent" must be taken to mean "complete legal acceptance"'.[5] Perhaps the most significant feature of the declaration is its statement that 'the doctrine of the Church of England' is set forth in the Articles, the Prayer Book and the Ordinal collectively, rather than in the Articles alone.

Doctrine Commission report, 1968

By the later 1960s there was growing anxiety within the Church of England about the requirement of assent to the Thirty-nine Articles. In 1967 the Archbishops of Canterbury and York appointed a Commission on Christian Doctrine, and it was asked, as its first task, to consider 'the place of the Articles in the Anglican tradition and the question of Subscription and Assent to them'. The commission was chaired by Bishop Ian Ramsey of Durham, and the 17 other members included Professors Henry Chadwick, Denis Nineham, Ninian Smart and Maurice Wiles, as well as two future bishops – John Austin Baker and David Jenkins. The commission worked quickly, publishing its report, *Subscription and Assent to the Thirty-nine Articles*, in July 1968, in time for the 1968 Lambeth Conference.

The commission observed in its report that while most Anglicans appeared unconcerned about subscription, two diverging tendencies could be discerned. On the one hand, there was increasing dissatisfaction with the requirement to subscribe to the Articles, which many felt was morally questionable in that ordinands were required solemnly to commit themselves to things which they (in common with many others in the church) did not actually believe. At the same time, however, others regarded attacks on the Articles as part of a general erosion of doctrine within the Church of England, and opposed any weakening of the requirement of assent to them.[6]

In Chapter 5 of its report the commission considered whether the Articles should cease to be printed with the Prayer Book, but did not recommend this course of action. Chapter 6, which discussed whether the Articles could be revised or replaced by a new statement of faith, was inconclusive. Chapter 7 therefore proposed that the problem should be addressed not by revising or replacing the Articles but by replacing the declaration of assent. It set out the conditions that a new declaration would need to satisfy 'if it is to win widespread acceptance' as follows:

(a)   It must recognize that the Articles are an historic document and should be interpreted only within their historical context.

(b)   It must leave room for an appeal to the Articles as a norm within Anglican theology.

(c)   It must not tie down the person using it to acceptance of every one of the Articles of 1571.

(d)   It must preserve the comprehensiveness characteristic of the Church of England.

(e)   It must not put the Articles in isolation, but must acknowledge that Bible, Creeds, Prayer Book, Ordinal, and the developing consensus of Anglican thought also have their own contributions to make to the doctrine of the Church of England. It must also indicate that these possess different degrees of authority.

(f)   It must not only declare in what ways the Church of England is distinctive, but must indicate the doctrines she shares with all Christians.

(g)   The possibility of fresh understandings of Christian truth must be explicitly left open.[7]

This, the commission suggested, would best be achieved by a brief form of assent preceded by a preface spelling out 'the context in which [it] was to be understood and given its meaning and implications'.[8] A proposed preface and form of assent were set out in paragraph 97 of the report.

The suggestion of 'a contextualizing homily prefacing a brief declaration' had been made by the Revd John Austin Baker (later Bishop of Salisbury) during the commission's third meeting, in February 1968.[9] He proposed a draft (which he later described as 'somewhat wordy'), and this was simplified and amended by the commission. After the meeting he proposed an amended version of the commission's draft preface to remedy 'a number of stylistic inelegancies', and this was further amended at the commission's next meeting, in May.[10] Interestingly, the commission was evenly divided over whether to list the historic formularies in the order Prayer Book – Ordinal – Articles (as in its earlier draft and John Austin Baker's amended version) or Articles – Prayer Book – Ordinal, the chairman giving his casting vote in favour of the latter order as representing the status quo in the 1865 declaration.[11] A further amendment to the preface was made at a meeting in July immediately prior to publication.[12]

At its September meeting, the commission gave further consideration to its report 'in the light of points raised not only by self-criticism but also in the Press and at the Lambeth Conference', and agreed an amended text of the preface 'to avoid misunderstanding of the original text and to improve it stylistically'.[13] The preface and form of assent proposed by the commission were as follows (brackets indicate deletion in the amended text, while inserted words and punctuation are underlined):

Preface

The Church of England is part of the Church of God, having faith in God the Father, who through Jesus Christ our only Lord and Saviour calls us into the fellowship of the Holy Spirit. This faith, uniquely [revealed] shown forth in the holy Scriptures, and proclaimed in the catholic Creeds, she shares with other Christians [throughout] in all parts of the world. She has been led by the Holy Spirit to bear a witness of her own to Christian truth, as in her historic formularies – the Thirty-nine Articles of Religion, *The Book of Common Prayer*, and the Ordering of Bishops, Priests and Deacons. [Now, as before, she has a responsibility to maintain this witness] Through her preaching and worship, the writings of her [confessors] scholars and teachers, and the utterances of her councils[.], the lives of her saints and confessors, she has sought, through her history, to further this witness to Christian truth. This responsibility remains.

You will therefore, in the profession you are about to make, [you will] affirm your loyalty to this inheritance of faith, as your inspiration and direction[,] under God[,] for bringing to light the truth of Christ and making him known to this generation.

Form of Assent

I, *A.B.*, profess my firm and sincere belief in the faith set forth in the Scriptures and in the catholic Creeds, and my allegiance to the doctrine of the Church of England.

The commission added that the form of assent could conclude with a promise to use only authorized forms of worship. The requirement of public reading of the Articles should be abolished.[14]

General approval

In 1969 the Church Assembly and the Convocations of Canterbury and York debated the report and asked for the necessary legislation to be prepared. Because it was thought that such a technical and complex subject should not come before the new General Synod at its first meetings, it was not until November 1972 that a draft Amending Canon containing the new Canon C 15 was introduced into the Synod, alongside the Worship and Doctrine Measure which would empower the Synod to regulate subscription and assent by canon. The Preface and Declaration of Assent (as they were now called) set out in the new Canon C 15 were in fact the preface and form of assent proposed in the amended version of the 1968 report, with the addition of the promise 'and in the public prayer and administration of the sacraments, I will use the forms of service authorised by Canon and none other'.

In the General Approval debate, the proposed preface and declaration were subjected to a number of criticisms. The Rector of St Aldate's, Oxford, Canon de Berry, and Bishop Maurice Wood of Norwich pleaded for retention of assent to the Articles, but 'in a general way', and extolled the benefits of public reading of the Articles. Other speakers argued that the reference in the declaration to 'the doctrine of the Church of England' lacked precision. The phrase might be expounded in Canon A 5 ('The doctrine of the Church of England is grounded in the Holy Scriptures, and in such teachings of the ancient Fathers and Councils of the Church as are agreeable to the said Scriptures. In particular such doctrine is to be found in the Thirty-nine Articles of Religion, *The Book of Common Prayer*, and the Ordinal'), but members of the congregation listening to the declaration being made were unlikely to be aware of this.[15]

The preface was also attacked on stylistic grounds. One speaker called it 'soporific both in length and substance': 'will this welter of words impress either the person called to make his assent or the listening congregation?'[16] Professor Geoffrey Lampe commented: 'It reminds me painfully of some of the less happy statements in the proposed reconciliation rite in the Anglican/ Methodist scheme. It is the kind of ecclesiastical language which my tutor taught me long ago to call guff, and I wish that it could be pruned and if possible omitted.'[17] A lay member added that 'the preface, because of its vagueness and verbosity, seems to me to be the sort of thing written by my great grandmother in one of her more lucid moments'.[18]

The Revision Committee

Most speakers had accepted the proposal of a preface and declaration, as had their predecessors in the Church Assembly and Convocations, but the wording clearly needed considerable amendment. This would be the task of the Revision Committee, under the chairmanship of the Venerable John Lewis, Archdeacon of Hereford.

When the committee met on 26 January 1973, it had before it proposals from 13 Synod members, 5 of whom attended the meeting. In addition, there were six letters from evangelical clergy or ordinands requesting retention of the 1865 declaration. Three asked that it should at least be available as an option, but a proposal to that effect by Dr Oliver Wright Holmes was rejected by the committee.[19]

(a) The Preface

Two of the proposals, from Professor Douglas Jones and the Revd Raymond Avent, Vicar of St Paul's, Tottenham, contained complete texts of a preface and declaration. The Preface proposed by Fr Avent read:

> The Church of England is part of the One, Holy, Catholic and Apostolic Church of Christ. As such it adheres to the Faith and Practice of the universal Church of all ages, uniquely shown forth in the Holy Scriptures and proclaimed in the catholic Creeds. To this faith and practice such formularies as the XXXIX Articles of Religion, the 'Book of Common Prayer and Administration of the Sacraments and other Rites and Ceremonies of the Church' and the 'Ordering of Bishops, Priests and Deacons', bear witness. In the declaration you are about to make you are therefore asked to affirm your loyalty to this inheritance of faith and practice as your inspiration and direction under God in bringing the 'grace and truth' of Christ to this generation.

Fr Avent explained that he preferred 'part of the One, Holy, Catholic and Apostolic Church of Christ' to the 1968 commission's wording 'part of the Church of God' because

> 'Church of God' is vague and is now the name of a certain sect. In such a preface it would be well to state categorically that the Church of England is a part of the one Church of Christ in which we declare our belief in the Nicene Creed. (See also Canon A1.)

In general he rejected the commission's wording as 'too insular and not set firmly enough in the wider context':

> It suggests a church founded in the 16th Century whereas the specific Anglican formularies were an attempt to interpret the essence of the Catholic Faith as handed down from the earliest days and grounded in the teachings of the ancient Fathers and Councils of the Church.

The original fourth and fifth sentences he omitted altogether as being tautological; he preferred the biblical 'grace and truth' (John 1.17) to the commission's 'bringing to light the truth of Christ', and pointed out that 'profession' should read 'declaration', since that is what it was.[20]

At the meeting a third member, Mr Bernard Stanley (a solicitor from the Diocese of Portsmouth), produced another text for the Preface, which drew both on the commission's wording and on Fr Avent's proposal.[21] It was Mr Stanley's text, with a few minor amendments, that the committee adopted (again, brackets indicate deletions and insertions are underlined):

> The Church of England is part of the One, Holy, Catholic and Apostolic Church worshipping the one true God, Father, Son and Holy Spirit. She [adheres to] professes the [one] faith [authoritatively] uniquely revealed in the Holy Scriptures and set forth in the [C]catholic creeds, which faith the [Universal] Church is called upon to proclaim afresh [to] in each [succeeding] generation. Led by the Holy Spirit, she has borne witness [of her own] to Christian truth in her historic formularies, the Thirty-[N]nine Articles of Religion, the Book of Common Prayer and the Ordering of Bishops, Priests and Deacons. In the declaration you are about to make [you] will you affirm your loyalty to this inheritance of faith as your inspiration and [direction] guidance under God in bringing the grace and truth of Christ to this generation and making Him known to those in your care?

Mr Stanley's text, like the other two, took the Doctrine Commission's 1968 text as its starting point and included its key themes. It began with the important description of the Church of England as 'part of' the Church, made a trinitarian reference, set out the relationship of the Scriptures and the creeds to the faith, spoke of the Holy Spirit leading the Church of England to bear witness to Christian truth in her historic formularies, and required the person making the declaration to affirm loyalty to the Christian faith.

Mr Stanley's text did not only shorten the preface and improve its style, however. He followed Fr Avent (and Professor Jones) in using the term 'One, Holy, Catholic and Apostolic Church', but without adding 'of Christ' or 'of God'. His trinitarian reference was not only much more succinct than that of the commission, but also replaced 'having faith in God' with 'worshipping the one true God' (a typically Anglican emphasis?). It was in the second sentence that Mr Stanley made what was perhaps his most original contribution. Replacing 'shown forth in the Holy Scriptures' with the commission's original 'revealed . . .', he added 'which faith the [. . .] Church is called upon to proclaim afresh to each [. . .] generation'. His object in this was 'to emphasise that our faith is divinely revealed and consequently unchanging but that the expression of that faith must be set in its historical context and re-interpreted from age to age'.[22] This was subtly different from the commission's aim (not really achieved in its own proposed wording) of explicitly leaving open 'the possibility of fresh understandings of Christian truth', but its effect was not dissimilar.

The third sentence, which followed the commission's proposal most closely, was not only four words shorter; it also emphasized 'led by the Holy Spirit' by placing it at the beginning, and by removing 'as' gave the historic formularies a distinctive place, rather than making them one example of the Church of England's bearing witness to the faith. Mr Stanley followed Fr Avent in dispensing with the commission's next two sentences as unnecessary. The final sentence again followed Fr Avent in speaking of 'the declaration' and of 'bringing the grace and truth of Christ' to this generation. The Revision Committee restored the commission's 'inheritance of' faith and reference to making Christ known (adding 'to those in your care').

In all of the subsequent correspondence and debates this version of the preface was never questioned – except for the use of 'she' for the Church taken over from the Doctrine Commission's original wording. With that exception, it remains in force today.

(b) The Declaration

Not surprisingly, the declaration, although much briefer, proved much more problematic. The Doctrine Commission had proposed the following wording for the first part of the declaration:

> I, *A.B.*, profess my firm and sincere belief in the faith set forth in the Scriptures and in the catholic Creeds, and my allegiance to the doctrine of the Church of England.

In the General Synod debate, this formulation was objected to because the text did not itself make clear what 'the doctrine of the Church of England' was or make any reference to the historic formularies. Professor Lampe suggested:

> I profess my firm and sincere belief in the faith set forth in the Scriptures and in the catholic Creeds, and in the historic formularies of the Church of England, the Thirty-nine Articles of Religion, *The Book of Common Prayer*, and the Ordering of Bishops, Priests and Deacons.[23]

The Revision Committee took this as its basis, beginning 'I, *A.B.*, do so affirm and accordingly declare my belief . . .'.[24] Fr Avent had pointed out that in a declaration one needed to 'declare', and Professor Jones that 'firm and sincere' was redundant ('Either you assent or you do not').[25] The committee omitted the listing of the historic formularies at the end (the term having been explained in the preface). The declaration continued: 'and in public prayer and administration of the sacraments I will use only the forms of service which are authorised or allowed by Canon'.[26] In response to Canon P. J. M. Bryan, who had suggested omission of the words 'and none other' as superfluous, the Revision Committee inserted 'only' and omitted 'and none other' as being 'unduly emphatic'.[27]

Following the meeting, Michael Elliott-Binns, the secretary of the Revision Committee, wrote to the chairman, Archdeacon Lewis, to express concern at the implications of the committee's adoption of Professor Lampe's suggestion.

> The new form of the declaration really restores the 1865 position over the historic formularies as against the policy of the Doctrine Commission . . . It seems to me (backed by legal opinions here) that the person making this declaration would declare his belief, not generally in the faith, but in the faith as set forth in the Scriptures, the creeds and the formularies. The Thirty-Nine Articles are the real problem . . . 'Declare belief in' seems to me to be stronger than 'assent', and belief in the Thirty-Nine Articles is required on the same basis as belief in the creeds. Belief in every article seems to me to be implied.[28]

He had drafted the relevant paragraph of the draft report of the Revision Committee (after a telephone discussion with the chairman), 'helping as far as I can the liberals who will now be in the greatest difficulties' and reflecting the committee's policy, but 'I do not believe that the wording of the declaration supports the paragraph'. 'My draft of the report I think conceals the issue and misleads, but I have no other instruction.' If the declaration were to be changed, he proposed, in line with the Preface, either 'witnessed in the historic formularies' or 'to which the historic formularies of the Church of England bear witness'. The following week he wrote again to suggest adopting a phrase inserted into the Worship and Doctrine Measure by its Revision Committee, requiring belief in the faith as 'grounded in' the Scriptures, creeds and formularies.[29] The draft amendments to draft Canon C 15, incorporating the latter change, were sent out to the members of the Revision Committee and to those Synod members who had submitted proposals for comment, together with a revised draft report.[30]

Two evangelical members of the committee objected to the words 'grounded in' as too weak. Michael Elliott-Binns reported this to the chairman and suggested two alternative solutions: his original proposal (keeping 'set forth' for the Scriptures and the creeds, and adding 'to which the historic formularies of the Church of England bear witness') and a much longer text based on Canon A 5.[31] The archdeacon, however, wrote to the two members with a slightly different suggestion, following the words of the Preface more precisely in the first part but adopting Michael Elliott-Binns's suggestion for the second: 'the faith as revealed in the Holy Scriptures, set forth in the catholic creeds and to which the historic formularies of the Church of England bear witness'.[32] The two members agreed to this version, which was duly circulated to the committee.[33]

Another member then objected that the new version was 'clumsy to read and will be more clumsy still to speak'; he also wished to insert 'Christian' before 'faith' and preferred 'set forth' for both the Scriptures and the creeds.[34] The chairman agreed to a tidying up of the grammar ('which is revealed . . . and set forth . . . and . . .') but not to the other changes, and thus the text of the declaration was fixed.

The Revision Committee's report explained the reasoning behind the wording of its declaration as follows:

> Belief is expressed in the faith, not in particular documents, but this faith is expressed by reference to certain documents. The Doctrine Commission specified the documents as the Scriptures and the catholic creeds and then referred to allegiance to the doctrine of the Church of England in a separate clause. We have added the historic formularies of the Church of England, and have followed the wording of the preface in a more precise form.

> We feel that in the Declaration of Assent, it is the faith of the Church which should have the key position, giving the Scriptures and the creeds as the source along with the particular witness of the later formularies of the Church of England. We desire to be definite in the sense that these sources are clearly

indicated, but we do not wish to suggest that we wanted to be narrowly rigid in our use of them.[35]

The synodical process

The Revision Committee's report was considered by the Synod in July 1973. An evangelical, Mr Hugh Craig, moved an amendment to replace the final version of the declaration with the penultimate one, which had referred to the faith 'as grounded in the Holy Scriptures'. It was pointed out that this phrase, which had been approved by the majority of members of the Revision Committee, had been removed at the request of two evangelical members. Mr Craig's amendment failed to attract sufficient support, as did another seeking to replace 'belief in' with 'commitment to'.[36]

Mrs C. M. Tebbutt (Peterborough) described the reference to the Church of England as 'she' as 'a bit old-fashioned': 'Perhaps it has something to do with "mother" Church and "father" priest.' She preferred to speak of the Church as 'it'.[37] No amendment to that effect was moved, but bishops who supported such a change had their opportunity in January 1975, when the House of Bishops considered the draft canon (as 'a provision touching doctrinal formulae') prior to its final approval, in accordance with Article 7 of the General Synod's constitution. The House changed 'she' to 'it' and ordered that 'Him' should be printed 'him'.[38]

It was in this amended form that the draft amending canon was considered for final approval in February 1975. There was no debate, and approval was given by overwhelming majorities, with just one priest and two lay people voting against – a remarkable achievement. The canon was promulged on 4 July 1975, and came into force on 1 September. (It was amended in 1992, without debate, to remove the requirement that the declaration be 'subscribed' (actually signed) as well as 'made' (read aloud).)

Recent developments

When this chapter was first published, it pointed to one aspect of Canon C 15 that was perhaps unfortunate. Whether for reasons of convenience or embarrassment, the oaths and the old declaration of assent were often made privately before institutions and licensings. The Doctrine Commission recommended that the preface and declaration should be used *publicly* on these occasions,[39] but Canon C 15 could not insist on this, because institutions and licensings may take place in private. Under the Clerical Subscription Act 1865, the congregation had still heard the old declaration even where it had been made in private, because it had to be repeated on the following Sunday when the Articles were read. However, when the new Canon C 15 was drafted, not only was the requirement for incumbents to read the Articles dropped, but the obligation to repeat the declaration was dropped with it. Ministers licensed to a stipendiary curacy continued to have to repeat the declaration,[40] but in parishes where the bishop did not have the Declaration of Assent made publicly at the institution and where there was no licensed stipendiary curate, this defining statement of the Church of England's identity was never heard by the people. This situation will be remedied in part by Amending Canon No. 24 (to be promulged in 2005), which will amend Canon C 15 so as to require that any cleric (rather than, as at present, stipendiary curates only) should, if instituted, installed, licensed or admitted to office in some place other than the place in which that cleric was to serve, publicly make the Declaration of Assent on the first Sunday on which he or she officiated in that place.

It still remains the case, however, that where the institution, installation, licensing or admission happens in the place where the cleric is to serve, the declaration may lawfully be made in private before a service rather than in public during it. This point was considered by the working group, set up by the House of Bishops, which produced the 2004 report *Clergy Discipline (Doctrine)*. While taking the view that practical considerations meant that a degree of latitude was required, it recommended 'that wherever practically possible the Declaration of Assent should be made publicly before a congregation in the context of a public act of worship'.[41]

Also in 2004, there was discussion of whether ordinands should make the declaration during the ordination service itself. Canon C 15 requires this in the case of ordination or consecration as a bishop, but allows those ordained deacon or priest to make the declaration privately before the service. In February 2004 the General Synod rejected an amending canon which would have removed the requirement that the declaration be made publicly at the consecration of bishops. Later in the year, the Revision Committee which revised the draft *Common Worship* Ordination Services considered whether to require those being ordained deacon and priest to make the declaration during the ordination service as well. In view of the disproportionate length of time this would take when up to 40 individuals are ordained at the same service, it decided not to do so (a decision supported by the General Synod in February 2005), but it did associate itself with the view expressed in the *Clergy Discipline (Doctrine)* report: 'For our part, we wish to underline the importance which we attach to the public making of the Declaration of Assent at institutions and licensings.' The Revision Committee also sought to raise the profile of the declaration in ordination services. The draft *Common Worship* services already included a new question, asking whether the ordinands had made the declaration, but the Revision Committee went further:

> We also consider it important that members of the congregation should know to what the question about the Declaration of Assent refers. We have therefore added a Note requiring that the Declaration of Assent should be printed at the front of the service booklet at all ordinations to the diaconate and priesthood, and have amplified the answer to the question about the Declaration of Assent so that it now includes a reprise of the Declaration itself.[42]

Concluding reflections

The story of the genesis of the Declaration of Assent is an interesting and in some respects surprising one.

The idea of a brief declaration preceded by a more extensive preface placing it in context was suggested by John Austin Baker, and the Preface follows, with some omissions, the outline suggested by him and the Doctrine Commission. The dignified, poetic and theologically sensitive final text of the Preface was not the work of academic theologians, however, but of two backbench Synod members – combining a parish priest's theological vision with a solicitor's skill in drafting – amended in minor details by a synodical revision committee at a single meeting. It is noticeable that of the three phrases from the Preface quoted by the House of Bishops in its response to *Ut Unum Sint*, one ('part of the One, Holy, Catholic and Apostolic Church') owes its formulation to Fr Avent and one ('which faith the Church is called upon to proclaim afresh in each generation') was contributed by Mr Stanley.

In the preface, the historic formularies of the Church of England are discussed in a separate sentence from the Scriptures and the creeds, which does not relate the formularies directly to the faith, but says that the Church of England has 'borne witness to Christian truth in' the formularies. It is the declaration proper that offers the succinct statement of the relationship between the faith, the Scriptures, the creeds and the formularies that has come to characterize the whole document ('the faith which was revealed in the Holy Scriptures and set forth in the catholic creeds and to which the historic formularies of the Church of England bear witness'). Similarly, it is the declaration proper that contrives to require belief in the faith in general (and not 'the doctrine of the Church of England') but at the same time demand affirmation of loyalty to the Church of England's inheritance of faith and acknowledgement that its historic formularies bear witness to the faith. Remarkably, the relevant formulation in the declaration was a last-minute production by the secretary of the Revision

Committee, Michael Elliot-Binns, refined by its chairman, Archdeacon Lewis, and another member, and only attempted because two members had objected to the previous solution.

Thus both the Preface and the Declaration of Assent can be said to be the product of a committee, and a fruit of the much-maligned synodical process.

As a statement of the identity of the Church of England, the Preface and Declaration of Assent are highly interesting. The Church of England is given no denominational or confessional description. The term 'Anglican' does not appear (it would essentially be tautologous),[43] and neither do the words 'protestant' or 'reformed' (whereas 'catholic' appears three times – of the Church and of the creeds). The only name given is a purely geographical one – 'of England'. The Church of England is thus defined first and foremost as a national part of the one holy, catholic and apostolic Church. The distinctions between revelation of the faith in the Scriptures, the setting forth of it in the catholic creeds, the witness of the historic formularies to it and the need (not to change it, but) 'to proclaim [it] afresh in each generation', make this a classic statement. The preface's culmination in the evangelistic and pastoral task with regard to 'the present generation' is another important and distinctive element. Finally, a comparison with equivalent continental protestant declarations is instructive. These tend to culminate in a promise to preach according to the confessional documents, whereas for the Church of England it is common prayer, the use of the liturgies authorized or allowed by canon, that defines a loyal Anglican. In the end, as the old adage would have it, *lex orandi* is indeed *lex credendi*: it is how the Church prays and worships that tells us what it believes.

5

Primacy in the Anglican tradition[1]

Recent developments in the Anglican Communion have thrown a spotlight onto the 'primates' of the Communion and onto the particular ministry within the Communion of the Archbishop of Canterbury. But what is a primate, and how has the Archbishop of Canterbury's role within the Anglican Communion developed to the point where he is regarded as its 'focus of unity'? This chapter, originally written as a contribution to ecumenical dialogue, offers some answers to those questions.

In his 1995 encyclical letter *Ut Unum Sint*, Pope John Paul II asked: 'Could not the real but imperfect communion existing between us persuade Church leaders and their theologians to engage with me in a patient and fraternal dialogue' on the primacy of the Bishop of Rome as a ministry of unity?[2] As a contribution to such a dialogue, this essay aims to describe and reflect on aspects of primacy in the Anglican tradition. Those who comment on the Roman primacy from an Anglican perspective often compare it with the position of the Archbishop of Canterbury within the Anglican Communion, and conclude that Anglican primacy differs from that of Rome in enjoying honour but not claiming jurisdiction. The first part of this chapter will seek to draw attention to the much older primacy of the Archbishops of Canterbury and York within England, in which jurisdiction goes hand in hand with honour, as a much more appropriate basis for discussions with Rome. The second will then examine how the Archbishop of Canterbury has come to enjoy a 'primacy of honour' within the Anglican Communion. In writing the original essay on which this chapter is based, it was necessary to limit the scope of the study, focusing on the canonical position in England and that expressed in the reports of the Lambeth Conferences; a study of how primacy has actually been exercised in practice would be a much greater undertaking. Similarly, no attempt is made to examine primacy within other churches of the Anglican Communion. However, in a new section at the end of the chapter, reference is made to some of the recent developments in relation to the Archbishop of Canterbury's 'primatial' role within the Anglican Communion, whereby his role is envisaged as going beyond a mere 'primacy of honour'.

A: The Church of England

> By virtue of their respective offices, the Archbishop of
> Canterbury is styled Primate of All England and Metropolitan,
> and the Archbishop of York Primate of England and
> Metropolitan. (Canon C 17.1)

The term *metropolitan*, first used by the Council of Nicaea (325), refers to a
bishop who has powers over a group of dioceses (called a province) and their
bishops (who came to be described as his suffragans[3]). The symbol of a
metropolitan's jurisdiction over his province is the pallium, a circular band with
two hanging strips, made of lamb's wool and marked with six black crosses,
which is worn on the shoulders. In 601 Pope Gregory the Great sent the pallium
to St Augustine, who had established the See of Canterbury four years earlier,
and to this day this symbol of metropolitical jurisdiction appears on the
Archbishop of Canterbury's arms. The letter that accompanied the pallium
envisaged the formation of a second province, with its metropolitical see in
York.[4] In the event, it was not until 735 that the See of York achieved lasting
archiepiscopal status. Ever since, the English Church has consisted of these
two provinces.

Although the title of *primate* (or 'bishop of the first see') was originally used of
all metropolitans, it was later applied to the chief bishop of a state or people.[5]
Thus in France the Archbishop of Lyon enjoys the (now purely honorific) style
Primat des Galles. When the precedence of the See of Canterbury over that of
York was finally accepted in 1353, it was agreed that the Archbishops of
Canterbury should be styled Primate of All England and those of York Primate
of England. Each archbishop was allowed to have his primatial cross carried
before him in the other's province (but Rome laid down that if their processions
should meet in a narrow road, that of the Archbishop of Canterbury should
pass first!).[6]

By this time, the senior bishops of the Province of Canterbury had come to be
seen as forming a provincial chapter (like a cathedral chapter), the Bishop of
London being dean, Winchester chancellor, Lincoln vice-chancellor, Salisbury
precentor, Worcester chaplain and Rochester cross-bearer.[7] Thus the
relationship between the archbishop and his suffragans (the other diocesan
bishops) was seen as in some sense comparable to that between a diocesan
bishop and his cathedral chapter. (The ancient titles are still used ceremonially
when the election of an Archbishop of Canterbury is confirmed.[8]) In the French
Church, the Bishops of Soissons and Chartres were described as deans of their
respective Provinces of Reims and Sens, just as the Bishop of London is Dean of
the Province of Canterbury, but there seems to have been no equivalent in
France of the Canterbury provincial chapter.[9]

Meanwhile, in the twelfth century the Irish Church had been divided into four provinces – Armagh, Dublin, Tuam and Cashel. A rivalry between the Sees of Armagh and Dublin came to be resolved in the same way as that between Canterbury and York, the archbishops being styled Primate of All Ireland and Primate of Ireland respectively. Eventually, the Province of Tuam was absorbed by that of Armagh and Cashel by Dublin under the Irish Church Temporalities Act of 1833.

Because in England both of the metropolitans are also primates (as are the two remaining Irish metropolitans), the distinction between a primate and a metropolitan is not immediately apparent to Anglicans in the British Isles today. Strictly speaking, however, the powers and responsibilities that belong to the Archbishops of Canterbury and York in their respective provinces are metropolitical rather than primatial.

Metropolitical jurisdiction

The description of the diocesan bishops of the Provinces of Canterbury and York as the suffragans of their respective archbishops is still current in English law,[10] and every bishop is required to 'take the oath of due obedience to the archbishop and to the metropolitical Church of the Province where he is to exercise the episcopal office in the form and manner prescribed in and by the Ordinal' (Canon C 14.1).[11] The oath reads:

> In the Name of God. Amen. I *N*. chosen Bishop of the Church and See of *N*. do profess and promise all due reverence and obedience to the Archbishop and to the Metropolitical Church of *N*. and to their Successors: So help me God, through Jesus Christ.

The jurisdiction that an English archbishop has over his province is set out in Canons C 17 (Of Archbishops) and G 17 (Of Visitations) of the present canons of the Church of England, which were promulged as recently as 1964/9. Although these two canons did not innovate, merely codifying existing law, their text stems not from the canons of 1604 (which did not deal with these matters) but from the 1947 report of the Archbishops' Commission on Canon Law,[12] and they therefore represent the considered view of the Church of England in the middle of the twentieth century.

As Canon C 17 makes clear, an archbishop has metropolitical jurisdiction 'at all times' – permanently rather than episodically:

> The archbishop has throughout his province at all times metropolitical jurisdiction, as superintendent of all ecclesiastical

matters therein, to correct and supply the defects of other bishops. (Canon C 17.2)

The Episcopal Ministry Act of Synod 1993 gives an interesting example of the metropolitical jurisdiction at work. Section 11 provides that where the bishop of a diocese has indicated that he is opposed to the ordination of women to the priesthood, and he has not made arrangements for the ordination of women to the priesthood and their licensing and institution to be carried out by another bishop, 'the ordination of women from the diocese and their licensing and institution shall be carried out by the archbishop concerned, either personally or through a bishop acting as his commissary'. The archbishop of the province 'shall act . . . either at the request of the diocesan bishop concerned *or in pursuance of his metropolitical jurisdiction*' (my emphasis). Thus an archbishop can (personally or through commissaries) ordain, license and institute throughout his province without being requested to do so by the diocesan bishop. Admittedly, the Act of Synod goes on to provide that 'the archbishop shall not so act unless he is satisfied that the diocesan bishop concerned has no objection', but one commentator has asked: 'How can an Act of Synod, which appears to have no legal force, yet claim to limit the authority of an archbishop?'[13] (The answer, presumably, is that the Act of Synod is only *morally* binding on the archbishop and does not claim to limit his legal authority.)

The archbishops' metropolitical jurisdiction is also exemplified by the fact that appeal lies from the consistory court of a diocese to the provincial court.

The Archbishops of Canterbury and York have decision-making powers throughout their provinces with regard to a range of matters, including cases of clergy (and episcopal) discipline, permissions to overseas clergy, and faculties under the Clergy (Ordination) Measure 1990 enabling divorced and remarried persons or those married to them to offer themselves for ordination. In some matters, clergy and others can appeal to the archbishop against decisions of their diocesan bishop.

In the nature of things, it is difficult to quantify the influence that the archbishops enjoy over the diocesan bishops of their provinces. Such influence must, in part at least, rest on the fact that they are not merely senior colleagues but metropolitans to whom the bishops have promised 'due obedience'. The bishops frequently seek advice from their archbishops about a range of matters. In responding, the archbishop has to be careful not to become involved in any matter which might later come to him on appeal. The archbishop and his bishops also exchange information (for example, the texts of major addresses). An important aspect of the relationship between an archbishop and the diocesans of his province is that the archbishop gives them pastoral care, for example in cases of illness or bereavement. The two archbishops consult and inform each other, and each has in the other a colleague who can give pastoral support.

Ordinary jurisdiction

In addition to their permanent metropolitical jurisdiction, the archbishops have a power of 'holding metropolitical visitations at times or places limited by law or custom' (Canon C 17.4). Furthermore,

> The archbishop has throughout his province . . . during the time of his metropolitical visitation, jurisdiction as Ordinary, except in places and over persons exempt by law or custom. (Canon C 17.2)

Canon G 5 (Of Visitations) reads:

1.   Every archbishop, bishop, and archdeacon has the right to visit, at times and places limited by law or custom, the province, diocese, or archdeaconry committed to his charge, in a more solemn manner, and in such visitation to perform all such acts as by law and custom are assigned to his charge in that behalf for the edifying and well-governing of Christ's flock, that means may be taken thereby for the supply of such things as are lacking and the correction of such things as are amiss.

2.   During the time of such visitation the jurisdiction of all inferior Ordinaries shall be suspended save in places which by law or custom are exempt.

(By custom, the Archbishop of Canterbury does not 'visit' the Diocese of London.)

Thus an archbishop can, for the period of a metropolitical visitation, exercise ordinary jurisdiction in the dioceses of other bishops of his province, and during that time their jurisdiction is suspended. Although metropolitical visitations were last held in England and Wales towards the end of the seventeenth century,[14] the important consideration is the fact that the canons promulged in the 1960s specifically provide for them.

Presidency

So far, we have been looking at the *application* of canons (jurisdiction). When it comes to the *making* of canons (legislation), the archbishops' role is much more one of presidency. Each is the president of his provincial Convocation, and they are joint presidents of the General Synod (Canon C 17.4). When a canon is promulged the archbishops, together with the prolocutors (chairmen of the House of Clergy) and the chairman and vice-chairman of the House of Laity, sign the instrument of enactment. In the case of an Act of Synod, the role of the archbishops is to ratify and confirm the Act of Synod for their respective provinces.[15] This reflects the canonical position that 'no Act is held to be an Act of the Convocation of the province, unless it shall have received the assent of the archbishop' (Canon C 17.5).

In terms of jurisdiction, the relationship between the bishop and his diocese is mirrored at the provincial level by the relationship between the archbishop and his province (and, more particularly, between the archbishop and the bishops of his province). In terms of synodical decision-making, however, the counterpart at provincial or national level of the bishop in his diocese is, for most purposes, not the archbishop(s) but the House of Bishops collectively.[16] (The choice of the name 'Archbishops' Council' for the central council of the Church of England – which came into existence in 1999 – tends to obscure this, since it might be taken to imply that the relationship between the archbishops and the Archbishops' Council is comparable to that of the bishop of a diocese and his bishop's council, which is not the case.)

Traditionally, the initiative in the making of canons lay with the House of Bishops, but their proposals were made in the light of the *counsel* offered by the clergy, and required their *consent*.[17] This is reflected in the requirement of the General Synod's constitution that a provision touching doctrine or worship 'shall, before it is finally approved by the General Synod, be referred to the House of Bishops, and shall be submitted for such final approval in terms proposed by the House of Bishops and not otherwise'.[18] It is also expressed in the seating arrangements in the General Synod, where by custom the bishops sit together at the centre of the Synod. They attend the Synod not as the leaders of delegations from largely autonomous dioceses, seated with them, but as members of the collective leadership of a church which has a corporate life at the provincial and national levels. They attend not to lead their dioceses in giving counsel and consent to the archbishops, but to receive, as a college of bishops chaired by the archbishops, the counsel and consent of the clergy and laity of their province or their church.

As well as exercising jurisdiction, 'the archbishop is, within his province, the principal minister' (Canon C 17.4). The sentence that follows mirrors a similar sentence about the diocesan bishop within his diocese (Canon C 18.4), but again, this should not mislead one into thinking that what is true of the bishop within the diocese is true of the archbishop within the province. The diocesan bishop has 'the right . . . of conducting, ordering, controlling and authorising all services', so that, for example, it can be said that a parish priest presides at the

Eucharist on the bishop's behalf. This is not true of the bishop in relation to his archbishop. The only liturgical duty that belongs as of right to the archbishop is that of being 'the chief consecrator at the consecration of every bishop'.

The Archbishop of Canterbury

What has been said so far is equally true of each archbishop in his own province. The Archbishop of Canterbury does, however, have a few powers which extend throughout the Church of England:

> By the laws of this realm the Archbishop of Canterbury is empowered to grant such licences or dispensations as are therein set forth and provided, and such licences or dispensations, being confirmed by the authority of the Queen's Majesty, have force and authority not only within the province of Canterbury but throughout all England. (Canon C 17.7)

The principal statute to which this canon refers is the Ecclesiastical Licences Act 1533 (25 Hen VIII c. 21), which conferred on the Archbishop of Canterbury the papal powers usually exercised by the pope through his legate (the 'legatine powers'). (By the Acts of Supremacy, the rest of the papal powers were vested in the Crown.)

The Archbishop of York

Nonetheless, the Archbishop of Canterbury remains one of two primates in the Church of England. In 1962 a Canterbury Convocation committee report commented that 'it is for the well-being of the Anglican Communion as a whole as well as of the Church of England in particular, that the two English primates should complement and balance one another, and that the see of Canterbury should not be allowed to develop into a patriarchate or papacy'. The committee saw the Northern Convocation as 'an important element in maintaining the status of the Archbishop of York'.[19] The then Archbishop of Canterbury, Michael Ramsey, endorsed these views:

> I believe that the dual Archiepiscopate in this country is something providentially given to us to prevent the See of Canterbury from ever becoming a sort of administrative papacy, which I believe in history it might have become but for our duo-archiepiscopal system. If there is to be an Archbishop of York and he is to be effectively a Primate he must be able to summon a Synod of bishops and clergy, otherwise he has a *cathedra* with no *corpus* around him. That, I think, is really important for the balanced health of our Church.[20]

Speaking in the General Synod in November 1997, the then Archbishop of York, Dr David Hope, complained that in the reports of three recent commissions 'the existing Provincial structure and character of our Church seems to have been set aside almost without further thought'. He argued, by contrast, for its retention, 'even perhaps to the extent of enhancing it to some degree', because 'our Church is immensely strengthened by the complementarity of the Provincial structure which it presently enjoys':

> I urge that we think much more imaginatively about ways in which the Provincial structures with which our Church of England is blessed might be developed to serve it all the more effectively, not only in the present, but also for the future.[21]

B: Canterbury's position in the Anglican Communion

The origins of primacy and metropolitical jurisdiction over Anglican dioceses outside the British Isles lie in the late eighteenth century, the first overseas diocese of the Church of England, that of Nova Scotia, having been established in 1787. Although that diocese and the many overseas dioceses that followed it were outside the Province of Canterbury, their bishops were subject to the Archbishop of Canterbury. For example, the letters patent which constituted the See of Australia in 1836 provided:

> The bishop of the said see of Australia and his successors shall be subject to the . . . Archbishop of Canterbury . . . in the same manner as any bishop of any see within the province of Canterbury, in Our Kingdom of England, is under the authority of the archiepiscopal see of the province of Canterbury and the archbishop thereof.

Every Bishop of Australia was to take an oath promising 'all due obedience' to the Archbishop of Canterbury and his successors.[22]

As time went on, the Archbishop of Canterbury relinquished metropolitical jurisdiction over most (though not all) of the overseas dioceses. This process began in 1835, when a second episcopal see, Madras, was founded in India. The Bishop of Calcutta was granted letters patent stating that 'the Bishop of . . . Calcutta for the time being shall be . . . the Metropolitan Bishop in India . . . and . . . the . . . Bishop of Madras shall be suffragan to the said Bishop of Calcutta and His Successors'. By the time of the first Lambeth Conference in 1867, there were also Metropolitans of Australia (Sydney, 1847), South Africa (Capetown, 1853), New Zealand (1858) and Canada (Montreal, 1860).

From 1867 onwards, successive Lambeth Conferences encouraged the gathering of extra-provincial dioceses into new provinces. A committee of the 1867 conference argued that provinces 'should follow the civil divisions' of the countries concerned, that the bishops should be subordinated to a metropolitan, and that 'it seems . . . most in accordance with primitive usage that the Metropolitical See should be fixed'.[23] Until the 1890s the overseas metropolitans of the Church of England remained bishops rather than archbishops (as the early occupants of the See of Canterbury had in fact been). The question of archiepiscopal status was raised but not resolved at the 1888 Lambeth Conference, though the relevant committee was inclined to favour it in some cases.[24] In 1893 the first meeting of the Canadian General Synod resolved that the two Canadian metropolitans should be styled archbishops. The Metropolitans of Australia, South Africa and the West Indies were also given the title by their synods, but refrained from using it pending endorsement by the Lambeth Conference.[25] This followed in 1897, when the conference resolved that 'recognising the almost universal custom in the Western Church of attaching the title of Archbishop to the rank of Metropolitan, . . . the revival and extension of this custom among ourselves is justifiable and desirable'.[26]

For almost 60 years, the Archbishop of Canterbury had retained an overall primatial role over what had remained overseas provinces of the Church of England. It had been laid down in 1835 that the Bishop of Calcutta was to exercise his metropolitical jurisdiction 'subject nevertheless to the general Superintendence and revision of the Archbishop of Canterbury for the time being . . . and subordinate to the Archiepiscopal See of the Province of Canterbury'.[27] The same applied to the Bishop of Sydney as Metropolitan of Australasia: the letters patent by which the Bishop of Australia became Bishop of Sydney and Metropolitan of Australasia in 1847 provided that the metropolitan should be 'subject nevertheless to the general superintendence and revision of the Archbishop of Canterbury'.[28] At the second Provincial Synod of the Province of Rupert's Land (Canada) in 1878, the metropolitan announced that the Archbishop of Canterbury had given his approval to the acts of the first Provincial Synod 'as Primate of the Province'.[29] In 1893, however, the Archbishop of Rupert's Land was elected to be the first Primate of All Canada, a development tacitly recognized by the 1897 Lambeth Conference when it resolved that 'the Archiepiscopal or Primatial title may be taken from a city or from a territory'.[30]

This development marked a change in understanding of the relationship of the overseas provinces to the Church of England. The 1861 constitution of the Province of Canada had stated: 'We desire the Church in this Province to continue, as it has been, *an integral portion of* the United Church of England and Ireland', but a subtle change took place in the constitution adopted by the

General Synod in 1893, which declared 'the Church of England in the Dominion of Canada' to be '*in full communion with* the Church of England throughout the world' (emphasis added in each case).[31] Other overseas provinces continued for much longer to be considered part of the Church of England: 'The Church of England in India' and 'The Church of England in Ceylon' did not become the Church of India, Burma and Ceylon until that church gained its own constitution in 1930, for example, and it was not until 1962 that the Anglican churches in Australia and Tasmania ceased to be 'organized upon the basis that they are not merely churches "in communion with" or "in connexion with" the Church of England, but are actual parts of that Church' – the name 'The Church of England in Australia' being retained until 1981.[32] In line with the Canadian development, however, the relevant committee of the 1908 Lambeth Conference was convinced that 'no supremacy of the See of Canterbury over Primatial or Metropolitan Sees outside England is either practicable or desirable'.[33]

'The Primacy of Canterbury'

Nonetheless, the same committee spoke of 'the universal recognition in the Anglican Communion of the ancient precedence of the See of Canterbury'.[34] With these words the same Lambeth Conference that recognized the end of any claim to primatial jurisdiction on the part of the Archbishop of Canterbury over the metropolitans of what had been (and in some cases still were) overseas provinces of the Church of England presaged the development of a new language of primacy – primacy of honour but not of jurisdiction – which, as the twentieth century progressed, was increasingly to be applied to the See of Canterbury in respect of the whole Anglican Communion, including churches (such as the Scottish Episcopal Church and the churches that stemmed from the Episcopal Church in the USA) that had never been part of the Church of England.

As early as 1924, a former Archbishop of Melbourne, Henry Lowther Clarke, could speak of the See of Canterbury enjoying a 'universal feeling of reverence and affection' as '*the* Primatial See of the Anglican Communion' (emphasis added):

> The Primacy of Canterbury stands to-day securely based upon constitutional usages and owes its far-reaching influence to the spirit in which its experience and wisdom have been placed at the service of the Church in every Province and Diocese throughout the whole Anglican Communion.[35]

It was to be more than 40 years before this could be reflected in official documentation. At the 1948 Lambeth Conference the Committee on the

Anglican Communion noted firmly that 'Former Lambeth Conferences have wisely rejected proposals for a formal primacy of Canterbury'.[36] In 1968, however, the Committee on Renewal in Unity argued that

> Within the college of bishops it is evident that there must be a president. In the Anglican Communion this position is presently held by the occupant of the historic see of Canterbury, who enjoys a primacy of honour, not of jurisdiction. This primacy is found to involve, in a particular way, that care for all the churches which is shared by all the bishops.[37]

The See of Canterbury was described as 'the focal point of our communion'.[38] The relevant section of the 1978 report went further: now the Archbishop of Canterbury personally was spoken of as *the* focus of unity – Anglican unity was 'personally grounded in the loyal relationship of each of the Churches to the Archbishop of Canterbury who is freely recognized as the focus of unity'.[39]

By 1997 the development was complete; the Virginia Report of the Inter-Anglican Theological and Doctrinal Commission advanced beyond the language of Canterbury as 'the primatial see' and its occupant 'enjoy[ing] a primacy' to speak of the Archbishop of Canterbury as 'the Primate of the Communion'. Indeed, the emphasis had shifted so much from the primacy of the See of Canterbury and its occupant to an office of 'Primate of the Anglican Communion' that the question could be asked: 'Does the Primate of the Anglican Communion need to be the occupant of the See of Canterbury?'[40]

If 'primate' means 'bishop of the first see', this question must be answered in the affirmative: it is the primatial see that is important and that confers significance on its occupant. The Porvoo Common Statement has recently given fresh emphasis to the ecclesiological significance of historic sees.[41] The question probably arises from the fact that in some Anglican churches the term 'primate' has been applied to bishops who do not occupy a primatial see. In Australia, one of the metropolitans is chosen as primate, while the Primate of Canada, like the Presiding Bishop of the Episcopal Church in the USA, is a bishop who does not have a diocese. There would seem to be a tension between this approach and the understanding of episcopacy contained in the Porvoo Common Statement, which affirms that 'The continuity signified in the consecration of a bishop to episcopal ministry cannot be divorced from the continuity of life and witness of the diocese to which he is called'.[42]

The role of the Archbishop of Canterbury in representing and speaking on behalf of the Anglican Communion means that primates of other Anglican churches turn to him for support in times of difficulty and invite him to attend occasions of great celebration. His advice is also regularly sought, especially by African primates and those in troubled areas, who see him as a source of wisdom and encouragement. On occasion, the archbishop has privately offered advice to other primates on his own initiative.

Metropolitans, Primates and Provinces

At the same time as the recognition of a primatial role for the Archbishop of Canterbury was developing, the ancient office of metropolitan and the meaning of the term 'province' as a group of dioceses under the jurisdiction of a metropolitan gradually came to be lost sight of in the deliberations of the Lambeth Conferences. Resolution 52 of the 1930 conference had been clear about the distinction between a province and a church, approving 'the association of Dioceses or Provinces in the larger unity of a "national Church"'.[43] In fact, however, all of the autonomous Anglican churches formed after 1930 consisted of single provinces, and as their number grew, so did the solecism of referring to each member church of the Anglican Communion as 'a province', however many provinces it actually comprised. The relevant subsection of the 1978 Lambeth Conference Report used the terms 'Churches of the Anglican Communion' and 'Provinces' interchangeably, the latter term predominating.[44] Writing in 1985, Bishop John Howe (Executive Officer of the Anglican Communion from 1967 and Secretary General of the Anglican Consultative Council from 1971 to 1983) defined the member churches of the Communion as 'Provinces'. (He did concede, however, that 'Some of the Provinces are themselves composed of smaller areas which . . . for convenience, and to accord with local terminology, may also be termed provinces'.[45])

The 1930 conference had been equally clear about the distinction between a metropolitan (who has jurisdiction) and a presiding bishop (who, as first among equals, does not): when a province was formed, 'The Metropolitan or Presiding Bishop should thereupon notify all Metropolitans and Presiding Bishops in the Anglican Communion'.[46] The 1968 Lambeth Conference could still refer to 'the Metropolitans',[47] and the 1978 report made one reference to 'metropolitical authority' (that of the Archbishop of Canterbury over extra-provincial dioceses),[48] but the index to the 345-page report of the 1988 conference, which lists 23 references to 'primate(s)' and 'primacy', does not include the word 'metropolitan' or any of its cognates. By 1978 the leading bishop of each member church was described as a primate, whether he was in fact a primate, a metropolitan or merely a presiding bishop, and the meeting of such bishops was referred to as the 'Primates Committee'.[49]

These changes were reflected in the lists of bishops printed in the successive Lambeth Conference reports. Until 1930 each report included a list of bishops 'arranged according to provinces', the senior bishop of each province being listed first and described as 'Metropolitan', 'Presiding Bishop', etc. In 1948, 1958 and 1968 the list was arranged by churches (except for the Provinces of Canterbury and York, which were still listed separately); in each case the senior bishop was listed first, followed by any other archbishops. In 1978, however, the bishops of each church were listed alphabetically by see, the archbishops being simply distinguished by (Abp) after their names. This development reached its culmination with the report of the 1988 conference, which contained a list of 'The Primates of the Anglican Communion' in which the names of the occupants of two of the Communion's oldest primatial sees, York and Dublin, were not to be found. The Church of England was listed as an 'Anglican Province', with two 'internal provinces', while an asterisk against the name of a bishop was said to indicate 'Head of Internal Province' (the term 'metropolitan' having been completely forgotten). Thus the 95th Archbishop of York, Primate of England and Metropolitan, was listed last among the diocesan bishops of the Church England, as 'York Y * J. S. Habgood'. In everyday parlance 'primacy' implies 'pre-eminence', but in the Anglican Communion, it seems, the first shall be last.

In fact, the single term 'internal province' has been used to describe quite different realities. The Episcopal Church in the USA (ECUSA) was, after its formation, divided for administrative convenience into internal provinces that have no ecclesiological significance and over which laypeople may preside. It has no metropolitan(s); diocesan bishops are consecrated by the presiding bishop but do not owe obedience to him or any other bishop. The groupings of dioceses in America are not 'provinces' in the traditional sense of a body of dioceses under the jurisdiction of a metropolitan, and are quite different from, for example, the Provinces of Canterbury and York, as ancient provinces of the catholic Church which combine to form the Church of England. Another complicating factor is that whereas in the past there were commonly a number of provinces within a single national church, some of the newer provinces of the Anglican Communion comprise several nations.

C: Ecumenical implications

The story of how the use of the term 'primacy' has changed and developed within the Anglican Communion may have some intrinsic interest, but it is also of relevance to the ecumenical discussion of the primacy of the Bishop of Rome for which Pope John Paul II has called. Anglican reflections on primacy have a tendency to be influenced by the recent usage of the word within the Anglican Communion. The 'primacy' currently enjoyed and exercised by the Archbishop of Canterbury in the context of the Anglican Communion makes it easy for Anglican commentators to sympathize with a primacy of honour and presidency, with the primate as the focus and even to some extent the spokesman of the churches. However, because the Archbishop of Canterbury has no jurisdiction over the autonomous churches that make up the Communion, concentration on his Anglican Communion role often makes the notion of primatial jurisdiction seem alien to what commentators might call 'the ethos of Anglicanism'. This tendency is strengthened by the fact that many of the bishops in the Anglican Communion who are described as 'primates' have a similar position within their own churches – one of presidency without jurisdiction.

It is here that the primacy of the Archbishops of Canterbury and York within England is of importance. As we have seen, they not only have a metropolitical jurisdiction 'at all times', with decision-making powers in certain matters, but canon law even makes provision for them in some circumstances to exercise ordinary jurisdiction in the other dioceses of their respective provinces. To be consistent with the polity of their own church, Anglicans who oppose the attachment of jurisdiction to universal primacy have to show why jurisdiction, and in some circumstances even ordinary jurisdiction, is appropriate at the provincial level but not at the universal level.

Another reason why national primacy and metropolitical jurisdiction tend to be neglected in Anglican–Roman Catholic discussions of primacy is that in the Roman Catholic Church today the provincial structure is weak and in some countries has effectively fallen into disuse. Structures at the national level remain underdeveloped, and ecclesiological significance is ascribed primarily to the individual dioceses and to Rome. In the Roman Catholic Church as presently constituted, it can seem that little of ecclesiological significance exists in the space between universal jurisdiction and the jurisdiction of the diocesan bishop. In many countries there is now no bishop who is perceived as being, by virtue of his see, the Roman Catholic primate.

The real area for debate with the Roman Catholic Church would therefore appear to be that of subsidiarity. Which primatial powers need to be exercised above the provincial and national levels? And on which occasions and for what causes is it appropriate for the ordinary jurisdiction that normally belongs to a diocesan bishop to be exercised by a superior ordinary, at whatever level? The Anglican experience of primacy in the Provinces of Canterbury and York is of a real but sparingly used metropolitical jurisdiction at the provincial level, with the *temporary* exercise of ordinary jurisdiction remaining a possibility (and thus part of what defines the relationship between metropolitan and diocesans) but one of which use is in practice never made. This would suggest that with properly developed provincial, national and perhaps even regional levels, jurisdiction at the world level would rarely be invoked, and ordinary jurisdiction – direct intervention in the affairs of a diocese – hardly ever. The jurisdiction of a universal primate would remain very much a 'longstop', but it would be real. The comment of the English House of Bishops on papal jurisdiction in its response to *Ut Unum Sint* reflects this position:

> The claim that the Bishop of Rome has by divine institution ordinary, immediate and universal jurisdiction over the whole Church is seen by some as a threat to the integrity of the episcopal college and to the apostolic authority of the bishops, those brothers Peter was commanded to strengthen. This is not an argument for a primacy of honour only, or for the exclusion from a universal primacy of the authority necessary for a world-wide ministry in the service of unity.[50]

For members of the Church of England the Anglican Communion can serve as 'a window into catholicity', and the ministry of the Archbishop of Canterbury as its focus of unity makes Anglicans sympathetic to the need for such a 'personal service of unity' at the world level. Nonetheless, in other ways the Archbishop of Canterbury's role as 'Primate of the Anglican Communion', like the use of the term 'primate' in Anglican Communion circles more generally, gives only a partial impression of what primacy involves. While the Primacy of Canterbury gives Anglicans an insight into the need for primacy internationally, in ecumenical discussions it might be more helpful (or at least less confusing) to take, as the Anglican example of what primacy entails, the Primacy of the Archbishop of York.

D: Developments since 1998

This chapter was first published in July 1998, just before the Lambeth Conference of that year. Already in the 1990s, requests from within other churches of the Anglican Communion had induced Archbishop Carey to intervene to some degree in the affairs of those churches. Following the genocide in Rwanda, for example, four diocesan bishops abandoned their dioceses and went into exile. Archbishop Carey joined the Provincial Synod of the Church of the Province of Rwanda in attempting to persuade them to either return or resign. When this failed, in 1996 the Anglican Consultative Council stepped in, effectively claiming jurisdiction to resolve the impasse within the province. It passed a resolution in which it 'recognise[d] that those sees are now vacant, and request[ed] the authorities in those dioceses to communicate this to their respective bishops, and to record this action in their records', and 'urge[d] the Church leadership, in consequence, in consultation as necessary with the secular authorities, to set in motion legal procedures to elect bishops to those four vacant sees; and as soon as possible after these elections and consecrations, to call a Provincial Synod'. The council's resolution not only explicitly 'applaud[ed] and support[ed] the initiatives which have been taken by the Archbishop of Canterbury, the Secretary General and the Archbishop's special envoy', but also offered

> our continued support and encouragement to them to take such future initiatives as they think necessary, consulting where possible the Primates of the Communion, the ACC Standing Committee, and other representatives of the Communion whose specialist knowledge of the situation may aid the process.[51]

The 1998 Lambeth Conference

Reflecting on these events, the 1998 Lambeth Conference passed the following resolution:

IV.13 This Conference:

(a)   notes with gratitude the ministry of support which the Archbishop of Canterbury has been able to give in Sudan and Rwanda, and recognises that he is called upon to render assistance from time to time in a variety of situations;

(b)   in view of the very grave difficulties encountered in the internal affairs of some Provinces of the Communion, invites the Archbishop of Canterbury to appoint a Commission to make recommendations to the Primates and the Anglican Consultative Council, as to the exceptional circumstances and conditions under which, and the means by which, it would be appropriate for him to exercise an extra-ordinary ministry of episcopé (pastoral oversight), support and reconciliation with regard to the internal affairs of a Province other than his own for the sake of maintaining communion within the said Province and between the said Province and the rest of the Anglican Communion.[52]

In its resolution on the Virginia Report (the report of the Inter-Anglican Theological and Doctrinal Commission),[53] the conference 'request[ed] the Primates to initiate and monitor a decade of study in each province on the report, and in particular on "whether effective communication, at all levels, does not require appropriate instruments, with due safeguards, not only for legislation, but also for oversight'".[54] More specifically, another resolution sought to locate powers of intervention with the Primates' Meeting (over which the Archbishop of Canterbury presides): the conference

    (b)   ask[ed] that the Primates' Meeting, under the presidency of the Archbishop of Canterbury, include among its responsibilities . . . intervention in cases of exceptional emergency which are incapable of internal resolution within provinces, and giving of guidelines on the limits of Anglican diversity in submission to the sovereign authority of Holy Scripture and in loyalty to our Anglican tradition and formularies.

    (c)   recommend[ed] that these responsibilities should be exercised in sensitive consultation with the relevant provinces and with the Anglican Consultative Council (ACC) or in cases of emergency the Executive of the ACC and that, while not interfering with the juridical authority of the provinces, the exercise of these responsibilities by the Primates' Meeting should carry moral authority calling for ready acceptance throughout the Communion, and to this end it is further recommended that the Primates should meet more frequently than the ACC.[55]

Section III of the conference, from which this latter resolution came, clearly had in mind not so much the sort of situation that had prompted intervention by the Archbishop of Canterbury in Rwanda and the Sudan in the 1990s, but rather one in which a member church of the Communion went beyond the limits of 'Anglican diversity'. It commented:

The Anglican Communion has developed an ecclesiology without a centralized authority which acts juridically on behalf of all its member churches. No single Province or group of Provinces has the right to arbitrate on behalf of other Anglican Provinces, or determine the shape of their faithful discipleship. Rather, the nature of Anglicanism must draw on the resources of the whole Communion. On the other hand, without any sense of connectedness or accountability to the wider Communion, individual churches will lose touch, not only with each other, but with the Anglican and Christian tradition from which they took their origin. They could then cease to be churches incarnating the gospel within their own culture, and become prisoners of that culture or to their own past. Their life will be static and fixed, rather than responding to a dynamic and living tradition.

The measure to which the Anglican Communion can be faithful to its koinonia will determine whether local churches can claim to incarnate the universal Church in their own life. It will also determine its capacity to retain its own integrity as a tradition, as well as its ability to walk together with other Christian communions on the shared pilgrimage towards visible unity and the reign of God.[56]

Initially, nothing was done in response to these resolutions. However, in 2002–3 developments in the Episcopal Church in the United States of America prompted action both by Archbishops Carey and Williams and by the primates.

The Diocese of Pennsylvania, 2002

In September 2002 the Bishop of Pennsylvania, Charles E. Bennison, deposed an opponent of the ordination of women to the priesthood, the Revd Dr David L. Moyer, from holy orders. Archbishop Carey wrote to the Bishop of Fulham, John Broadhurst:

Thank you so much for your letter of 20 August concerning the impending deposition of Fr David Moyer, Chairman of Forward in Faith North America. As you are aware, I am watching these events with great anxiety and even now hope that we might persuade the bishop not to take this drastic action. I can confirm gladly that I have the highest regard for David and would have no hesitation in giving him permission to officiate in the Diocese of Canterbury. Indeed, I will go one step further to say that were he to seek a licence to officiate in the Province of Canterbury, I would be glad to offer it.[57]

His designated successor, Archbishop Williams of Wales, replied to a letter from Fr Geoffrey Kirk in similar vein:

As you probably know, I have spoken with Fr David on the phone and expressed my concern about the situation in which he has been placed. From what I know of him, I could see no objection to my granting Permission to Officiate in this diocese or considering him for a licence here if the circumstances arose. All I know of him suggests that he is not guilty of any moral or doctrinal delinquency, and is respected as a priest of disciplined life, personal spirituality and great teaching capacity . . . I hope this is some help. It is a worrying situation, and Fr David is in my prayers.[58]

In writing these letters, both archbishops had effectively intervened in the affairs of the Diocese of Pennsylvania, repudiating the expected deposition by the bishop of that diocese of one of his priests.

New Westminster, New Hampshire and the Windsor Report, 2003-4

The following year, five years after the 1998 Lambeth Conference, events began to unfold which, in the eyes of many, demonstrated the need for the Archbishop of Canterbury to exercise an international primatial ministry of unity, enunciating the consensus of the primates of the individual Anglican churches and exercising a degree of oversight over arrangements within them. First the Diocese of New Westminster (Canada) authorized a public rite for blessing of those in committed same-sex relationships; then the Diocese of New Hampshire elected as its new bishop Canon Gene Robinson, a priest in such a relationship, and his election was confirmed by the 74th General Convention of the Episcopal Church in the USA.

The Archbishop of Canterbury responded by calling an emergency meeting of the primates of the Anglican Communion and the moderators of the United Churches, which met at Lambeth Palace on 15 and 16 October 2003. In their statement[59] the primates commented 'that recent actions in New Westminster and in the Episcopal Church (USA) do not express the mind of our Communion as a whole, and these decisions jeopardise our sacramental fellowship with each other'. The primates went on to express 'a particular concern for those who in all conscience feel bound to dissent from the teaching and practice of their province in such matters'. In this connection, the statement (whose signatories included the Presiding Bishop of ECUSA) for the first time gave the Archbishop of Canterbury a specific role in the internal affairs of a church other than the Church of England:

> We call on the provinces concerned to make adequate provision
> for episcopal oversight of dissenting minorities within their own
> area of pastoral care *in consultation with the Archbishop of
> Canterbury on behalf of the Primates.* (italics added)

(The primates nonetheless re-affirmed 'the teaching of successive Lambeth Conferences that bishops must respect the autonomy and territorial integrity of dioceses and provinces other than their own'.) Finally, the primates renewed the 1998 Lambeth Conference's request to the Archbishop of Canterbury (in resolution IV.13 'to establish a commission to consider his own role in maintaining communion within and between provinces when grave difficulties arise', and asked that its remit be extended 'to include urgent and deep theological and legal reflection on the way in which the dangers we have identified at this meeting will have to be addressed'.

Such a commission began work in February 2004 under the chairmanship of the Archbishop of Armagh, Lord Eames. It became known as 'the Lambeth Commission on Communion'. Its terms of reference called upon it to report first on (1) the legal and theological implications of the developments in the USA and Canada, with (2) practical recommendations for maintaining the highest degree of communion possible. After making such a report, the commission was then

> 3. thereafter, as soon as practicable, and with particular reference to the issues raised in Section IV of the Report of the Lambeth Conference 1998, to make recommendations to the Primates and the Anglican Consultative Council, as to the exceptional circumstances and conditions under which, and the means by which, it would be appropriate for the Archbishop of Canterbury to exercise an extraordinary ministry of episcope (pastoral oversight), support and reconciliation with regard to the internal affairs of a province other than his own for the sake of maintaining communion with (*sic*) the said province and between the said province and the rest of the Anglican Communion.[60]

This wording repeated the relevant part of the resolution IV.13 of the 1998 Lambeth Conference (quoted on page 73 above) – except that in what was probably a typographic error 'with' was substituted for 'within' towards the end.

The commission's report on the first two of its terms of reference was published in October 2004 as *The Windsor Report*. This first report did also briefly address the role of the Archbishop of Canterbury within the Anglican Communion, ascribing to the occupant of the See of Canterbury not only a ministry as '*the* significant focus of unity' within the Communion (italics in original), but also an important teaching ministry on its behalf:

> The Commission believes . . . that the historic position of the Archbishopric of Canterbury must not be regarded as a figurehead, but as the central focus of both unity and mission within the Communion. The office has a very significant teaching role. As *the* significant focus of unity, mission and teaching, the Communion looks to the office of the Archbishop

to articulate the mind of the Communion especially in areas of controversy. The Communion should be able to look to the holder of this office to speak directly to any provincial situation on behalf of the Communion where this is deemed advisable.[61]

To avoid this leading to the archbishop feeling 'exposed and left to act entirely alone', the commission further recommended that a Council of Advice be established to support him in the development of this particular ministry.

This initial response by the commission to the 1998 Lambeth Conference's request to the Archbishop of Canterbury, renewed by the primates in October 2003, that he 'establish a commission to consider his own role in maintaining communion within and between provinces when grave difficulties arise' met with a somewhat lukewarm response from the primates when they considered the Windsor Report at the Primates' Meeting held in February 2005. While their *communiqué* welcomed 'the general thrust of the Windsor Report', it expressed hesitation about the commission's recommendations concerning the role of the Archbishop of Canterbury:

> We also have further questions concerning the role of the Archbishop of Canterbury, and of a Council of Advice (The Windsor Report, paragraphs 108-112). While we welcome the ministry of the Archbishop of Canterbury as that of one who can speak to us as *primus inter pares* about the realities we face as a Communion, we are cautious of any development which would seem to imply the creation of an international jurisdiction which could override our proper provincial autonomy. We ask the Archbishop of Canterbury to explore ways of consulting further on these matters.[62]

Thus there continues to be a lack of agreement as to whether the Archbishop of Canterbury's international role should be enhanced, and if so how. None the less, it seems clear that the issue will remain on the agenda, whether for consideration by the Lambeth Commission in fulfilment of the third of its terms of reference, or in the 'ways of consulting further' which the Archbishop has now been asked to explore – or by the next Lambeth Conference, when it reviews the implementation of the resolutions of 1998, including Resolution IV. 13.

6

Territoriality, communion and parallel episcopates[1]

Both in the context of the events in the USA and Canada which led to the establishment of the Lambeth Commission and in the debates about the ordination of women to the priesthood and episcopate, the Anglican Communion and the Church of England are confronted by a complex of issues involving territoriality (the Church's territorial nature), communion (the relationship between parts of the Church in different territories), and the possibility of parallel episcopates (the presence of two bishops, or two separate groups of bishops, within the same territory). These include the following:

- What does being 'in communion' mean?
- Can individuals, or individual parishes or dioceses, declare themselves to be in or out of communion with others?
- How has the Church of England entered into communion with other churches, and what do those precedents suggest about the possibility of withdrawing from communion?
- Is it acceptable for there to be two separate sets of bishops, albeit in some degree of communion with each other, within the same territory?
- If the ordination of women to the episcopate were judged to require the provision of episcopal oversight alternative to that of the diocesan bishop, or even a third province, how could this be squared with the territorial nature of episcopacy in the Church of England? Would this involve 'parallel episcopates', and if so, what would be the degree of communion between them?

This chapter seeks to illuminate these and other related questions from the perspectives both of the history and law of the Church of England and also of ecumenical discussions about the visible unity of the Church.

A: Territoriality

The extent of the Church of England and its Provinces

To set the context for an examination of 'territoriality' as the Church of England understands it, it will be well to begin by considering the extent of the territory of the Church of England as a whole and of its two provinces. In law, the Church of England is 'that branch of the Holy Catholic and Apostolic Church which was founded in England when the English were gradually converted to Christianity between the years 597 and 686'.[2] (The Church was, of course, present in England before St Augustine's mission, but it is to that mission that the identity of the Church of England as a corporate entity may be traced back.) In the 1530s Henry VIII nationalized that English branch of the Church catholic. (He then proceeded to privatize many of its assets, but that is another story.) The preamble to the Act in Restraint of Appeals (1533) asserted that 'this realm of England is an empire', and furthermore that 'that part of the said body politic called the spirituality, now being usually called the English Church', possessed such 'knowledge, integrity, and sufficiency of number' that it was 'also at this hour sufficient and meet of itself, without the intermeddling of any exterior person or persons, to declare and determine all such doubts and to administer all such offices and duties as to their rooms spiritual doth appertain'; there was no need for appeals to Rome.[3] Thus the island church was viewed as being entire of itself, rather than 'a piece of the Continent, a part of the main'; juridicially, it was self-sufficient. It was no longer to be subject to the pope.

The Supremacy of the Crown Act 1534 declared the king 'the only supreme head in earth of the Church of England called *Anglicana Ecclesia*'.[4] (Elizabeth I's Act of Supremacy 1559 replaced this with the statement that the queen was 'the only supreme governor of this realm and of all other her Highness's dominions and countries, as well in all spiritual or ecclesiastical things or causes as temporal'.[5]) The term 'Church *of* England' was not novel: this is how '*Ecclesia Anglicana*' was normally translated from the later fourteenth century onwards.[6] What was new was not the church or its name, but its structural separation from continental Christianity; in this sense, Henry VIII had 'taken the Church of England out of Europe'.[7] Yngve Brilioth commented:

> 'The separation of the English Church from Rome in the
> sixteenth century is rather a phase of the nationalist movement
> of breaking away from the undivided Latin Church, which began
> in the last centuries of the Middle Ages, than part of the great
> continental Church Reformation.'[8]

Henry VIII did not use his newly acquired supremacy to enforce major liturgical change. He died in 1547, more than 17 years after the meeting of the Reformation Parliament, never having heard Mass other than in Latin. It was under his son, Edward VI, that two successive Books of Common Prayer were to be enforced by Acts of Uniformity. The concluding paragraph of Article XXXIV of the Thirty-nine Articles of Religion, formulated in 1563, explained the authority for liturgical changes as follows: 'Every particular or national Church hath authority to ordain, change, and abolish, ceremonies or rites of the Church ordained only by man's authority'. There was no claim that the English Church's way of worshipping was right for other nations; these were things that every national church should decide for itself. Similarly, there was no attempt to export the English Reformation. Unlike the German and Swiss Reformers, who accepted invitations to reform the Church in other territories and kingdoms, the English Reformers did not seek to spread 'Anglicanism' into continental Europe or beyond.[9] Indeed, not only was there no attempt to export the English Reformation; there was also at that time no such concept as 'Anglicanism' to be exported: Diarmaid MacCulloch remarks of the distinctive strand of western Christianity called 'Anglicanism' that 'it is very doubtful whether one can find it at all in the English Reformation of the sixteenth century'.[10] Thus the Church of England was not expansionist.

Nonetheless, the Church of England was never confined to England – nor even to the realm of England, which from 1536 included Wales (already part of the Province of Canterbury); royal dominions beyond the kingdom were also included. As the courts confirmed in 1521,[11] the Isle of Man was not part of the realm of England, yet the Diocese of Sodor and Man, formerly in the Province of Nidaros (Trondheim, Norway), became part of the Province of York in 1541.[12] The Channel Islands, which continued to belong to the English sovereign as Duke of Normandy but were similarly not part of the realm of England, were definitively and finally detached from the Diocese of Coutances in 1569, though their annexation to the Diocese of Winchester was for many years a dead letter. (Presbyterian church government and worship held sway in the islands, and episcopacy was restored in Jersey only in 1620 and in Guernsey not until 1662.[13]) The Channel Islands continue to be 'annexed to' the Diocese of Winchester, not part of it; presumably, their relationship to the Province of Canterbury is the same. Under Henry VIII and Edward VI, the separated English church even had toe-holds in continental Europe in the shape of Calais (which was not lost to the English Crown until 1558) and, briefly, Boulogne (held from 1544 until 1550).[14]

As we saw in Chapter 3, from the eighteenth century onwards the Church of England included overseas dioceses;[15] though this Colonial Church was, initially, under the jurisdiction of the Archbishop of Canterbury, it did not form part of the Province of Canterbury. As mentioned in Chapter 5, the letters patent that constituted the See of Australia in 1836 provided:

> The bishop of the said see of Australia and his successors shall be subject to the . . . Archbishop of Canterbury . . . in the same manner as any bishop of any see within the province of Canterbury, in Our Kingdom of England, is under the authority

of the archiepiscopal see of the province of Canterbury and the archbishop thereof.[16]

Thus the jurisdiction of the Archbishop of Canterbury extended beyond his Province of Canterbury. This indicates that the Province of Canterbury is not defined as consisting of those people, parishes and clergy that are under the metropolitical jurisdiction of the Archbishop of Canterbury; rather, it is a territory which today simply comprises part of England but in the past also included the whole of Wales.

Almost all of the dioceses that formerly comprised the Colonial Church have become independent of the Church of England and ceased to be under the jurisdiction of the Archbishop of Canterbury. One exception is the Diocese of Gibraltar. Founded in 1842 as a colonial diocese for Anglicans living on the shores of the Mediterranean, it has gone in the opposite direction from the others. In 1980 it was united with the Jurisdiction of Northern and Central Europe (the chaplaincies in that area which were under the jurisdiction of the Bishop of London and the direct episcopal oversight of his suffragan, the Bishop of Fulham) to form the Diocese in Europe. Under its constitution, the diocese is 'deemed to be part of the Province of Canterbury'.[17] Again, this indicates that the Province of Canterbury is a territory; that territory does not include continental Europe and the Diocese in Europe is therefore not part of the Province of Canterbury but is 'deemed to be' part of it. (It may be noted, in passing, that the name of the diocese reflects a view that the other dioceses of the Church of England are not 'in Europe'.)

Thus, since its separation from Rome, the Church of England has always extended beyond England and indeed beyond the realm of England. However, while the Province of York includes the Isle of Man, the Province of Canterbury actually consists today only of the southern part of England, though the Channel Islands are annexed to it and the Diocese in Europe is deemed to be part of it.

Territoriality and parallel jurisdictions

Though it has never been confined to a single territory, the Church of England is a territorial church. An English diocese is defined as consisting of a certain territory; it is, in law, not a body of people who worship in Anglican churches or whose names appear in Anglican electoral rolls, but a geographical area. Thus, for example, the Diocese of Truro is defined in the *Church of England Year Book* as comprising 'Cornwall; the Isles of Scilly; one parish in Devon'. Similarly, the bishops are not, and do not see themselves as, only the bishops of those who worship in their churches. This is reflected in the language of Canon C 18

'Of Diocesan Bishops': 'Every bishop is the chief pastor of *all* that are within his diocese, as well laity as clergy . . . Every bishop has within his diocese jurisdiction as Ordinary *except in places* and over persons exempt by law and custom.'[18] Furthermore, in England every ecclesiastical parish has a defined (and mapped) geographical boundary, so that it can be said with certainty to which parish every street and every field in England belongs.

Again, the Diocese in Europe is the exception that proves the rule. Unlike the English dioceses, the Diocese in Europe does not consist of an area (or indeed of territorial parishes) but of chaplaincy congregations within an area. Its constitution says that

> The Diocese . . . incorporates the former Diocese of Gibraltar and the Jurisdiction of Northern and Central Europe and consists of the chaplaincies and congregations in that area which shall be designated from time to time by the Diocesan Bishop.[19]

Writing in 1917, the then Bishop of Gibraltar, Henry Knight, described his diocese as 'a diocese of persons, not a geographical area'.[20] Indeed, even the use of the term 'diocese' for the collection of congregations under that bishop's jurisdiction was not uncontroversial. Bishop Knight wrote that it was necessary for Charles Sandford (bishop from 1874 to 1903) to 'consistently set forth that he was a Diocesan Bishop, and that his charge was a "Diocese". He did not use the word "Diocese" as implying territorial jurisdiction. His episcopal charge was one of souls, not of places or territory.'[21] Therefore, the comment attributed to a pope meeting a Bishop of Gibraltar: 'Bishop, I believe I am in your Diocese!',[22] may have been humorous but it was not accurate: in Rome, only the members of the English chaplaincy congregation were in the Bishop of Gibraltar's diocese.

In continental Europe there are no fewer than four Anglican jurisdictions. Three of them are under the metropolitical jurisdiction of the Archbishop of Canterbury: the Diocese in Europe, the Lusitanian Church (Portuguese Episcopal Church) and the Spanish Reformed Episcopal Church. The fourth is the Convocation of American Episcopal Churches in Europe. These four jurisdictions are 'parallel jurisdictions' in that they exist side by side in the same territory. (More precisely, each of the three others exists side by side with the Diocese in Europe in part of the territory which the latter covers – two of the churches are present only in Portugal and Spain respectively, while the American Convocation has eight 'parishes' and four 'missions' in Belgium, France, Germany, Italy and Switzerland.) They are 'parallel jurisdictions' but they are not 'overlapping jurisdictions' (as is sometimes claimed), since the Diocese in Europe claims jurisdiction only over the chaplaincies that comprise it and not over the territory in general.

Enclaves and peculiar jurisdictions

Today, the English dioceses form compact and self-contained territories; their boundaries may appear odd, in that they no longer match civil boundaries or correspond to social realities, but in most cases there is a single boundary and everywhere within that boundary is part of the diocese. It is therefore sometimes assumed that it is somehow in the nature of a territorial diocese that all of its parishes should be contiguous. This is not the case. In the past, it was not unknown for parishes or groups of parishes belonging to one diocese to be entirely surrounded by the parishes of another diocese or other dioceses. Perhaps the largest and latest example of this was the 32 parishes of the Archdeaconry of Croydon, which, even though they were situated between the Diocese of Rochester and the Diocese of Southwark, formed part of the Diocese of Canterbury until they were transferred to Southwark on 1 January 1985.

Parishes, places and institutions may also be exempt from the jurisdiction of the ecclesiastical unit in which they are situated. This is known as a 'peculiar jurisdiction'.[23] The most minor example is that of 'extra-parochial places', which are outside the jurisdiction of the parish in which they are located (though under that of the diocesan bishop, and therefore arguably not strictly peculiars at all, in that they and the parishes in which they are situated are both under the jurisdiction of the same Ordinary).[24] At the other end of the spectrum are the royal peculiars, which are not only extra-diocesan but also extra-provincial, and are subject only to the Crown. They are therefore 'like mini-provinces in their own right, with the Ordinary being in an equivalent position to the archbishop in his province'.[25] The most well-known examples are Westminster Abbey and St George's Chapel, Windsor. A 'peculiar' need not be a physical place or even a building; it may be an institution. An example of this is the Chapel Royal (the body of clergy, singers and vestry officers appointed to serve the spiritual needs of the sovereign, which is distinct from the physical 'Chapels Royal' such as that at St James's Palace).

Most peculiar jurisdictions were abolished by Orders in Council made between 1836 and 1852,[26] and anomalies such as the Archdeaconry of Croydon have been resolved. When discussing issues of territoriality it is important to remember, however, that for most of its history the map of the Church of England would have been more of a patchwork than it is today. The consolidation of dioceses' territory so that all of their parishes are contiguous is the product of modern rationalization, and the royal peculiars remain as testimony that in a territorial church it is perfectly possible for a church, institution or district to be exempt from the jurisdiction of the diocesan bishop and archbishop whose diocese and province surround it. Thus, leaving aside whether such a development would be desirable on other grounds, it would by no means be unprecedented for parishes physically situated in one diocese to form part of another diocese and thereby fall under the jurisdiction of its diocesan bishop.

B: Communion

Much has been written in a theological vein about the concept of communion. Expositions of it may be found, for example, in the paper *Being in Communion*,[27] which was published in 1993 as a supporting document to what became the Episcopal Ministry Act of Synod, and in the House of Bishops' Occasional Paper *Bishops in Communion: Collegiality in the Service of the Koinonia of the Church.*[28] There is no need to try to repeat or summarize that theology here, but it should be noted as part of the context in which questions of communion must be viewed. It may be useful to draw attention to one distinction, however. In its broadest sense, 'communion' is the relationship of *koinonia*, or fellowship, in which all the baptized (in this world and the next) stand with each other by virtue of their baptism. This relationship is described in the creeds as 'the communion of saints' and referred to in the Collect for All Saints' Day ('O Almighty God, who hast knit together thine elect in one communion and fellowship, in the mystical body of thy Son Christ our Lord . . .'). In this book, however, the term 'communion' refers not to this baptismal communion but to the (related but distinct) concept of ecclesial communion.

Ecclesial Communion

It is important to remember that (as the term itself suggests) ecclesial communion is a relationship between churches, because this shows that it is not for individuals or pressure groups to declare themselves to be in or out of communion either with other individuals or groups or with whole churches. People are 'in communion' in this sense because of their membership of a church that is 'in communion'. The only way for individuals to change the relationships of communion that they are in is to leave the church to which they belong and join another church with whose relationships of communion they are more in agreement. While it is true that individual Christians are in communion with Christians beyond their own diocese through their diocesan bishop, in the Church of England diocesan bishops are not independent operators but members of the college of bishops of a province and a national church, whose canons bind them to corporate decisions in matters of communion. Thus, as far as the Church of England is concerned, 'ecclesial communion' is about relationships between the Church of England and other churches, and not in the first instance between local churches (dioceses), still less between the congregations of parish churches. As will be shown below, it is clear from both history and law that the Church of England is in communion as a church, and that it is in communion not with individual dioceses but with other churches (the Church of Norway, the Church in Wales, etc.). Parishes cannot declare themselves to be in or out of communion with overseas churches and dioceses, and though diocesan bishops are the 'vehicles' of ecclesial communion, they too cannot individually declare their dioceses to be in or out of communion with overseas churches.

Reduced to the minimum, the 'cash value' of ecclesial communion may be said to consist in an interchangeability of members and ministers. If members of a church that is in communion with the Church of England move to England, they are automatically treated as members of the Church of England, and may receive the sacraments, without needing to be 'received into the Church of England'. (This goes beyond mere eucharistic hospitality, whereby members of one church are admitted to communion in the other as guests.) Similarly, bishops of such a church may (if given archiepiscopal and episcopal permission) minister as such in the Church of England without needing to be ordained afresh; bishops of such a church may (if invited to do so) participate in the consecration of bishops in the Church of England. Furthermore, the relationship is mutual: the other church accords the same rights to members and clergy of the Church of England.

There is increasing support for the view that ecclesial communion should involve more than this basic minimum. It should, it is argued, also involve 'bonds of communion' – structures for consultation and, indeed, joint decision-making by the representatives of the individual churches (especially their bishops, who are the representatives *par excellence* of their local churches). In order to be 'bonds', these bonds need to have some 'binding' character; the representatives and the churches they represent need to be 'bound' by the decisions – discussions should not, as the Germans would say, be *unverbindlich*. The structures of the Anglican Communion are widely believed to be deficient in this regard. In 1997 the Virginia Report of the Inter-Anglican Theological Commission noted that 'Questions are asked about whether we can go on as a world Communion with morally authoritative but not juridically binding decision-making structures at the international level'.[29] (Such questions were not new: in his opening address to the Lambeth Conference back in 1988, Archbishop Runcie challenged Anglicans to consider 'a minimum structuring of our mutual interdependence – that which is actually *required* for the maintenance of communion and no more'.[30]) The questions intensified in 2003 when the Presiding Bishop of the Episcopal Church (USA) consecrated Canon Gene Robinson as Bishop of New Hampshire despite a statement by the Primates Meeting of the Anglican Communion that 'if his consecration proceeds . . . the future of the Communion itself will be put in jeopardy'.[31]

The terminology of Communion

The report of the 1958 Lambeth Conference's Committee on Church Unity and the Church Universal rightly commented that 'since 1931 the terminology to describe various degrees of inter-Church relationship has been inconsistent and confusing'.[32] That confusion persisted into the 1980s. Terms such as 'communion', 'full communion', 'intercommunion' and 'full intercommunion' have been used, with a shifting variety of meanings. As we shall see, however, English law simply refers to churches as being 'in communion' (or 'not in communion') with the Church of England.

In recent years, use of the term 'full communion' has also been avoided in the Church of England's ecumenical work. It does not appear in the Porvoo Common Statement, for example.[33] One reason for this is that the term 'full communion' has become problematic because of the ordination of women to the priesthood and *a fortiori* the episcopate in some Anglican churches. Thus there are priests of some Anglican churches who are effectively not recognized as priests in other Anglican churches, and women ordained to the episcopate in other Anglican churches cannot minister as bishops in England, nor are those ordained deacon or priest by them allowed to minister as such here (because to allow them to do so would be to pre-empt the Church of England's own discussion of the rightness or otherwise of the ordination of women to the episcopate).[34] These developments mean that the communion between the Church of England and churches with women bishops cannot be said to be 'full'. These churches are 'in communion' with the Church of England, but that communion is 'impaired' by their ordination of ministers whose orders cannot be recognized in England. Indeed, following the ordination of women to the priesthood in England, accompanied by provisions permitting parishes and individuals to refuse their ministrations, the communion within the Church of England itself may similarly be said to be 'impaired'. (Another reason for avoiding the term 'full communion' is a recognition that communion on earth is always likely, in a broader sense, to be imperfect; looked at in this way, 'full communion' is an eschatological concept.) The term 'intercommunion' is also problematic, since today it is usually heard as implying mutual eucharistic hospitality (welcoming members of other churches to receive communion) without necessarily involving an interchangeability of ministries (allowing ministers of other churches to preside at Holy Communion).

The legal position regarding Communion

The Church of England has no law that addresses the question of ecclesiastical communion in its own right, but aspects of two elements of the 'cash value' of communion are addressed in the Overseas and Other Clergy (Ministry and Ordination) Measure 1967 (which deals with the interchangeability of ministries) and the Church Representation Rules (which touch on the interchangeability of members). The Overseas Clergy Measure refers to 'a Church in Communion with the Church of England' and provides that 'if any question arises whether, for the purposes of this Measure, a Church is in Communion with the Church of England . . . it shall be determined by the Archbishops of Canterbury and York, whose decision shall be conclusive'.[35] The Church Representation Rules similarly provide that 'if any question arises whether a Church is a Church in communion with the Church of England, it shall be conclusively determined for the purposes of these rules by the Archbishops of Canterbury and York'.[36] Although in both instances the determination is made only for the purposes of the legislation in question, since the right to determine rests with the archbishops in each case, and since interchangeability of ministries and interchangeability of members taken together are the 'cash value' of ecclesial communion, it may be said that for all practical purposes it is for the Archbishops of Canterbury and York to determine which churches the Church of England is in communion with, and that their determination is conclusive. The archbishops must, nonetheless, have some basis for making a determination. That basis is now provided by resolutions of the General Synod.

Entering into communion: twentieth-century precedents

On five occasions during the twentieth century (the first in which such questions arose) the Church of England decided to enter into communion (as we would now call it, though various terms were used) with other churches. In each case, communion was established by (or as a result of) resolutions of the Convocations of Canterbury and York (before 1970) or resolutions of the General Synod (since 1970, when the Convocations' powers to regulate relations with other churches passed to the General Synod). These instances were as follows:

1.   *Old Catholic Churches of the Union of Utrecht:* separate resolutions of the four Houses of the Convocations, 20–22 January 1932:

     That this House approves of the following statements agreed on between [Old Catholic and Anglican representatives] . . . And this House agrees to the establishment of Intercommunion between the Church of England and the Old Catholics on these terms.[37]

2.   *Philippine Independent Church, Spanish Reformed Episcopal Church, Lusitanian Church (Portuguese Episcopal Church)*: separate resolutions of the two Houses of the Convocation of Canterbury and of the Convocation of York in respect of each church, 8 October 1963:

That this House (*York*: Convocation) agrees to the establishment of Full Communion between the Church of England and [*name of church*] on the basis of mutual acceptance of the following Concordat.[38]

3. *Church of North India, Church of Pakistan*: resolution of the General Synod, 3 May 1972:

That the proposal to enter into full communion with the Church of North India and the Church of Pakistan be finally approved.[39]

4. *Mar Thoma Syrian Church of Malabar*: resolution of the General Synod, 7 November 1974:

That this Synod, noting that the Mar Thoma Church is a true part of the Church Universal, holding the catholic faith and possessing the apostolic ministry of bishops, priests and deacons, resolves to enter into Communion with that Church and requests the Presidents to communicate this decision to the Metropolitan Mar Juhanon Mar Thoma.[40]

5. *Evangelical-Lutheran Church of Finland, Evangelical-Lutheran Church of Iceland, Church of Norway, Church of Sweden, Estonian Evangelical-Lutheran Church, Evangelical-Lutheran Church of Lithuania*: resolution of the General Synod, 9 July 1995:

That the Porvoo Declaration be finally approved.[41]

(The Archbishops of Canterbury and York had indicated that they would take final approval of the declaration as their basis for treating those churches named in the preamble to the declaration which themselves approved the declaration as 'churches in communion with the Church of England'.[42])

The Church of South India: A special case

The case of the Church of South India (CSI) was more complex than the first four of these five cases because of the presence in that church of non-episcopally ordained ministers (we shall return briefly to the case of the Porvoo Agreement below). Convocation resolutions about the CSI were passed in 1950.[43] These were replaced in July 1955 by further, more generous, resolutions.[44] Resolution 3 of the 1955 resolutions regulated the (incomplete) interchangeability of ministries and members between the two churches. The resolutions did not categorize the relationship, but using present-day terminology it could be categorized as one of 'restricted' communion (because the CSI's non-episcopally ordained ministers were excluded from the interchangeability of ministries).

In 1972 Archbishop Michael Ramsey wished the General Synod to consider the Church of England's relationship with the CSI in advance of that church's Silver Jubilee in the autumn of that year. In November 1972 the Synod duly gave final approval to a resolution which for the first time described the relationship established by the Convocation resolutions as one of 'communion' and adjusted the details of the resolutions.[45] (The resolution purported to permit episcopally ordained CSI presbyters to minister in other churches in England while also ministering as priests in the Church of England, but it may be doubted whether in view of the terms of the Overseas Clergy Measure and the canons the Synod in fact had the power to do this.) The Synod resolution did not use the term 'full communion', the Board for Mission and Unity having rejected that term on the grounds that it would be ambiguous to speak of 'full communion' and then qualify this by saying that non-episcopally ordained ministers of the CSI would not be able to exercise their ministry in the Church of England.

However, at the general approval stage in July 1972 the Synod had also passed an amendment, moved by Robert Runcie (then Bishop of St Albans), to a preliminary motion. The amendment requested the House of Bishops 'to consider how the Church of England and the Church of South India may now be joined in a relationship of Full Communion'.[46] The House's report (GS 134) was debated by the Synod in February 1973. The House did not feel able to recommend legislation allowing non-episcopally ordained CSI presbyters to minister as priests in the Church of England 'for reasons which are theological, pastoral and practical' (para. 9). Motions were nonetheless moved on behalf of the House by Bishop Runcie. One of these (arguably otiose in view of the November 1972 resolution quoted above) was that

> This Synod resolves to enter into communion with the Church of
> South India subject to regulations, which may from time to time
> be made by the General Synod.

A further motion set out regulations governing the relationship, (a) allowing members of the CSI to be placed on electoral rolls and hold office, (b) allowing episcopally ordained CSI ministers to minister in the Church of England, and (c) stating that non-episcopally ordained CSI ministers were prevented by canon law and the law of England from celebrating Holy Communion in the Church of England. However, it was pointed out in debate that the proposed regulations did not change the existing position in any way, but that unlike the earlier resolutions, which mentioned only the positive permissions, part (c) had the effect of 'rubbing in' the bar on non-episcopally ordained ministers. In view of this, Bishop Runcie withdrew the motion.

The matter was reopened in November 1984, when Runcie, by now Archbishop of Canterbury, presented to the Synod *Relations with the Church of South India: A Report by the House of Bishops* (GS 650). Noting that there were still non-episcopally ordained presbyters in the Church of South India and that there were now also women presbyters, this sought to redefine the term 'full communion' as involving interchangeability of ministers subject to the canon law of the churches concerned. Archbishop Runcie accordingly moved 'That this Synod now declares the Church of England to be in Full Communion with the Church of South India in accordance with the terms of the definition set out in paragraph 7 of this Report'. However, the Synod resisted this attempt to resolve the problem of the lack of full communion by redefining the term 'full communion', and instead passed an amendment moved by the Ven. Peter Dawes (Archdeacon of West Ham, later Bishop of Derby) to replace the words after 'now' with

> desires the Church of England to enter into Full Communion with the Church of South India in accordance with the traditional meaning of that term (as expressed in the 1958 Lambeth Conference Report).[47]

To 'enter into Full Communion with the Church of South India in accordance with the traditional meaning of that term' would have involved a change in the law to allow non-episcopally ordained presbyters and women priests to minister as priests in the Church of England. Not surprisingly, nothing further was done.

The controversies of 1972–84 about the classification of the relationship with the Church of South India now seem arcane and trivial. The ordination of women to the episcopate in certain Anglican churches means that the relationship between them and the Church of England can no longer be described as one of 'Full Communion . . . in accordance with the traditional meaning of that term'. That situation arguably made it easier for the Church of England in 1995 to enter into a relationship (described as 'communion', not 'full communion') with Lutheran churches, some of which have ministers who are not eligible to minister in the Church of England (a small number of ministers ordained by cathedral deans in Norway, a small number of ministers originally ordained in non-episcopal Lutheran churches and a relatively small but growing number of ministers ordained by women bishops).

Ceasing to be in communion: past instances

There has been no instance of the Church of England withdrawing from communion with another church. The archbishops have, however, from time to time determined that certain churches are not in communion with the Church of England. The example of this that most readily comes to mind is the case of the Church of England in South Africa. The Church of England in South Africa claims identity with the Church of England in Natal, which originated in the schism between Bishop Colenso of Natal and his followers and the Church of the Province of South Africa. After the schism, the Church of England continued to be in communion with the Church of the Province. Accordingly, by ceasing to be part of the Church of the Province, this group ceased to be in communion with the Church of England. Thus this is not a case of the Church of England breaking with a church, but of a bishop and his followers ceasing to be part of a church in communion and thereby ceasing to be in communion. Another instance of the ending of communion with the Church of England came about in 1947, when four dioceses withdrew from the Church of India, Burma and Ceylon to join in forming the Church of South India. The dioceses concerned automatically ceased to be in communion with the Church of England, because they were no longer part of the church with which the Church of England was in communion. Eventually, however, as we have seen, the Church of England entered into communion with the Church of South India.

Withdrawing from communion

Neither of these cases offers a precedent for the Church of England deciding to withdraw from communion with another church, but some conclusions may be drawn from twentieth-century history. The main one is that on each occasion in the twentieth century when the Church of England entered into communion with another church or group of churches, it did so as a result of a resolution of the Convocations or of the General Synod. If a comparable procedure were adopted in the case of withdrawing from communion, the archbishops would not declare a church to be no longer in communion with the Church of England without obtaining a General Synod resolution calling for this. That said, however, legally it is quite clear that the decision as to whether a church is or is not in communion with the Church of England rests with the archbishops and not with the Synod.

A second conclusion is that all the precedents involve entering into communion with churches, rather than with individual dioceses. The Overseas Clergy Measure and the Church Representation Rules speak only of 'churches in communion with the Church of England' or 'churches not in communion with the Church of England'. It is churches and the orders of churches that are recognized, not individual dioceses or individual bishops. This does not mean that the archbishops are bound to give permissions under the measure to any particular bishop, priest or deacon, but it does mean that there is no basis in law or precedent for declaring an individual diocese or a number of individual dioceses to be no longer in communion with the Church of England (unless those dioceses withdraw from the church with which the Church of England is in communion).

Thirdly, were dioceses to withdraw from a church with which the Church of England is in communion other than to join another church with which the Church of England is already in communion, it would accord with the precedent of the Church of South India case if the archbishops did not declare any new church formed by those dioceses to be in communion with the Church of England without obtaining a Synod resolution on which to base that decision.

Consequences of withdrawing from communion

It ought to be borne in mind that ecclesial communion is by its very nature mutual in character. Therefore, withdrawing from communion with another church may have consequences for members and ministers of the Church of England who are living in the country concerned or ministering in the church concerned. What those consequences were would depend on the law and policy of the church concerned.

For members and ministers of that church residing in or visiting England, the consequences may not be as serious as might be imagined. The Overseas Clergy Measure allows the archbishops to give permission for ministry to those ordained in a church *not* in communion with the Church of England whose orders are recognized and accepted by the Church of England. Whether such clergy would be required to go through some form of reception into the Church of England (as a Roman Catholic priest, for example, would) might be judged to be a matter of policy rather than of law. Similarly, baptized members of other churches may declare themselves to be members of the Church of England and then have the right to be enrolled on electoral rolls and stand for office. Such persons would be 'members of the Church of England . . . who have been otherwise episcopally confirmed', and under Canon B 15A would be entitled to receive communion as such. Thus it might be said that withdrawing from communion with another church would make little practical difference to members and ministers of the church concerned, but might have consequences for members and ministers of the Church of England abroad. It would essentially be a gesture or statement of the Church of England's disapproval of the church concerned as a whole.

C: Parallel episcopates and the unity of the Church[48]

Thus far we have considered questions concerning the territorial nature of the Church of England and its episcopate and the matter of communion between the Church of England and churches in other territories. What, then, of the possibility of a relationship of communion between two distinct episcopates within the same territory? The acceptability of this possibility depends, as will become clear, on what vision one has of the unity of the Church. It is in ecumenical discussions about the 'goal of unity' that questions of territoriality, communion and parallel jurisdictions come together.

Unity within the same territory

The Church of England believes in one Church, it believes in a visible Church, and it believes that the unity of that one Church should be made visible 'so that the world may believe'; during the 1990s the General Synod repeatedly affirmed the vision of 'full, visible unity' (as it did again in February 2004 when considering a report of the Anglican–Roman Catholic International Commission[49]). The goal of 'visible unity' is, moreover, not just the official ecumenical policy of the Church of England, but also that of the Anglican Communion, endorsed by the Lambeth Conferences of 1988 and 1998.[50]

All of the relationships of communion mentioned in the second section of this chapter are relationships between the Church of England and churches in other countries. What of relationships between churches in the same country? For there to be in the same country parallel episcopates displays disunity to the world; even if those episcopates were in communion with each other, it would not be that communion that the world would see, but the fact of two episcopates meeting in separate conferences while exercising jurisdiction over the same territory (or at least over churches within the same territory). Such a situation would, of course, also contravene the provision of Canon 8 of the Council of Nicaea – a canon specifically formulated in the context of reunification of the Church after schism – that there should not be two bishops with separate jurisdictions in the same city. Successive Lambeth Conferences have sought to overcome parallel or overlapping jurisdictions within the Anglican Communion precisely because they appear, at least, to fly in the face of this Nicene prohibition.

The establishment of communion with interchangeable ministries between churches with bishops in different countries – for example between the Church of England and the Episcopal Church in the USA in the nineteenth century or between the Church of England and the Nordic and Baltic Lutheran churches in the twentieth century – contributes to the unity of the Church without conflicting with the principle of 'one bishop in one place'. The establishment of communion with interchangeable ministries between churches with bishops in the same country, by contrast, would not only fail to achieve visible unity (if there are 'rival' bishops in the same place, the Church is not seen by the world to be united), but could even be viewed as entrenching and legitimizing disunity. Furthermore, if it is held (as increasingly it is) that ministry is only rightly understood in the context of the Church that it serves, then it might seem anomalous to unite the ministry while leaving the churches disunited. Arguably, the emphasis should be on uniting the Church and then uniting the ministry within the context of a united Church, rather than approaching things the other way round. Such an approach would involve creating a single structure of episcopal oversight before attempting to create a single priesthood.

For reasons such as these, the Church of England is not open to ecumenical proposals that have communion between it and another church in England as their *goal*. (The parallel or overlapping jurisdictions involved in communion with another episcopal church in the same country might possibly be regarded as one of the 'temporary anomalies' which the 1998 Lambeth Conference believed '*may* be bearable *when there is an agreed goal of visible unity*' (my italics), but the conference underlined that 'there should always be an impetus towards their resolution'.[51]) The English House of Bishops said in 1995:

> The House can only imagine entering into a relationship of visible unity with another church in England if that entailed a unity in faith, sacramental life, a single presbyteral ministry with a common episcopate in the historic succession and common structures: in short a single Church for the sake of strengthening a common mission and service to all.[52]

Unity and diversity in the Anglican–Moravian Conversations

This does not mean that for the Church of England, proposals for unity in England must involve integrating the other church into the hierarchy of the Church of England. Unity with a sizeable partner could not mean the integration of one church into the existing structure of the other; both churches would be changed profoundly. The issue of integration did arise, however, in the Church of England's conversations with the Moravian Church in the early 1990s. The difficulty here was the Moravian Church's small size: in 1995 it had 4,090 members in Great Britain and Ireland,[53] the number in England itself being even smaller. It was difficult to see how unity between such a small body and the Church of England (1995 electoral roll: 1,468,000[54]) could be other than the incorporation of the smaller church into the larger. Unity is not uniformity, however. The Porvoo Common Statement, agreed by representatives of the British and Irish Anglican churches and the Nordic and Baltic Lutheran churches in 1992, while noting that 'all existing denominational traditions are provisional', affirmed:

> Visible unity should not be confused with uniformity. 'Unity in Christ does not exist despite and in opposition to diversity, but is given with and in diversity' ... Both the unity and the diversity of the Church are ultimately grounded in the communion of God the Holy Trinity.[55]

It was against this background that the Anglican–Moravian conversations called for further work on 'how within a united church the particular gifts and distinctive ethos of both traditions could be sustained and enrich each other' and on 'the role of the episcopate within a "united" church to express the unity of the whole Church while at the same time to safeguard the distinctive identity of the traditions'.[56] This agenda would be about showing how absorption (which seemed inevitable only because of the disparity in size) might not mean extinction but rather the flourishing of a distinctive tradition nurtured within a larger whole. In a world that values diversity as never before but arguably also needs unity more than ever before, such an ecumenical experiment could have great value not only for those involved but also more widely. However, given the great difference in size of the two churches, it was understandable – though still very disappointing to those who long (as the present author does) for unity between the two churches – that the Moravian Church feared that absorption would mean extinction and therefore did not at that point feel able to move into unity with the Church of England.

Overlapping jurisdictions in the Porvoo Agreement

In the conversations which resulted in the Porvoo Agreement, the issue of overlapping jurisdictions did not loom so large, since the churches concerned were all in separate territories (most of them being the historic national churches of the countries concerned). Nonetheless, it needed to be considered, since there are Church of England chaplaincies in most of the Nordic and Baltic states and Nordic chaplaincies in the British Isles. The Porvoo Declaration therefore included a commitment 'to welcome diaspora congregations into the life of the indigenous churches, to their mutual enrichment'.[57] This was explained as follows:

> The last phrase does not imply the absorption of diaspora congregations such that they would lose their distinctive identities, language and traditions. On the other hand it would

be anomalous for diaspora congregations of churches in communion with a local church to have no structured relationship with that local church and its bishop.[58]

This commitment has resulted in Finnish, Icelandic, Norwegian and Swedish chaplains in England being given either a licence or permission to officiate in English dioceses and participating in the life of the deaneries where their churches are situated. Similar arrangements have been agreed between the Nordic and Baltic bishops and Church of England chaplains working in their dioceses. The attention given to this point testifies to a consciousness that the position of these 'diaspora congregations' constitutes an anomaly – albeit one that is necessary for pastoral reasons, given the differences of language, culture and rite.

The Church of England and ECUSA: Differing approaches

The Porvoo Agreement, in which overlapping jurisdictions are effectively recognized as an anomaly that requires special arrangements, may be contrasted with the recent Concordat between the Episcopal Church in the United States of America (ECUSA) and the Evangelical-Lutheran Church in America, which provides for 'full communion' between the two churches which retain their separate, parallel episcopates. It must be recognized, however, that the present situation and past history of the Church of England and ECUSA are very different. Factors which colour the Church of England's view of the goal of unity include the following:

- The Church of England is a territorial church in a stronger sense than is true of ECUSA. An English diocese is, in law, not just a body of people who worship in Anglican churches or whose names appear in Anglican electoral rolls *within* a defined territory; it *is* a geographical territory. ('Diocese' was a geographical term before it was adopted by the Church: it derives from the name for the twelve regions into which Diocletian divided the Roman Empire for administrative purposes.) Similarly, the bishops are not, and do not see themselves as, only the bishops of those who worship in their churches.[59]

- In many English parishes 'the parish church' is the only place of Christian worship (in most cases, the only place of worship of any faith), and as the protestant free churches decline and withdraw both from the inner cities and from the countryside, this is increasingly the case.

- For the first 1,000 years and more of the Church of England's existence, its bishops were the only bishops in England; the existence of rival episcopates, be they Roman Catholic, nonjuring or Moravian, is of very recent origin by comparison. Only since 1850 has there been another territorial hierarchy in England.

- Furthermore, the Church of England is today a very diverse church in its worship and theology – more so, perhaps, than many of the other churches of the Anglican Communion.

In such a context, the idea that there might again be a single Christian church in England, with a single college of bishops and a common ministry but with a great diversity of styles of worship and theological positions, for all it may seem a remote prospect, is not an incredible one. This helps to explain why the Church of England holds to the goal of 'full, visible unity', understood as necessarily involving the creation of a single structure of episcopal oversight within England.

The history and present situation of the Episcopal Church in the United States of America are very different. ECUSA is not a territorial church in the same manner as the Church of England: its bishops are not in any sense, and are not seen as, the bishop for everyone who lives within the bounds of their dioceses; and there were bishops of other churches in the USA before ECUSA's inception. There are no areas in which the Episcopal Church is the only church: everywhere there is a plethora of churches of all sorts. There never has been a single Christian church in the USA, and the multiplicity of churches and sects that gives rise to the attitudes collectively known as 'American denominationalism' makes the idea that there ever could be one scarcely credible. In such a context, surely, the full, visible unity of the whole Church is simply not a realistic goal.

Visible unity or reconciled diversity?

In his important article '"Reconciled Diversity" and the Visible Unity of the Church',[60] the American Lutheran ecumenist Michael Root weighs the historical and doctrinal arguments for the alternative goal of 'reconciled diversity' (which involves the continuance of parallel ecclesial structures in the same territory), and finds them wanting: 'Unity in reconciled diversity represents an historical innovation and the doctrinal arguments in its favour are usually insufficient.'[61] He is all too conscious of the danger that 'unity in reconciled diversity' could involve little more than amicable separation:

> In a situation of 'friendly division with porous borders', in which persons move freely between churches with little sense of what divides them but also with little sense of any need to overcome their division, the danger is of a peaceful coexistence on the model of market competition.[62]

Nonetheless, he concludes that:

> The strongest and, in my estimation, convincing arguments for
> some version of unity as reconciled diversity are not those that
> appeal to history or to a general doctrine of the Church, both of
> which should make us suspicious of this model. Rather, the
> decisive arguments arise out of a consideration of the concrete
> ecumenical situation of the Church today.[63]

In a further article[64] Root points to modern social, cultural and, indeed,
ecclesiastical diversity as making unity in territorial parishes no longer a
realistic goal: 'Many Christians value unity, but they also value the liturgy and
typical theology, the customs and habits of their churches, which they are not
willing simply to abandon.'[65] (These factors, it should be noted, apply to the
English situation as much as they do in the United States of America.) At the
same time, Root warns that 'the network of communion agreements now being
put into place could degenerate into mere "status quo ecumenism", an
ecumenism that leaves division in place but calls it union, unless there is the
will to realize such a truly common life'.[66] He affirms that 'the unity of the
Church must not only be visible to those who wish to see it'. Therefore, 'conciliar
structures at every level are necessary, capable . . . of corporate (and thus
binding) decision-making and consequent action'. Such binding structures for
decision-making, he suggests, are essential as a means of addressing the fact
that if, in a relationship of communion, the oversight of the diverse
congregations within a single city rests with different bishops, the unity
between them is not necessarily visible.

Territorial episcopacy and the ordination of women to the episcopate

The question of whether a territorial understanding of episcopacy, based on the
Nicene principle of 'one bishop in one place', is any longer sustainable is not
only an ecumenical issue. Such an understanding was crucial to the
arrangements adopted by the English General Synod in 1993 in order to
mitigate the effects of the ordination of women to the priesthood. The
preamble to the Episcopal Ministry Act of Synod 1993, 'passed by the General
Synod to make provision for the continuing diversity of opinion in the Church
of England as to the ordination and ministry of women as priests', stresses as a
fundamental point that 'The bishop of each diocese continues as the ordinary
of his diocese'. Therefore, the 'provincial episcopal visitors' (appointed by the
archbishops to provide 'extended pastoral care and sacramental ministry' to
congregations whose relationship with their bishop has been impaired by his
having ordained women to the priesthood) carry out in the parishes committed
to their care only 'such episcopal duties . . . as the diocesan bishop concerned
may request'.[67] All priests in the diocese continue to owe canonical obedience
to the diocesan bishop.

It is widely accepted that the consecration of women to the episcopate would create a new situation not catered for by this Act of Synod. If the diocesan bishop were a woman, how could those who do not believe that a woman could or should be a bishop swear the oath of canonical obedience to her or recognize her as having ordinary jurisdiction over them? Could the provincial episcopal visitors accept commissions from a woman bishop to ordain, institute and license, and perform other episcopal duties on her behalf? In responses to a recent survey 'it was widely acknowledged that the Act of Synod would be rendered unworkable in its present form if both women and men were included in the episcopate, since the Act hung crucially on a mutual recognition of orders among the bishops as the guarantee of continued communion'.[68]

In 2004 the then Archbishop of York, Dr David Hope, indicated that the Act of Synod could not 'bear the weight of this further development' and additional arrangements would be needed:

> It would not only be a tragedy if the Act of Synod were to be rescinded; it would be an act of betrayal and trigger a new crisis for our Church. But then given the fact that the ordination of women to the episcopate is now on the agenda – the question which ought in any case to have been addressed in the very first instance – the question needs to be asked whether the Act can continue to bear the weight of this further development having in mind its main premise of 'extended' episcopal care. Plainly it could not. Any such arrangements in respect of the ordination of women to the priesthood must surely be at least 'alternative' rather than merely 'extended', and that these same arrangements be in respect of 'oversight' rather than 'care' – arrangements ranging from a further development of the Act of Synod to an altogether more distanced Third Province. Discussions will no doubt further continue both as to what might be most desirable as well as the realism of what might actually be achievable.[69]

In an interview shortly before the confirmation of his election, the present Archbishop of Canterbury similarly recognized that if women were consecrated as bishops, the Act of Synod would no longer be adequate:

> I would find no personal difficulty in consecrating a woman bishop, but if we go down this road there are large questions about what happens to the substantial minority for whom this would be the last straw – people for whom the Act of Synod would no longer be an adequate resort.

Q: 'It sounds as if you are thinking about the Third Province idea quite seriously.'

A: 'With some sympathy, partly because I don't see that the Act of Synod style of provision will do anything here, and because I take seriously what people on both sides of the debate have said: you can't indefinitely perpetuate a situation in which, in one body, the ministry of some is regarded wholly negatively.'[70]

A third province is one of the options discussed in *Women Bishops in the Church of England?* (the report of the House of Bishops' working party, chaired by the Bishop of Rochester).[71] Such a third province need not involve overlapping jurisdictions in the strict sense (as indicated in the first section of this chapter, it could consist of territorial parishes forming enclaves within the territory of their former dioceses). However, if, for example, there were parishes within a cathedral city which belonged not to that cathedral's diocese but to a new 'third province' diocese, the question would arise as to whether the Church of England was still living in 'visible unity' with itself: in the world's eyes and to the casual observer there would effectively be two bishops in one city. The people of a single district would no longer belong to a single diocese. (If some belonged not only to a different diocese but also to a different province, possibly with its own conciliar and synodical structures, in which the orders of the bishop of the first diocese and her priests might not be recognized, to the casual observer there might appear not just to be two bishops but also two churches.)

Concluding reflection

By allowing for the existence of two parallel episcopates in the same territory, both the American understanding of 'full communion' and discussion of a third province in England (however practical or likely an outcome that might or might not be) seem to place a question mark against the Nicene principle of 'one bishop in one place' and territorial understandings of episcopacy. Secular culture seems to do the same. Many people today, in great cities at least, live in one place, work in another and spend their weekends visiting family and friends elsewhere. They belong to various non-geographical communities – formed by work, interest and relationship – and maybe only to a limited extent to communities formed by common residence in a place where they sometimes do little more than sleep. The Internet begins to create 'virtual communities' totally unrelated to geographical location.

In such a context, can a territorial understanding of episcopacy any longer be regarded as absolute? Given the diversity of society and of the Church today, should the acceptance of 'overlapping jurisdictions' no longer be limited to situations such as those of expatriate congregations worshipping in a language other than that of the country in which they live (as in the Porvoo context, or in the Orthodox diaspora) or according to a different rite (as with the Eastern rites in the Roman Catholic Church, or, again, Anglican congregations in 'Porvoo' Lutheran dioceses and vice versa), but extend to cover whole churches of different traditions in the same country, or communities stemming from a common tradition but with differing beliefs (for example, about the ordination of women as priests and bishops)? Or, alternatively, is a witness to the importance of 'rootedness' in place and local community – and to the need for unity in such local communities – made more important, not less, by the context in which the Church finds itself? Is this another instance in which its calling is, as the Epistle to the Romans says, 'Do not be conformed to this world but be transformed'?[72] These are some of the real and pressing questions that confront and challenge traditional Anglican understandings of the Church and its unity today.

7

Synodical government in the Church of England: History and principles[1]

This chapter offers an introduction to the history of synodical government in the Church of England, how it works and what principles underlie it. Synodical government is often contrasted with episcopal governance, and sometimes it is suggested that the former is modern and protestant while the latter is ancient and catholic. The historical survey with which the chapter begins shows synodical government in the Church of England to be rooted not in the protestant Reformation but in the medieval Church, and the second section, which looks at how the General Synod works, shows how the episcopate is central to the Synod; the third section looks briefly at diocesan and deanery synods. The chapter concludes by drawing out ten principles of synodical government which emerge from the preceding account and which help to explain the rationale for the Church of England's synodical structures.

A: History of synodical government to 1970

Continuity and adaptation

Compared with the history of other countries, England's history is marked by a remarkable continuity. This continuity has nonetheless been accompanied by development and adaptation. Although there has been a great reluctance to abolish institutions, they have been adapted to the needs of the time. Under a surface characterized by continuity and stability of form, substance and practice have been able to change greatly without the need for radical breaks. The history of the Church of England and its institutions is a classic example of this English way of doing things.

The Reformation is a case in point. The historic episcopal succession and the three orders of bishop, priest and deacon were retained, and the system of parishes, deaneries, archdeaconries, dioceses and provinces remained essentially unchanged, as did the constitutions and functions of the non-monastic cathedrals and the ecclesiastical courts. Much the same is true of the medieval canon law. Those parts of the general and provincial canon law ('canons, constitutions, ordinances and synodals provincial') that were in force in England in 1534, and did not conflict with the laws, statutes and customs of England, remained in force,[2] and if they have been 'continued and uniformly recognised and acted upon in England since the Reformation'[3] they remain in force today. A revision, the *Reformatio Legum Ecclesiasticarum*, was prepared between 1551 and 1553, but failed to gain the approval of Parliament.[4] The canons that were eventually passed in 1604 did not abrogate the medieval canon law in those areas that they did not address. Thus, the very significant changes in doctrine and worship, practice and ethos at the Reformation took place in a context of structural continuity. With the notable exception of the monastic foundations, the *Ecclesia Anglicana* (English Church or 'Church of England'[5]) continued intact.

The primary change effected in the 1530s was the cutting off of the Provinces of Canterbury and York from the rest of the Western Church and the substitution of the authority of the Crown - the king in council and in Parliament - for that of the pope. Even here it can be argued that the new situation in many cases continued what had been the reality of royal power (not only in England but also in other countries) in the medieval period; that reality was formalized and set in concrete by its embodiment in statute law. As Yngve Brilioth commented,

> The separation of the English Church from Rome in the sixteenth century is rather a phase of the nationalist movement of breaking away from the undivided Latin Church, which began in the last centuries of the Middle Ages, than part of the great continental Church Reformation.

As a result of this combination of continuity with the medieval Church and separation from Rome in the sixteenth century, the Church of England's internal structure today is much closer to that of the medieval Church than is that of the modern Roman Catholic Church. The reason for this is that because of its separation from Rome, the Church of England was unaffected by the Counter-Reformation and subsequent changes in the structures of the Roman Catholic Church. This closeness to the medieval Church was even more true before the changes that began to be made in the nineteenth century. Bishop Eric Kemp has said of historical research about the medieval English Church: 'I have found . . . that it is often possible to use evidence of eighteenth century practice as a reasonably reliable guide to what was being done in the fourteenth and fifteenth centuries.'[7] Despite this high degree of continuity with the medieval Church, the Church of England is not simply imprisoned in medieval practices and structures. This is because of the development and adaptation that are characteristic of the history of English institutions. Where medieval structures have been retained, they have usually been adapted to the needs of the age.

The origins of synodical government

Among the structures that the Church of England has inherited from the Middle Ages are the Convocations of Canterbury and York – the provincial synods of the two provinces, which still exist today and now also combine to form the House of Bishops and the House of Clergy of the General Synod of the Church of England, which has inherited most of the Convocations' functions. The Church of England's synodical structures are therefore an example of catholic ecclesiology, albeit in a distinctive and developed form, and are not derived from the Reformed tradition. Unlike the synods of the Reformed tradition, the synods of the Church of England do not have disciplinary jurisdiction (which belongs to the bishops and the ecclesiastical courts or tribunals). The history of the Convocations is set out by Eric Kemp in his book *Counsel and Consent,* on which the following account of the early history of the Convocations is based.[8]

The organization of the English Church in two provinces was envisaged as early as 601 – by Pope Gregory the Great in a letter to St Augustine (who came to England in 597 and founded the See of Canterbury) – but the Province of York was not permanently established as a separate province until 735. By the end of the eighth century the metropolitans who presided over the provincial councils of the two provinces as *primus inter pares* had become archbishops, to whom their suffragans (the bishops of the province) took an oath of obedience at their consecration, as they still do today. From the eleventh century papal power increased, and as a result spiritual and doctrinal matters lay less and less within the competence of the provincial councils or synods.

In the thirteenth century a variety of councils, synods and ecclesiastical assemblies, some provincial and some national, were held in England. The councils – sometimes national, sometimes provincial – were, of course, primarily gatherings of bishops, but they were sometimes also attended by dignitaries (abbots, priors, deans and archdeacons), though not by the lower clergy. The ecclesiastical assemblies, summoned to consider royal requests for taxation of the clergy, were sometimes attended by proctors (representatives) of the lower clergy; in other cases the lower clergy were consulted in diocesan and local assemblies.

By the mid-fourteenth century these ad hoc meetings had become formalized into two bodies, the provincial *Council* and the provincial *Convocation* (an ecclesiastical assembly equivalent to Parliament for taxation purposes). The membership of both bodies now consisted of the archbishop and bishops, the abbots and priors, the deans and provosts of cathedrals and collegiate churches, the archdeacons, two proctors for the clergy of each diocese and one for the chapter of each collegiate church.

By the beginning of the fifteenth century these two bodies with identical membership had in each of the two provinces fused into a single synod, and the names Convocation and Provincial Council had become interchangeable. The prominence of the lower clergy in these synods might have seemed strange to people from continental provinces. This fusion of the two types of assembly had a very important consequence. In a provincial council the clergy had given their bishops *counsel* (advice), but in the Convocation their *consent* was needed for taxation. In time, the fusion of these two bodies into one Convocation in each of the two provinces removed the distinction, and the clergy (in the shape of the Lower House of the Convocation) exercised a right to give or withhold their consent to the whole range of proposals of the Upper House (the House of Bishops). Such, then, was the synodical government of the two provinces that made up the Church of England before the Reformation.

Gibson's Synodus Anglicana

In 1702 a dispute between the two houses of the Convocation of Canterbury prompted Edmund Gibson (later Bishop of London) to publish an account of the English Convocations under the title *Synodus Anglicana.*[9] Some quotations from this work will illustrate both the continuity of the Convocations, whose structure was unaffected by the Reformation, and the relationship between the two houses.

Gibson argued that despite the existence of an upper and a lower house, which gave it a superficial resemblance to Parliament, an English Convocation was essentially an ecclesiastical synod and not just an imitation of Parliament: 'as to their independence in acting, or any degrees of it, there is no such resemblance as has been pretended between the proceedings of parliament and convocation'[10] Gibson's reason for emphasizing this was that

> The rights and privileges of the house of commons, if vested in the lower house of convocation, would give the clergy a coordinate power with their bishops, and so remove our church still further from primitive practice.[11]

In order to prove that in Convocation the Lower House (of clergy) did not have equal powers to the Upper House (of bishops), Gibson examined the practice of the Convocations before the Reformation as well as after. He defended this as follows:

> A scruple has been raised by some members of the lower house, how far the registers before the reformation are to be regarded in the methods of holding an English synod. But as nothing passed then, which could any way affect the usual intercourse

between the two houses when met and entered upon business, so after the reformation, they continued the self-same ways of acting, that were established before.[12]

Gibson concluded his work as follows:

> The authors . . . of some late schemes have done manifest injustice to the constitution of our protestant church in contending, against law and practice, that the reformation put an end to the ancient canonical ways of transacting ecclesiastical matters, and introduced a new model inconsistent with the primitive distinctions between presbyters and bishops, and unknown either to this or any other episcopal church. The foregoing chapters, I hope, may vindicate our reformation from the late aspersions of that kind, as well as the ecclesiastical government thereof from any such repugnancy to the primitive rules; and may withal make it more easily understood, whether they who have carried on those new measures, or they who have opposed them, are the truer friends to the rights, liberties, and honour of our reformed church.[13]

Although he proved that the Lower House did not have an equal power with the Upper House, Gibson strongly reaffirmed the Lower House's right to veto proposals of the Upper House:

> The greatest power enjoyed by the English clergy in a provincial synod, beyond the presbyters of other nations, is a negative upon the metropolitan and bishops, none of whose resolutions, either in part or in whole, can be passed into synodical acts without the previous approbation of the inferior clergy.[14]

This, then, was the situation (as described by Gibson in 1702) when the Reformation Parliament assembled in 1529. The English Church had two provincial synods, each consisting of an Upper House of bishops (which had the right to initiate proposals) and a Lower House of clergy (which possessed a right of veto over the decisions of the Upper House). What impact did the Reformation have on the government of the Church of England?

The Reformation

The Reformation made no change to the structure or procedures of the Convocations (except for the very important change that three-quarters of the members of the Canterbury Convocation and half of the York Convocation – the abbots and priors – disappeared), but the royal supremacy, which replaced that of the pope, brought with it important changes in the powers of the Convocations. On 15 May 1532 the Convocation of Canterbury agreed the Submission of the Clergy, which was embodied in an Act of Parliament of 1534. Thereafter the Convocations could only meet when a royal writ for them to be summoned was issued. They could make no canons without the royal licence, and canons could not come into effect without royal assent. Canons which conflicted with the royal prerogative, with English customs and laws or, importantly, with statute law could not be put into effect.[15] Thus the canon law made by the Convocations was effectively subordinated not only to the Crown but also to the statute law made by Parliament. Interestingly, one of the arguments for these changes advanced by members of the House of Commons was that the laity had no voice in the Convocations. Through the House of Commons they would now have a veto over the decisions of the Convocations. Like the pre-Reformation system, the Reformation changes remain in force today. However, the underlying practice (as distinct from the superficial form) is much altered.

Restoration and suppression

In the seventeenth century there are just two dates of long-term significance in the history of the Convocations. In 1664, after the restoration of the monarchy and episcopacy (and also of the Convocations), Archbishop Sheldon, by an oral agreement with Lord Chancellor Clarendon, surrendered the right of the clergy to tax themselves in Convocation. Now that the Crown no longer needed to summon the Convocations in order to obtain taxation, it felt no need to summon them at all. The next time they were allowed to discuss serious business was in 1689, after the Glorious Revolution, but there was disagreement between the two houses of the Convocation of Canterbury, so the king's ministers preferred not to summon them again. Protests led to permission for the Convocations to transact business in 1701, but disputes between the two houses erupted again (prompting Gibson to write his *Synodus Anglicana*, as we have seen). Even greater controversy in 1717 meant that apart from an isolated meeting in 1741 the Convocations were allowed to transact no business until the middle of the nineteenth century.

The nineteenth century

The increasing pace of social change in the nineteenth century created a corresponding need for ecclesiastical legislation. From 1820 to 1870 Parliament passed an average of twenty-five statutes covering ecclesiastical matters each year, compared with an average of less than two and a half between 1530 and 1760 and ten between 1760 and 1820. Many in the church were disturbed that so much change was now being undertaken by Parliament, especially when protestant dissenters (from 1828) and Roman Catholic laymen (from 1829) became eligible to sit in the House of Commons. From the 1830s onwards, demands for the Convocations to be allowed to transact business increased. The Convocation of Canterbury began to do business again in 1852, that of York in 1861.

Lay participation

The Convocations, of course, consisted entirely of clergy and bishops. However, in 1886 an advisory House of Laymen was established by the Convocation of Canterbury, and one for York followed in 1892. Provision for the two lay houses to meet jointly was made in 1898, and in 1903 a Representative Church Council, consisting of the two Convocations and the two Houses of Laymen, was formed. This still had no legislative or executive powers. By now, however, Parliament could no longer cope with the volume of ecclesiastical legislation needed, and criticism of the situation whereby a Parliament that included non-Anglicans was legislating for the church continued to grow. In 1919, therefore, the Church of England Assembly (Powers) Act was passed. This 'enabling act' established a national assembly of the Church of England – the Church Assembly.

The Church Assembly

The Church of England Assembly (Powers) Act provided that the Church Assembly could approve measures. These measures would be considered by a joint Ecclesiastical Committee of both Houses of Parliament, which would produce a report on the measure's nature and legal effect and its 'expediency, especially with relation to the constitutional rights of all His Majesty's subjects'. Parliament would not be able to amend a measure, but it would need to be approved as a whole by resolutions of both houses. It would then receive the royal assent and become part of the statute law of England, just as if it were an Act of Parliament. This system of legislation by measure remains unchanged today.

The Church Assembly consisted of the Convocations together with a House of Laity, and its constitution and procedures were under the control of the Convocations. The Convocations continued to exist alongside the Church Assembly, retaining their traditional powers. The Church Assembly's first act was to pass a measure enabling the Convocations to reform the membership of their lower houses by canon. This they did, increasing the representation of the parochial clergy at the expense of the other categories, so that they now had large majorities in both lower houses.

However, the resulting system was cumbersome. Statute law was made by the Church Assembly, but canon law continued to be made by the Convocations (meeting and voting separately), which also passed Acts of Convocation which had moral but not legal force. When the canons of the Church of England were completely revised from 1947 onwards (a process completed in 1969), the laity had no constitutional part in the process. Therefore, after each draft canon had been considered by the Convocations it was sent to the House of Laity for comment. The process was repeated at a second revision stage before the canon was finally approved. There was no procedure whereby the two Convocations and the House of Laity could discuss the canon together. The problems of coordination and the time taken were great indeed. As a result, moves to create a General Synod incorporating the Convocations and the House of Laity began in 1953.

B: The General Synod of the Church of England

The General Synod and its powers

This movement resulted in the Synodical Government Measure 1969, which established the General Synod with effect from 1970.[16] The General Synod consists of the Convocations of Canterbury and York together with a House of Laity. The upper houses of the Convocations combine to form the House of Bishops and the lower houses combine to form the House of Clergy. The Convocations also continue to exist separately, and although most of their powers were transferred to the General Synod, they do retain some residual rights. The powers of the General Synod can be described under five headings, as follows.

1. Legislation by Measure and Canon

The General Synod has inherited the powers of the Church Assembly to pass measures which, if approved by resolution of each House of Parliament, receive royal assent and thereby become part of the law of England. It has also inherited the powers of the Convocations to legislate by canon, subject to royal licence and assent. Because of the precedence of statute law created by the Act for the Submission of the Clergy in 1534, new canons often require a measure giving the Synod power to legislate by canon on the subject concerned. It is important to note that in the case of a measure, it is the royal assent that gives it the force of law, whereas in the case of a canon the royal licence and assent only empower the Synod to 'promulge and execute a canon' – it is the action of the Synod (not of the Crown) that gives a canon its legal validity.

2. Relations with other churches

The General Synod has also inherited the Convocations' power to regulate the Church of England's relations with other churches and to make provisions for matters relating to worship and doctrine. It can make provision by Act of Synod,[17] regulation or other instrument in cases where legislation by or under a measure or canon is not necessary.

3. Liturgy and doctrinal assent

The Worship and Doctrine Measure 1974 gave the General Synod power to approve, amend, continue or discontinue liturgies and make provision for any matter (except the publication of banns of marriage) to which rubrics of *The Book of Common Prayer* relate. These powers are exercised without reference to Parliament and no measure is required. Similarly, the Synod now decides the form in which ministers and officers of the Church of England are required to assent to the doctrine of the Church of England (the Declaration of Assent).[18] Again, no measure or reference to Parliament is required.

The Synod is required to 'ensure that the forms of service contained in *The Book of Common Prayer* continue to be available for use in the Church of England'. At first sight its powers appear to be further limited by the fact that canons, regulations and liturgies approved under the Worship and Doctrine Measure must be 'such as in the opinion of the General Synod is neither contrary to, nor indicative of any departure from, the doctrine of the Church of England in any essential matter'.[19] However, the measure also says that 'the final approval by the General Synod of any such Canon or regulation or form of service or amendment thereof shall conclusively determine' that the Synod is of that opinion.[20] So the Synod may not approve liturgies or forms of subscription unless it believes them to be in accordance with the doctrine of the Church of England, but if it does approve them, that test is automatically deemed to be met.

4. Deliberation

As well as being a legislative body, the General Synod is also a deliberative one. It has power 'to consider and express their opinion on any other matters of religious or public interest'.

5. Finance

Finally, the General Synod has the power to approve (or reject) the central budget of the Church of England each year.

Composition

The presidents of the General Synod are the Archbishops of Canterbury and York, and the Synod has three houses – the House of Bishops, the House of Clergy and the House of Laity.

The House of Bishops comprises the upper houses of the Convocations and consists (from 2005) of the 44 diocesan bishops, the Bishop of Dover (the suffragan bishop who in practice is the bishop for the Diocese of Canterbury) and 7 elected representatives of the other suffragan and assistant bishops.[21] The Archbishop of Canterbury is chairman and the Archbishop of York vice-chairman. The House of Bishops has a considerable number of functions in its own right and therefore meets separately about three times a year, between sessions of the General Synod.

The House of Clergy comprises the lower houses of the Convocations and consists (from 2005) of 205 members, including 5 cathedral deans, the Dean of Jersey or Guernsey, 6 proctors of the university clergy, 2 representatives of the religious communities (all elected by their constituencies), 3 elected Forces' chaplains and the Chaplain General of Prisons.[22] The remainder are proctors elected by all the licensed clergy in each diocese, with room for five co-options. The house is chaired by the prolocutors (chairmen) of the lower houses of the two Convocations.

From 2005, the core membership of the House of Laity is 207. Apart from two elected representatives of the religious communities, three lay members of the armed forces and the first and second Church Estates Commissioners, all the members are representatives of the laity in each diocese, elected by the lay members of deanery synods, with room for five co-options.[23] There are up to twelve further members of the Synod who sit in the appropriate house, depending on whether or not they are ordained. These are eleven *ex officio* members (the Dean of the Arches, the vicars-general of the two provinces, the Third Church Estates Commissioner, the Chairman of the Church of England Pensions Board and the six appointed members of the Archbishops' Council) and a seventh elected representative of the armed forces. In 2005 the ten *ex officio* members who are not otherwise members of the Synod are laypeople and are therefore additional members of the House of Laity.

The House of Laity and the House of Clergy only occasionally meet separately, and when they do, it is normally in conjunction with a meeting of the General Synod. From 2005 the total potential membership of the General Synod is 476, compared with 581 before 2005; the Church Assembly had 746 members. The Convocation of York has a higher level of representation per diocesan elector than the Convocation of Canterbury, in order to ensure that in numerical terms it remains a viable provincial synod.

Meetings

A new General Synod is elected every five years. All elections take place according to the single transferable vote system. So far, each new General Synod has been inaugurated by Her Majesty the Queen after a service of Holy Communion in Westminster Abbey. The Synod meets at least twice each year – in Church House, Westminster, for the inside of a week in February, and at the University of York over a long weekend in July. It sometimes meets in London for two or three days in November as well. The London sessions run from 9.30 (or even 9) a.m. to 1 p.m. and 2.30 to 7 p.m.; the York sessions continue until 10 p.m. with an evening break from 6 to 8.30.

Business and procedure

The primary task of the Synod is to legislate by measure and canon and to make rules, regulations and schemes under existing measures. Measures and canons go through a number of stages, the main ones taken in full Synod being first consideration, the revision stage (at which the draft may be amended) and final approval. (Chapter 8 gives an illustration of how the process of legislation by measure and canon works.) The procedure for synodical consideration and approval of draft forms of service similarly involves three stages in full Synod.

The Synod also votes money, to be paid by the dioceses, for the Church of England's central administration, for training for the ministry and for Anglican Communion and ecumenical bodies, as well as for the pensions of clergy employed by mission agencies and for housing assistance for retired clergy. It considers the annual report of the Archbishops' Council and sometimes also those of other bodies. A significant opportunity for the Synod to keep the central work of the Church of England under review is provided by Question Time. On one evening – usually the first of each group of sessions – between 75 and 90 minutes are devoted to the oral answering of questions submitted in advance by members. Supplementary questions may be asked without prior warning. Question Time also provides an opportunity for members to raise issues of concern in the church in general, which can also be done to a certain extent in the debate on the Business Committee's report on the Synod's agenda.

The rest of the Synod's time is spent on its deliberative function – considering issues of concern in the church and the world. Often this is done on the basis of a written report, at the initiative of a board or council, or of the Archbishops' Council or the House of Bishops, but general concerns can also be raised in two other ways:

- Any member of the Synod may put down a private member's motion. Members sign the motion and the most popular of those that achieve more than 100 signatures are debated in turn according to the number of signatures they attract.

- Any diocesan synod may send a motion up to the General Synod. These must be debated, and they are taken in chronological order according to the date they were submitted.

The three houses of the Synod sit as a single assembly. There are reserved seats for the House of Bishops and the Synod's officers (the presidents, the prolocutors, and the chairman and vice-chairman of the House of Laity), but the clergy and laity sit together rather than as two separate 'orders'. Normally votes are taken by a show of hands, the hands only being counted if the result is unclear. Sometimes, however, the voting is too close for certainty or the number of votes needs to be recorded exactly. In these cases, a division of the whole Synod is ordered, and members are counted leaving the chamber. Thus, voting is public and open, rather than by secret ballot. How members vote can be observed both by their fellow members and by members of the public sitting in the public gallery. However, no record is taken or kept of how members vote; there are no 'division lists'.

Special provisions and safeguards

There are several safeguards to protect the rights of the individual houses and the Convocations, and generally to ensure that substantial changes are not approved by small majorities.

Any 25 members of the Synod can require a vote to be taken by a division by houses. In this case a majority is needed in each house for the motion to be passed. The clergy and laity vote by leaving the chamber by separate doors marked 'clergy ayes', 'clergy noes', 'laity ayes' and 'laity noes', while the bishops vote by going up onto the platform on one side or the other. The final approval of any measure or canon must be by a majority in each house.

Article 7 of the Synod's constitution safeguards the prerogatives of the House of Bishops and of the Convocations (especially the York Convocation, being the smaller of the two). It states that 'a provision touching the doctrinal formulae or the services and ceremonies of the Church of England or the administration of the sacraments or sacred rites thereof' has to be referred to the House of Bishops before final approval and can only be submitted for final approval in terms proposed by the House of Bishops. This applies, for example, to all liturgies. The House of Bishops is entitled to amend the text at this penultimate stage, it can only proceed if the House of Bishops approves it, and the Synod can only give it final approval in the form in which the House of Bishops has already approved it. After the House of Bishops has approved the text, either of the Convocations or the House of Laity can also require that the provision be referred to the Convocations and the House of Laity. They cannot change the text, but if such a reference is required, the provision cannot be submitted for final approval unless each house of each Convocation and the House of Laity separately approve it. (If one of the four Convocation houses rejects it, it can be referred back to them, and if only one house rejects it a second time, it can be referred to a joint meeting of the Houses of Bishops and Clergy. If it receives a two-thirds majority it can then go for final approval.)

Article 8 of the constitution safeguards the services of Baptism and Holy Communion and the Ordinal, and the identity of the Church of England. Under this article, measures and canons providing for permanent changes in the services of Baptism or Holy Communion or in the Ordinal, and church unity schemes involving another church a substantial number of whose members reside in England, have to be approved by a majority of the diocesan synods. (The presidents can also direct that this article should apply to schemes involving churches whose members mainly live outside England, and they used this power in respect of the Porvoo Agreement between the British and Irish Anglican churches and the Nordic and Baltic Lutheran churches.) Changes in the services of Baptism, Holy Communion and the Ordinal require a two-thirds majority in each house of the General Synod, and in the case of a scheme, the Synod may resolve that special majorities in each house or overall will be required. (In the case of the Porvoo Agreement, the Synod decided that a two-thirds majority in each house should be required.) The Synod's standing orders require a majority of two-thirds in each house for the final approval of all liturgies.

Role of the House of Bishops

The House of Bishops is the only house of the Synod that meets separately between groups of sessions of the General Synod, and the only house with powers not enjoyed by the other houses. Its position therefore deserves special attention.

The ability of any 25 members of the Synod (note that 25 is just under half the membership of the House of Bishops) to require a vote by houses means that if a majority of the House of Bishops presses its opposition to any proposal, it cannot be passed. Of course, the other houses have a veto too, but the important point here is that the role of the bishops in leading the Church is preserved. Article 7 means that proposals affecting the doctrine or worship of the Church of England can only be given final approval if they have previously been approved by the House of Bishops, and can only be approved in the precise terms in which the House of Bishops has approved them. Here the bishops' role as guardians of the faith and liturgy is preserved. Thus the Church of England remains an episcopally led as well as a synodically governed church.

C: Diocesan and deanery synods

Reference has already been made to the diocesan and deanery synods. These too were created in their present form by the Synodical Government Measure 1969.

Diocesan synods were an important feature of church life in England before the Reformation, electing proctors of the clergy to the Convocations, receiving and publishing decrees from higher authorities and supplementing the general and provincial ecclesiastical law with diocesan constitutions. They consisted either of the whole clergy of the diocese or of their representatives, and on occasion, lay *testes synodales* were also summoned. There were a few sporadic meetings of diocesan synods in the seventeenth century, but thereafter they ceased to exist.[24] Calls for the revival of diocesan synods began to be made in the 1830s, and the first diocesan synod of modern times was held by Bishop Henry Phillpotts of Exeter in 1851.[25] Following the reactivation of the Convocations, diocesan conferences began to be held from the mid-1860s.[26] In 1867 a committee of the Upper House of the Convocation of Canterbury recommended that (clerical) synods promulgating decrees that would be binding on the clergy should be avoided, but that from time to time there should be assemblies of clergy and laity, 'convened, presided over and directed by the Bishop'. The report, which was adopted by the Upper House in February 1868, established an important principle which has applied ever since: that if a vote is taken 'the Clergy and Laity should have an equal voice'.[27] (This principle is now expressed both by the practice of voting by houses and by the number of clergy and lay members of synods being approximately equal.) By 1881 all but three dioceses had some form of diocesan assembly.[28] The Church Assembly had as its counterpart in each diocese a diocesan conference. Since these included at least one representative of every parish and an equivalent number of clergy, their size could be very large (ranging from 150 to 1,300 members, with the average lying between 500 and 900) – too large to be effective. Under the Synodical Government Measure diocesan conferences were replaced by much smaller diocesan synods.

Ruridecanal chapters (meetings of the clergy of a rural deanery) were revived from 1839, and by 1870 they had been established in almost all dioceses.[29] In the era of the Church Assembly, most (but not all) dioceses had not only diocesan conferences but also ruridecanal conferences, in which the clergy were joined by representatives of the laity.

Deanery synods

Because (unlike the pre-1970 diocesan conferences) the diocesan synods do not include a representative of every parish, it was thought important for deanery synods, in which every parish is represented by at least one member, to be a mandatory part of the new system. Deanery synods consist of a house of clergy and a house of laity and are jointly chaired by the rural dean (or 'area dean') and a lay chairman. Their membership normally ranges from 50 to 150.[30] The functions of a deanery synod are:

(a) to consider matters concerning the Church of England and to make provision for such matters in relation to their deanery, and to consider and express their opinion on any other matters of religious and public interest;

(b) to bring together the views of the parishes of the deanery on common problems, to discuss and formulate common policies on those problems, to foster a sense of community and interdependence among those parishes, and generally to promote in the deanery the whole mission of the Church, pastoral, evangelistic, social and ecumenical;

(c) to make known and so far as appropriate put into effect any provision made by the diocesan synod;

(d) to consider the business of the diocesan synod, and particularly any matters referred to that synod by the General Synod, and to sound parochial opinion whenever they are required or consider it appropriate to do so;

(e) to raise such matters as the deanery synod consider appropriate with the diocesan synod:

Provided that the functions referred to in paragraph (a) hereof shall not include the issue of any statement purporting to declare the doctrine of the Church on any question.[31]

Additionally, diocesan synods may delegate functions to deanery synods; one such function may be the apportionment of the quota to be subscribed towards diocesan expenditure by the parishes. Arguably, however, the most important function of the deanery synods is that their members elect most of the clergy and nearly all of the lay members not only of the diocesan synods but also of the General Synod.

Diocesan synods

Diocesan synods consist of three houses: a house of bishops (consisting of the diocesan bishop, the suffragan bishops (if any), and other assistant bishops nominated by the diocesan with the concurrence of the archbishop of the province), a house of clergy and a house of laity.[22] The diocesan bishop is the president of the diocesan synod and it is customary for there to be a clerical and a lay vice-president elected by their respective houses, of which they are also the chairmen.[33] Diocesan synods have between 120 and 270 members, the numbers of clergy and lay members being approximately equal.[34] They must meet at least twice a year.[35] The functions of a diocesan synod are:

(a) to consider matters concerning the Church of England and to make provision for such matters in relation to their diocese, and to consider and express their opinion on any other matters of religious and public interest;

(b) to advise the bishop on any matters on which he may consult the synod;

(c) to consider and express their opinion on any matters referred to them by the General Synod, and in particular to approve or disapprove provisions referred to them by the General Synod under Article 8 of the Constitution;

(d) to consider proposals for the annual budget for the diocese and to approve or disapprove them;

(e) to consider the annual accounts of the diocesan board of finance of the diocese:

Provided that the functions referred to in paragraph (a) hereof shall not include the issue of any statement purporting to declare the doctrine of the Church on any question.[36]

The measure says that 'it shall be the duty of the bishop to consult with the diocesan synod on matters of general concern and importance to the diocese.'[37] Each diocese is also required to have a bishop's council, which is also the standing committee of the diocesan synod, and this body may discharge the synod's advisory functions on its behalf, though either the bishop or the bishop's council may require any matter to be referred to the diocesan synod.[38]

Diocesan synods normally vote as a single body, though either the diocesan bishop or any ten members may require a vote to be taken by houses.[39] Furthermore, the Church Representation Rules state that 'nothing shall be deemed to have the assent of the diocesan synod unless the three houses which constitute the synod have assented thereto', and that 'if . . . the diocesan bishop . . . so directs, that question shall be deemed to have the assent of the house of bishops only if the majority of the members of that house who assent thereto includes the diocesan bishop'.[40] Thus the diocesan bishop can require a vote by houses on any issue and then require that the matter will not be deemed to have been passed in the house of bishops if he has not voted in favour of it.[41] However, this safeguard for the diocesan bishop is balanced by a safeguard for the clergy and people of the diocese: Canon C 18 of the canons of the Church of England states that 'Where the assent of the bishop is required to a resolution of the diocesan synod it shall not lightly nor without grave cause be withheld'.[42]

There is communication in both directions between the synods at different levels. A motion passed by a deanery synod can be sent on for debate by the diocesan synod, and if passed by the diocesan synod it can be sent forward for debate by the General Synod. Most notably, the resolution passed by the General Synod in November 1984, 'That this Synod asks the Standing Committee to bring forward legislation to permit the ordination of Women to the Priesthood in the Provinces of Canterbury and York', began as a motion passed by the Wandsworth Deanery Synod which was then passed by the Southwark Diocesan Synod and finally moved in the General Synod by the then Bishop of Southwark on behalf of his diocese. In the other direction, the General Synod refers some matters to the diocesan synods before coming to a final vote on them (in some cases, such a reference is required by Article 8 of the constitution), and the diocesan synods often refer the matter in turn for debate in their deanery synods before voting on it. Diocesan synods are required to 'keep the deanery synods of the diocese informed of the policies and problems of the diocese and of the business which is to come before meetings of the diocesan synod' and to 'give opportunities of discussing at meetings of the diocesan synod matters raised by deanery synods and parochial church councils'.[43]

D: Principles of synodical government in the Church of England

It is typical of the English and Anglican way of doing things that we lack a grand statement of the principles of synodical government. Instead, the principles must be deduced from practice, or, in this case, from the rules that govern that practice. In what follows, I therefore offer a list of ten key principles which I deduce from what is stated above. I should stress that what I say below applies to the Church of England but does not necessarily apply to other Anglican churches. The ecclesiology of the Episcopal Church in the USA, in particular, differs significantly from that of the Church of England in important respects.

1. Synods are a necessary and permanent feature of the life of the Church. In the Church of England their existence continues between their meetings (at the end of which they are prorogued, not dissolved), and when they are finally dissolved at the end of an electoral period new synods are immediately elected. It is the duty of each diocesan bishop to consult with his diocesan synod on matters of general concern and importance to the diocese.

2. A synod is a representative gathering of the whole Church at the level concerned, and thus necessarily involves representatives of the clergy and of the laity as full members. (The involvement of the clergy in the English provincial synods dates from the Middle Ages. The principle of lay representation originated with the Reformation, when it was expressed through the role of the House of Commons in Parliament, and was gradually established in ecclesiastical assemblies between the 1860s and 1920, though only since 1970 have ecclesiastical assemblies with lay membership been termed 'synods'.) There is, admittedly, an issue as to how far those who are elected – especially the members of the House of Laity of the General Synod – are actually representative of the churchgoing laity as a whole.

3. The Church is not a democracy, however. Synods therefore do not simply represent the members of the Church in numerical proportion (which would result in a huge majority of lay members); instead, the partnership between clergy and laity is expressed by the clergy and the laity having approximately equal numbers of members. Furthermore, important or controversial proposals need the support of all three houses (bishops, clergy and laity) voting separately.

4. Synods can exist at every level of the Church's life above that of the parish (in the Church of England every diocese except the Diocese in Europe has deanery synods for all its parishes; the Diocese in Europe has archdeaconry synods instead; the Diocese of London additionally has synods for its episcopal areas). Synods must exist at the level of the diocese, the province and the national church. At present it is not possible for the Church of England to be represented at a synod with binding authority at any level above the national level. Thus, although

the Anglican Consultative Council (an international representative body of episcopal, clerical and lay representatives) expresses the principle of synodality that is an important feature of the life of the Anglican churches, it cannot be described as a synod. (The Lambeth Conference, to which all Anglican bishops are invited every ten years, and the Primates Meeting, which is attended by the senior bishop of each of the member churches of the Anglican Communion, are expressions of episcopal collegiality. They too lack canonical authority and cannot make binding decisions, though they possess a certain moral authority.)

5.   The fact that synods, and not mere conferences, exist at the provincial and national levels is an indication of 'ecclesial density' at those levels. The Church of England has a corporate identity at the national level. Its bishops attend meetings of the General Synod not just at the head of the representatives of their own dioceses but also as members of the Church of England's corporate episcopal leadership at the national level. The importance of this is symbolized by the fact that the bishops mainly sit together, rather than sitting with members from their dioceses. The General Synod is not a federal conference at which largely autonomous dioceses are represented by delegations casting 'block votes'. Each member speaks and votes as an individual member of the whole Synod (or of his or her house within the Synod), and exercises those responsibilities on behalf of the whole church at the national level.

6.   By the same token, the powers of a diocesan synod are limited. It may not issue any statement purporting to declare the doctrine of the Church on any question. A diocesan synod cannot unilaterally take actions which touch the faith and order of the Church. Many consider it to be a great weakness of the Church of England's position that the General Synod effectively does possess such competence. In particular, those opposed to the ordination of women to the priesthood argued that, while the General Synod was *legally* empowered (subject to the approval of Parliament) to make such a change, *morally* it should not have done so in the absence of a consensus on the matter within the universal Church.

7.   A synod is a gathering of the whole church around (and, indeed, under) its bishops, never over against them. (This is symbolized when the Synod meets in Church House, Westminster, by the fact that the bishops sit in the centre of the circular Assembly Hall.) The diocesan bishop is the president of his diocesan synod and the archbishops are

the presidents of their provincial synods (the Convocations) and of the General Synod. A diocesan synod cannot pass a resolution against the will of the diocesan bishop, nor can the General Synod do so against the will of the House of Bishops. (It should be noted that although the archbishops are the presidents of the General Synod and of their Convocations, in synodical terms it is not the archbishops but the House of Bishops (or Upper House) that is the equivalent at the national and provincial levels to the diocesan bishop at the diocesan level.[44]) However, a diocesan bishop is enjoined not to withhold his consent 'lightly nor without grave cause', and the House of Bishops' veto is one that the house wisely exercises very sparingly.

8.   Within the General Synod, the bishops have a particular role as the guardians of the faith and order of the Church and of its liturgy. Draft liturgies are introduced into the Synod by the House of Bishops. The Synod can only finally approve a liturgy if the House of Bishops has previously approved it, and can only finally approve a liturgy in the form proposed at that final stage by the House of Bishops.

9.   A synod is concerned not just with the internal life of the Church but also with the needs and issues of the world and with the Church's mission in that world. The synods of the Church of England are public bodies established under a measure approved by Parliament. Thus it is one of the functions of deanery and diocesan synods, as well as of the General Synod, 'to consider and express their opinion on any . . . matters of religious and public interest'.

10.   Finally (and this emerges not from what has been said above but from the synods' life), a synod is a liturgical – indeed, a eucharistic – and spiritual body. It enjoys a certain formality and order. Each day's session of the General Synod begins with prayer and ends with a blessing given by one of the presidents; the inauguration of a new General Synod begins with a celebration of the Eucharist in Westminster Abbey, there is a big celebration of the Eucharist in York Minster on the Sunday morning of the July group of sessions in York, and about once a year there is also a celebration of the Eucharist in the Synod chamber; in addition, there are celebrations of the Eucharist each day outside the session for those members who wish to attend. When final decisions are taken about weighty and controversial matters, it is customary for the chairman to call for a period of silent prayer before the Synod votes, and for the result to be heard in silence.

These ten principles combine to produce a distinctive synthesis between episcopal governance and synodical representation of the whole church, including the laity, that is unusual if not unique. The Church of England has neither the type of episcopal system of governance in which the clergy and laity have at most a purely advisory role, nor the sort of representative, quasi-democratic governmental system to which episcopacy can appear to have been 'bolted on' as an additional adornment. There is an equality between the laity and the clergy in the synods of the Church of England; both houses have real decision-making power, including a power of veto. However, this does not mean that there is an equality between laity, clergy and episcopate, still less that bishops are now somehow subordinated to synods. On the contrary, the Church of England remains a truly episcopal church. It is still led and governed by its bishops, but the bishops act not in isolation but in partnership and constant dialogue with the clergy and laity through the synods of the church, and with their consent.

8

Synodical government in the Church of England, illustrated by the case of the ordination of women to the priesthood[1]

This chapter uses the case of the ordination of women to the priesthood to illustrate how the General Synod works.[2] At the time of writing it has not yet been decided whether the General Synod will embark on the process of legislation to permit the ordination of women to the episcopate, but this survey indicates how such a legislative process would unfold.

The early stages

Discussion of the ordination of women to the priesthood can be traced back to 1962, when the General Synod's predecessor, the Church Assembly, called for a study of the subject. The report *Women and Holy Orders* was published in 1966 and debated in 1967. *Women in Ministry: A Study* was published in 1968. In 1971 the Anglican Consultative Council asked the member churches of the Anglican Communion to consider the question and express a view. As a basis for discussion, the Church of England's Advisory Council on the Church's Ministry published in 1972 *The Ordination of Women to the Priesthood* (GS 104), a consultative document by Miss (later Dame) Christian Howard, a leading advocate of women's ordination.[3] Because the question included matters of doctrine, the General Synod referred it to the diocesan synods in 1973. Thirty diocesan synods passed the motion 'That this Synod considers that there are no fundamental objections to the ordination of women to the priesthood', but only 15 approved a second motion calling for the removal of legal and other barriers.[4] In 1975 the General Synod, in the light of the diocesan synod voting, approved the first motion. A motion calling for legislation to remove the legal and other barriers failed in the Houses of Bishops and Clergy, but a motion inviting the House of Bishops to bring such proposals before the Synod 'when, in the light of developments in the Anglican Communion generally as well as in this country, they judge the time for action to be right' was carried, as was a motion requesting the presidents to inform the Roman Catholic and Orthodox authorities of the decision and to invite them to share in 'an urgent re-examination of the theological grounds for including women in the Order of Priesthood'.[5] Three years later the House of Bishops considered that the time for action was right, and invited the Bishop of Birmingham, Dr Hugh Montefiore, to move a motion in November 1978 calling for legislation to remove the barriers to the ordination of women to the priesthood and episcopate. *A Supplement* (GS Misc 88) to the earlier consultative document, again by Miss Howard, was circulated. The motion, which was opposed by the Bishop of Truro (Dr Graham Leonard, later Bishop of London), was defeated in the House of Clergy.[6] In 1984 a *Further Report* (GS Misc 198), once again by Miss Howard, was circulated.

Preparation of legislation (1984–88)

The system of synodical government allows a deanery synod to send a motion to the diocesan synod for debate, and diocesan synods can send motions to the General Synod for debate (normally in the order in which they are received, one or two at each group of sessions). In November 1984 a motion 'That this Synod asks the Standing Committee to bring forward legislation to permit the ordination of Women to the Priesthood in the Provinces of Canterbury and York', having been passed by the Wandsworth Deanery Synod and the Southwark Diocesan Synod (and similar motions having been passed by seven other diocesan synods), was moved in the General Synod by the Bishop of Southwark – and carried.[7]

A new General Synod is elected every five years, so nothing was done until October 1985, after the synodical election, when the Standing Committee established a group, roughly equally divided between supporters and opponents of the legislation, to consider what it might include (an unusual step). The group's report, published in June 1986, set out possible safeguards for bishops and parishes unable to accept women priests, financial provisions to relieve the hardship of those who felt obliged to resign, and five possible ways of providing for those who remained in the Church of England but felt unable to accept the ministrations of a bishop who ordained women (ranging from the delegation of episcopal ministry to a bishop designated by the archbishop of the province to complete separation into two churches). In each case, the Synod was invited to consider which, if any, of these provisions should be included.[8] The House of Bishops responded with a memorandum saying that the bishops wished to reflect on the report 'bearing in mind . . . "their special responsibility to maintain and further the unity of the Church, to uphold its discipline and to guard its faith"'.[9] In July the Synod debated the report, but passed an amendment moved by the Archbishop of York, Dr John Habgood, which postponed further consideration to enable the House of Bishops to report to the Synod.[10]

A unanimous report by the House of Bishops was published in February 1987.[11] This set out the principal theological issues concerned, 'principles on which the legislation should be based', and a framework for legislation and safeguards. It supported safeguards for bishops and parishes and a separate measure making financial provisions, but rejected any provision for those unable to accept the ministry of bishops who ordained women; other matters should be covered by a House of Bishops' code of practice. The General Synod resolved that the legislation should be based on this report, and invited the bishops to begin work on their code of practice.[12] The draft legislation was not ready for general approval until July 1988.[13]

Since the Submission of the Clergy (agreed by the Convocation of Canterbury in 1532 and embodied in an Act of Parliament in 1534), canon law has been subordinated in England to statute law. Therefore, when the General Synod wishes to legislate by canon in an area (such as the ordination of women to the priesthood) not previously covered by canon law, this has to be sanctioned by Parliament. Today, however, the General Synod can pass measures which, if approved by Parliament (which can approve or reject, but not amend them), receive the royal assent and become part of the law of England. The main items of legislation were therefore the Priests (Ordination of Women) Measure and Canon C 4B (Of Women Priests). Clause 1 of the measure made it lawful for the General Synod to legislate by canon for the ordination of women to the priesthood (but stated that 'Nothing in this Measure shall make it lawful for a woman to be consecrated to the office of bishop'). Most of the remaining clauses were taken up with safeguards for those opposed. A General Synod measure 'may relate to any matter concerning the Church of England, and may extend to the amendment or repeal in whole or in part of any Act of Parliament',[14] so this measure could include a provision that the Sex Discrimination Act 1975 should not apply to decisions about the ordination, appointment or licensing of women priests. Canon C 4B contains just two clauses:

1. A woman may be ordained to the office of priest if she otherwise satisfies the requirements of Canon as to the persons who may be ordained as priests.

2. In the forms of service contained in *The Book of Common Prayer* or in the Ordinal words importing the masculine gender in relation to the priesthood shall be construed as including the feminine, except where the context otherwise requires.

The measure also provided that it should not come into force until another measure had received the royal assent, providing for the relief of hardship incurred by people resigning from ecclesiastical service because of their opposition to the promulgation of the canon. It was therefore accompanied by an Ordination of Women (Financial Provisions) Measure. Amending Canon No. 13 contained necessary amendments to other canons. The two measures and two canons all went through the synodical process at the same time.

The synodical process: 1988–92

Second Report of the House of Bishops and General Approval, July 1988

In July 1988 the Synod debated the second report of the House of Bishops.[15] This substantial (140-page) report set out in detail the theological arguments for and against the ordination of women to the priesthood. In doing so, it nuanced the claim in the 1975 Synod resolution that 'there are no fundamental objections to the ordination of women to the priesthood'; from now on, there was official acceptance that fundamental objections did exist, even though they were not shared by the majority of the Synod's members.

The Synod then went on to debate the measures and canons. The Archbishop of Canterbury, Dr Robert Runcie, said that he believed that 'the theological arguments now tip the balance in favour' of the principle, but expressed disquiet that the House of Bishops had had no opportunity to consider the draft legislation, which had been prepared on behalf of the Standing Committee (which alone could initiate legislation; now legislation is introduced on the instructions of the Archbishops' Council or the Business Committee). Fearing that 'debate on this legislation occupying so much time in our dioceses and parishes with such uncertain prospect of success will not serve the cause of women's ordination or the spiritual health of the Church', and that it would divide the Church of England, he was unable to vote for it. General approval was given, but by much less than the two-thirds majorities that would be required for final approval (Bishops: 28–21; Clergy: 137–102; Laity: 134–93).[16] (The general approval stage is now known as 'first consideration'.)

Revision, 1988–90

The legislation was then committed to a Revision Committee consisting of the Steering Committee of members in charge of the legislation and 15 other members (five of them – a bishop, a priest, two laymen and a lay woman – opposed to the measure). This met seven times to consider 392 amendments proposed by 54 individuals and by the Steering Committee, and produced revised drafts.

On 7 and 9 November 1989 the General Synod had general debates on the revision of the main measure, and went on to debate it and the two canons clause by clause – over 13 hours of debate.[17] Seven new clauses and 23 amendments to the measure were moved, and for each clause or group of clauses the Synod had to vote positively that it should be included in the measure. Many of the amendments could be dealt with speedily, because after an amendment has been explained by the person moving it, and commented on by the Steering Committee, it lapses unless 40 members stand up to request a debate. Most votes were taken by a simple show of hands (in three cases where the voting was too close for certainty, the hands were counted); only on two amendments, and on the principle of women priests (clause 1 of the measure and Canon C 4B) did 25 members require a vote by houses. None of the new clauses and only two substantive and five consequential amendments were carried.

There was, however, one very important change. The Revision Committee had inserted a clause putting a time limit of 20 years on the safeguards. The Synod postponed a decision on this until the second day, after they had been finalized. The Steering Committee then proposed, in the light of the earlier debates, that the clause should be dropped. After two speeches for the time limit (by a laywoman and a bishop) and one against (by a priest), the Archbishop of York (Dr Habgood) intervened to say that opponents of women priests saw the time limit as a threat and it should be rejected. The Synod took his advice.[18] As a result, the safeguards can only be removed by a two-thirds majority in each house (and parliamentary approval). This may be seen as a turning point in the whole process, marking the beginning of a concern to assure those opposed to the ordination of women to the priesthood of a permanently protected position in the Church of England.

Reference to the dioceses and final drafting, February 1992

Under Article 8 of the Synod's constitution a measure or canon providing for permanent changes in the services of Baptism or Holy Communion or in the Ordinal must be approved by a majority of the diocesan synods before the General Synod can give it final approval. After revision of the Financial Provisions Measure in February 1990 two booklets were published in April, one containing the text of the legislation, an explanatory note and the House of Bishops' draft Code of Practice, the other a digest of their second report.[19]

The dioceses had until 30 November 1991 to respond. During those 18 months, the legislation was debated by the deanery synods (although members often did not have copies of the texts) and then by the diocesan synods. Approval by both the House of Clergy and the House of Laity in 23 of the 44 diocesan synods was required; in fact, 38 approved it in this way. The voting in the deanery synods was significant, because their membership includes all the beneficed and licensed clergy of the Church of England and representatives of every parish. In them, only 62.5 per cent of the clergy and 66.1 per cent of the laity supported the legislation, whereas in the diocesan synods the figures were 67 per cent and 68 per cent.[20]

Reference to the House of Bishops, the Convocations and the House of Laity, 1992

In February 1992 the Synod debated the report on the reference to the dioceses and made minor and technical amendments to the legislation.[21] Under Article 7 of the constitution 'a provision touching doctrinal formulae or the services or ceremonies of the Church of England or the administration of the Sacraments or sacred rites thereof' must be referred to the House of Bishops before it is finally approved, and can only be submitted for final approval in terms proposed by the House of Bishops. This safeguards the role of the bishops as the guardians of the church's faith and liturgy. The house approved the legislation in June.

When the General Synod was established, the two Convocations continued to exist and meet occasionally. This was due not only to veneration of institutions older than Parliament itself, but also to concerns that without its own Convocation the smaller northern province (14 dioceses) would be dominated by the southern province (30 dioceses), and that 'the Northern Convocation is an important element in maintaining the status of the Archbishop of York': 'If there is to be an Archbishop of York and he is to be effectively a Primate then he must be able to summon a Synod of bishops and clergy.'[22] Either Convocation or the House of Laity may require business covered by Article 7 to be referred for approval by each house of each Convocation and by the House of Laity; this protects the northern province (although a repeated rejection by one house of one Convocation can be overruled by a two-thirds majority in the General Synod Houses of Bishops and Clergy). This right was claimed, and the legislation was approved at separate meetings of the five houses in York in July 1992. In 1990 the legislation had been the main issue in the synodical election; this was the first opportunity for the members of the new Synod to vote on it. Under Article 8 of the constitution, final approval of the measure would require a two-thirds majority in each house, but in July the House of Laity (half of whose members were women) approved it by only 148 votes (61.41 per cent) to 93 (38.59 per cent). In the ensuing months members of the Synod were lobbied intensively – especially, it is said, members of the House of Laity who had been seen to vote against in July.

Final approval, November 1992

On 11 November 1992 the chamber and galleries were full, crowds waited outside Church House, and the Synod's proceedings were broadcast live on radio and television.[23] It was a solemn occasion. Normally, debates are chaired by one of a panel of chairmen, but when an Article 7 or 8 measure is considered for final approval, one of the archbishops must be in the chair. The Archbishop of York chaired in the morning, the Archbishop of Canterbury (now Dr George Carey) in the afternoon. The motion was moved by the Bishop of Guildford and opposed by the Prolocutor of the Convocation of Canterbury; both archbishops spoke in favour. In a final approval debate every member who wishes must be allowed to speak, but after five hours the archbishop asked those who had not yet spoken not to insist on doing so. After concluding speeches on each side, he invited the Synod to stand for a prayer, followed by the giving of the Peace. The registrar then called on the Synod to 'divide'. In a division by houses, clergy and laity vote by leaving through different doors, the bishops by ascending the platform on one side or the other; those voting are counted by members of their own house. One female member who was elected as an opponent but felt obliged to abstain remained seated, quietly weeping; she was comforted by a bishop who also abstained. When the Synod reassembled, the archbishop reminded the Synod of its custom of receiving the result of controversial votes in silence, and announced the results: Bishops: 39 (75 per cent) – 13; Clergy 176 (70.4 per cent) – 74; Laity: 169 (67.3 per cent) – 82. The measure had been approved by the narrowest of margins; had two lay members (or five bishops) voted differently, it would have been defeated. The Synod went on to approve the other measure and the canons without debate, divisions by houses being required. Outside, supporters of the legislation celebrated jubilantly, while opponents slipped away into the night.

Parliamentary approval and the Episcopal Ministry Act of Synod, 1993

Almost immediately, media attention focused on those opposed to the ordination of women to the priesthood. The measures (but not, of course, the canons) now had to be presented to Parliament for approval, and Parliament's Ecclesiastical Committee, consisting of 15 members of each House of Parliament, had the task of reporting on 'the nature and legal effect of the measure[s] and its views as to the expediency thereof, especially with regard to the rights of all Her Majesty's subjects'.[24] The committee met eleven times between March and July 1993, four times with Synod representatives (including, unusually, an opponent of the legislation) and once with the Synod's whole Legislative Committee. The committee's deliberations focused particularly on the expediency of the legislation (how much it would cost in terms of division and financially) and on the rights of those opposed to the ordination of women to the priesthood.[25]

The parliamentary process gave an interval in which arrangements to limit the number of opponents who would leave and provide for those who would stay could be worked out. A group of five bishops, chaired by the Archbishop of York (Dr Habgood), had been meeting since early in 1992 to plan the way forward, whichever decision was taken in November. In January 1993 the House of Bishops met for four days with the rest of the bishops. When a statement was finally agreed unanimously, many of the bishops were in tears and began singing a hymn. In June the House of Bishops met again to agree the details. Pressure both from those opposed and from the Ecclesiastical Committee led the house to agree that the proposals should be embodied in an Act of Synod, which although it is not legally binding has great moral force and can only be revoked by the Synod.[26] This was published in a document entitled *Bonds of Peace*, which stated that 'those who . . . cannot conscientiously accept that women may be ordained as priests will continue to hold a legitimate and recognised position within the Church of England' and that 'the bishops, corporately and individually, are pledged to maintain the integrity of both positions'.[27] The document was supported by a theological paper entitled *Being in Communion*.[28] The Act of Synod was debated by the General Synod on 13 July 1993.[29] The day before, the Ecclesiastical Committee had voted (by 16 to 11 and 17 to 10) that the measures were expedient. The House of Commons and House of Lords went on to approve the measures in October, and they received the royal assent on 5 November.

The purpose of the Episcopal Ministry Act of Synod 1993 is 'to make provision for the continued diversity of opinion in the Church of England as to the ordination and ministry of women as priests'. Section 1 states that 'No person or body shall discriminate against candidates either for ordination or for appointment to senior office in the Church of England on the grounds of their views or positions about the ordination of women to the priesthood'. The Act of Synod goes on to set out arrangements for episcopal ministry to those opposed, including the appointment of up to three additional suffragan bishops, called provincial episcopal visitors, who also act as spokesmen and advisers for those opposed and assist the archbishops in monitoring the operation of the Act of Synod. Where a diocesan bishop is not willing to ordain women to the priesthood or commission another bishop to do so, he may allow women to be ordained by the archbishop or by a bishop commissioned by him.

On 9 November the General Synod debated the draft Act of Synod, which had been revised following the July debate, clause by clause.[30] Apart from four small drafting amendments proposed by the Steering Committee, all amendments were defeated. One amendment stated that no one 'who holds that it is impossible for a woman to be a priest' would in future be ordained or appointed to senior office; this was defeated overwhelmingly, confirming that there would be no limits to the diversity of opinion. The Act of Synod was approved on 11 November (Bishops: 39–0; Clergy: 175–12; Laity: 194–14); some militant campaigners for the ordination of women protested from the public gallery and had to be removed. Synodical approval was also given to the creation of up to three new suffragan sees for the provincial episcopal visitors. The House of Bishops published its Code of Practice in January 1994. It is striking that by the end of the process the measure, Act of Synod and Code of Practice contradicted in a number of important respects the House of Bishops' first report on the principles that should underlie the legislation, while the provision of provincial episcopal visitors resembled one of the options in the original report that the bishops rejected.

Promulgation of the canons and proclamation of the Act of Synod, 1994

A final stage remained. Since the Submission of the Clergy, the making of canons has required the royal licence and assent. Statutes become law when the royal assent is given, but canon law is made by the Synod, not the Crown, so it is after the royal licence and assent has been received that a canon is promulged. Thus on 22 February 1994 the Archbishop of Canterbury took the chair of the Synod (the promulgation of a canon must be moved by one of the archbishops from the chair). He announced that the royal licence and assent had been received, and asked the registrar to read the Instrument of Enactment. He then moved 'That the Canon entitled "Canon C 4B" be promulged and executed'. This motion cannot be debated, and only a simple majority is required. The motion having been passed by a show of hands, the instrument was signed by the archbishops, the prolocutor and the chairman and vice-chairman of the House of Laity. The amending canon was similarly promulged. A motion that 'The Episcopal Ministry Act of Synod be solemnly affirmed and proclaimed an Act of Synod' was passed without debate and the registrar read the Act of Proclamation. These formalities concluded the process of legislation.[31]

Concluding reflections

Reflections on whether or not the decision was right would be out of place here, but this survey prompts some questions about the process. Was it right that a report on the contents of the legislation could be published before it was seen by the House of Bishops,[32] or that the Synod could give general approval to such controversial legislation without the House of Bishops having considered it[33] (and against the advice of the Archbishop of Canterbury and 20 of his episcopal colleagues)? Especially given the narrow margin by which final approval was given, some have asked whether legislation that will require a two-thirds majority in each house for final approval should require similar majorities for general approval (or 'first consideration', as the initial stage is now called)? More fundamentally, some commentators have suggested that legislation, which in the view of a significant minority affects the identity of the Church of England, should require a higher overall majority – perhaps 75 per cent (as was required for the Anglican–Methodist unity proposals in 1969).[34]

Whatever the answer to these questions, the Church of England can take pride in its synodical system. No one could claim that the Synod acted hastily or without due consideration. Only after 22 years of debate and discussion was a motion calling for legislation passed, and the process from then until the promulgation of the canon took more than nine further years. The legislation was prepared and revised with great care and attention to detail, and debated not only in the General and diocesan Synods but in each deanery synod. The final approval debate was widely praised for its tone and quality by those who heard a Synod debate for the first time on radio or television. The laity and the clergy, but also in the end the bishops, were able to play their proper and distinctive roles in discerning the way forward.

9

The choosing of bishops in the early Church and in the Church of England: A historical survey[1]

The means by which bishops[2] are chosen has varied throughout history, in response to changes in the balance of power within church and state. Within the Church of England, as this chapter will show, the system has outwardly remained the same over the last 1,000 years – in the twenty-first century bishops are still elected by the canons of the cathedral on the nomination of the Crown, as they were in the eleventh century and indeed before that. Yet that continuity of form masks great change, albeit an evolutionary change which has taken place gradually without a radical alteration at any one point. Over the years the personal role of the sovereign gradually became a formal one, with the real decision lying with the prime minister; more recently, the prime minister's role has been reduced to that of choosing between candidates proposed by the church. This illustrates the nature of change in the Church of England, and indeed in England generally: continuity of form on the surface, combined with gradual adaptation in the underlying reality to match the different circumstances of succeeding ages.

The early Church and developments in East and West

In the earliest times, bishops were elected by the whole diocese - clergy and people together. However, the person elected needed to be accepted by the bishops of neighbouring churches, who came together to ordain him. Canon 4 of the Council of Nicaea (325) required the presence of at least three of the bishops of the province and the written consent of the remainder, and allocated the confirmation of the election, and thus a potential veto, to the metropolitan.[3] Once ordained, the bishop was regarded as married to his diocese. Translation to another see was viewed as akin to adultery and outlawed by Canon 15 of Nicaea - although the canon was never rigorously adhered to and translation became common in the Middle Ages. Dioceses clung to the right to choose their own bishop, despite the attempts of both emperors and provincial synods to interfere. The Council of Ancyra (c.314) upheld the right of a diocese to reject a bishop chosen and consecrated for it by a provincial synod, but as the fourth century progressed, Eastern canons attempted increasingly to restrict the local church's rights in favour of the provincial synod of bishops.[4] Popular election not infrequently gave rise to malpractice, faction and disorder, however. People were often bribed to shout for one candidate rather than another, and riots could occur. At the papal election of 366, an attack by supporters of the eventually successful candidate on those of his rival left 137 dead in the basilica where the consecration was taking place. Malpractice and disorder contributed to the abandonment of the election of bishops by the whole diocese, clergy and people.

In the East, the Emperor Justinian (527–65) eventually restricted the local electorate to the clergy and notables, and limited their role to nominating three candidates, of whom the metropolitan would select one. The role of the general laity was confined to that of assenting to the election by acclamation. At this stage, emperors were involved only in elections to the patriarchal See of Constantinople. By the fifteenth century, Eastern bishops came to be chosen by the bishops of the province either unanimously submitting a single name for confirmation by the metropolitan or offering him a choice of three. From the tenth century the emperor claimed a right of veto, and from 1317 the bishops also recognized an imperial right to nominate (while reserving their right to reject a candidate and await a further nomination).[5]

In the West, royal control was exercised more completely and much earlier. In the sixth century the Frankish kings often rejected those elected by the local church and appointed their own candidates, and by the end of the seventh century bishops in Spain were appointed by the king and the metropolitan. According to a canon of the Twelfth Council of Toledo (681), the Archbishop of Toledo was to consecrate 'whomsoever the royal power chooses', providing he considered the candidate worthy.[6] However, the theory that bishops should be elected by the clergy and people survived longer in the West than in the East, compromised as it was by royal control. In the mid-ninth century the principle came once again to be honoured in practice in France. A compromise agreed by the Synod of Valence in 855 preserved the right of clergy and people to elect, but made it subject to royal permission, which came to be known as the *congé d'élire*. This arrangement did not preclude very strong suggestion by the king as to who should be elected.[7] In the eleventh century, 'election by clergy and people' became a slogan of reformers. The principle was reaffirmed in 1049 by the Council of Rheims ('Nobody should be promoted to government in the Church unless he has been elected by the clergy and the people') and by Gregory VII at the Synod of Rome in 1080. By about 1140, however, the role of the laity was no longer seen as equal to that of the clergy: Gratian's *Decretum* says 'The clergy is to elect, the people to consent'. At the same time, the clerical electorate became narrower. A constitution of the Second Lateran Council (1139) restricted the right of election to the canons of the cathedral chapter, though the other clergy were to have a consultative voice and their consent was still held to be necessary. By the thirteenth century the cathedral chapter alone elected, and the right of the people to consent was no longer upheld.[8]

Anglo-Saxon England

Practice in Anglo-Saxon England seems not to have been consistent, but however the appointment was formally made, in practice the choice rested in the hands of the king and his close advisers. Once the kingdom was united, election by a provincial synod or national council of the Church did not imply freedom from royal influence, since the distinction between such synods or councils and the *witenagemot* or council of state was unclear, the king and noblemen as well as bishops being present at both.[9]

In the 960s a new phenomenon arose in England, that of the monastic cathedral; Winchester and Worcester were reorganized on monastic lines, and Sherborne and Canterbury followed by the turn of the century. The *Regularis Concordia*, rules for monastic life in England approved by the Synod of Winchester between 970 and 973, provided that the cathedral monastic communities should elect their bishop with the advice and consent of the king and in accordance with the provisions of the Rule of St Benedict concerning the election of an abbot. If no monk from the cathedral community was suitable, a monk from another distinguished monastery could be chosen.[10] These provisions were generally followed in Worcester and Sherborne, and between 1006 and 1049 Dorchester had three successive bishops from Ramsey Abbey, with which it was closely connected. Winchester and Canterbury, however, were too important for the king to allow the monks to choose their own bishop.

If the monastic cathedral communities were only partially successful in securing a real voice in the election of their bishops, it was hardly likely that the unreformed bodies of clergy who served the secular cathedrals would be able to do so. On the eve of the Conquest, these bodies, which seem to have consisted of between five and seven clerks or canons, were generally poor, and by definition they lacked the sense of corporate identity and relative independence that the monastic cathedral communities enjoyed. In the confusion following the Viking conquests the clergy of St Cuthbert's remote foundation were able to elect their own bishop at Chester-le-Street and even at Durham in 1020, but thereafter royal power reasserted itself. Elsewhere, it is safe to say that at this time, as earlier, bishops were appointed by the king, whether acting of his own volition or at the instigation of his stronger courtiers. The *witan* (the king's council) is occasionally mentioned, but it does not seem to have had a formal role. Nor is it clear that an election by the local church took place in every case.

Even where there was such a ceremony, it is important that the term 'election' should not be taken to imply a contest between rival candidates. It has been pointed out that in the mid-eleventh century generally (not just in England)

> *Electio* had a predominantly passive sense. It was a procedure for giving legal validity to a decision which had usually already been taken. It was only when the demand arose for '*libera electio*', and by new bodies of electors, that an active force was created capable of opposing the will of the king.[11]

Furthermore, in considering canonical elections, it is important to be clear that the word 'election' did not carry its modern, democratic meaning. Indeed, *electio* means 'choice', rather than 'election' in the modern sense, and it could denote choice by a single individual;[12] in the words of the German historian Albert Hauck, 'appointment is not the antithesis of election'.[13]

From the beginning, English archbishops received from the pope, as a sign of their metropolitical jurisdiction, the pallium (a narrow scarf of wool which loosely encircles the neck and hangs down in front and behind, forming the letter Y - as depicted on the arms of the Archbishop of Canterbury). From 927 (1026 in the case of York) there was an established custom that the archbishops went to Rome to receive the pallium, whereas previously it had been sent.[14] The election of an archbishop was in a sense confirmed by the pope in his bestowing of the pallium. The first attempt by the papacy to obtain control over episcopal elections came in the case of Stigand, who was appointed Archbishop of Canterbury while his exiled predecessor was still alive. He had to obtain the pallium from an antipope in 1058. William I refused to be crowned by him and he was deposed by papal legates in 1070.[15]

The English Church from the Conquest to Magna Carta

From the mid-eleventh century the Church began to assert its distinctiveness from the state. In 1075 Pope Gregory VII outlawed the custom whereby newly ordained bishops were invested with ring and staff, the symbols of their office, by the secular ruler. At the same time, and with papal encouragement, cathedral chapters claimed the right to elect their bishops. Especially in larger dioceses, election by the whole clergy of the diocese would be impractical; the members of cathedral chapters were normally on the spot when their bishop died and could easily be gathered together for an election. By the middle of the twelfth century the legal right of the cathedral chapter to elect was everywhere established.[16]

In England, neither the abandonment of royal 'investiture' nor capitular election (election by the cathedral chapter) was conceded without a struggle. In 1085 three bishops were elected at a Christmas synod, all of them royal clerks, and even when capitular election was conceded, this did not necessarily imply freedom from royal control. In 1107 Henry I made an agreement with Anselm, the Archbishop of Canterbury, in which he gave up the investiture with the ring and staff while continuing to require bishops to do homage for the temporalities of their see before they were consecrated. He also conceded capitular election, but the agreement provided that the election by the chapter should be made in the king's chapel with his assent and in the presence of his ecclesiastical advisers.[17] Capitular elections held in such circumstances could hardly be described as 'free'. However, when the king was weak, free election was possible, and of the 14 elections held between 1143 and 1154, in the latter part of Stephen's reign, at least six reflected a free choice by the chapter.[18] Under Henry II, Richard and John it was exceptional for a bishop-elect actually to gain possession of a see in England or Wales if the king preferred another candidate.

Whereas in the Church at large free election by cathedral chapters meant more disputed elections and therefore a great increase in appeals to Rome, in England royal influence was so strong that disputes and appeals to Rome remained rare.[19] One disputed election which did result in an appeal to Rome was that for the See of Canterbury in 1205. Fifteen monks summoned to Rome for the appeal elected Stephen Langton as archbishop, and in 1207 he was consecrated by the pope. King John's refusal to accept him resulted in England being placed under an interdict (whereby no religious services could be performed) until 1213. On 21 November 1214 John granted a charter to the church, the provisions of which were in turn confirmed by the pope the following year. This granted freedom of election to cathedral and conventual chapters, but made this subject to recognition of the king as founder and patron of the churches concerned. Before proceeding to an election, the chapter was to apply to the king for a *congé d'élire* (permission to elect), as was already customary, but the election would then be held in the chapter house and not in the king's chapel, the king's views being signified by letter. His assent was, however, required. This would be given in letters patent addressed to the metropolitan or, in the case of an archbishop, the pope, requesting him to proceed to confirm the election and consecrate the bishop-elect. After consecration, the bishop would do homage and receive in return the temporalities (the properties, revenues and ecclesiastical patronage) of his see.[20] This agreement settled procedures which (with the exception of the papal role in confirming the election of an archbishop) essentially remain in force today.

From Magna Carta to Henry VIII

The opening chapter of Magna Carta, the Great Charter of 1215, promised that the Church of England should be free ('Quod anglicana ecclesia libera sit'), but in the matter of episcopal elections this freedom was to be short-lived. Free elections meant disputed elections, and this was especially so because of the rules for canonical elections set down in the constitution *Quia propter*, published at the Fourth Lateran Council in 1215. This set out three methods of canonical election: *quasi per inspirationem* (where all agree to elect the same person), *per compromissum* (where all agree to delegate the election to a small committee) and *per scrutinium* (whereby each elector gives his vote for his preferred candidate orally or in writing to three scrutineers, and the candidate chosen by all, or the majority, or the *senior pars*, is declared elected).[21] Of the third method, Geoffrey Barraclough commented: 'It is striking enough that the Church had the wisdom to reject the democratic fallacy of "counting heads", and to attempt an estimate of the intelligence and enlightened good faith of the voters.'[22] Election was an exercise in identifying not the candidate preferred by the majority, but the candidate chosen by God; elections were held above all with a view to a manifestation of the divine will.[23]

The third method, which was most commonly used, gave ample scope for argument as to whether the majority or the minority of a chapter was the *senior pars*.[24] Disputed elections resulted in appeals to Rome (for a decision as to which part had the sounder judgement), and there was a great increase in these. In some cases the king sought to overturn elections in favour of his own candidate, in others chapters sought to defend their freedom to elect. The number of appeals and their resolution in Rome (sometimes by the pope appointing a fresh candidate) naturally tended to increase the involvement of the pope in the choice of English bishops. In the thirteenth century papal involvement generally served to maintain the freedom of chapters as electoral bodies against royal power,[25] but ultimately the effect was the opposite.

The thirteenth century was, in any case, a time of centralization in the Western Church as well as one of reform; indeed, some of the most active reformers were also the most active centralizers. It was at this time that the practice of reservation of benefices for papal provision (direct appointment by the pope) began. Initially, this might be a special reservation of a particular benefice or a general reservation of a class of benefices. In 1265 the papacy reserved all benefices which fell vacant when their holders died at the papal court, and by the end of the century this was extended to those who died within two days' journey. In the first half of the fourteenth century sees vacated by the translation (by the pope) of their existing bishop were added, and finally all sees whatsoever.[26]

During the reign of Henry III (1216–72) there were only six direct provisions to English bishoprics (although six of the seven men appointed to Canterbury in the thirteenth century were in effect designated by the pope[27]). The turning point was the reign of Edward II (1307–27), in which 13 out of 28 appointments were by papal provision, and after 1344 all bishoprics were filled in that way.[28] It should not be thought, however, that in the long run this resulted in an increase in papal power over the English Church and a corresponding decline in royal power. That was only so when a weak king was confronted by a strong pope. Thus, of the 13 papal provisions under Edward II, only six were more or less against the king's wishes, and all of these came after 1316 (when the king was weakest), by John XXII (1316–34). It was under Clement VI (1342–52) that papal provision became the norm, but by then it was accepted that the pope would act on the king's nomination. By 1345 Clement was saying that if the King of England asked him to make an ass a bishop, he would do so. It is also important to stress that papal provision did not mean the appointment of alien bishops. In the fourteenth century, for example, only two foreigners were appointed by papal provision, both in the latter part of Edward II's reign, and one of them was a royal nominee. Another change which occurred in the fourteenth century was the growth of translation. In the first half of the century only 9 out of 70 appointments were made by translation of an existing bishop from another see, but between 1351 and 1400 the proportion was 31 out of 86, and it remained at much the same level.[29]

A renewed struggle with Rome in the middle years of the century resulted in the Statute of Provisors (1351), which outlawed the introduction of bulls of provision on pain of forfeiture and imprisonment. If a chapter was unwilling to elect in the face of a papal provision, the statute empowered the Crown to make a direct appointment. In practice, however, the statute was not applied if the pope appointed the king's nominee to an episcopal see by papal provision. The Statute of *Praemunire* (1353) prevented electors who ignored a papal provision being cited to Rome on appeal. This was extended by the Great Statute of *Praemunire* (1393, 16 Richard II, c. 5), which provided that anyone who should procure, bring into the realm, receive or execute any bulls, excommunications or other instruments from Rome would be put outside the king's protection, their lands and property would be forfeit to the king, and they would be imprisoned during the king's pleasure.[30]

The system of negotiation, compromise and agreement between Crown and pope over episcopal appointments, which persisted until 1534, generally suited both sides. It exalted the popes' office within the Church, but at the same time in practice it was easier for the kings to get the appointments they wanted through this system than when elections were disputed. When popes did try to appoint their own candidates, the Statutes of Provisors and *Praemunire* could be renewed and brought into play. Occasionally, a royal nominee might be rejected, but the matter was usually settled by compromise. Generally, appointments were made by mutual agreement between the king and the pope.[31] Throughout this period, the practice whereby the cathedral chapter, on receipt of a *congé d'élire* from the Crown, elected the candidate nominated by the Crown in an accompanying letter persisted. The only difference was that instead of the bishop-elect seeking confirmation of the election from the metropolitan, the Crown instead sought provision by the pope, which made confirmation of the election unnecessary. Confirmation by the metropolitan was revived between 1415 and 1417, when the See of Rome was itself vacant.[32]

Sixteenth-century changes

In the course of the separation of the Church of England from Rome in the 1530s under Henry VIII, two statutes which touched on the appointment of bishops were enacted. The first, passed in 1532, required the pope to act upon Crown nominations without delay; otherwise the nomination would be submitted for confirmation to the archbishop of the province. The second was the Act in Restraint of Annates (25 Hen. 8 c. 20), now known by the short title The Appointment of Bishops Act 1534, which is still in force today.[33] The act enshrines the traditional practice in statute law. The king grants a *congé d'élire* to the prior and convent or dean and chapter of the cathedral, which is sent together with 'a letter missive containing the name of the person which they shall elect and choose'. When the election has been made, the king sends letters patent to the archbishop of the province informing him of the election and requiring him to confirm it and invest and consecrate the bishop-elect, without reference to Rome. In the case of an archiepiscopal see, the letters patent are sent to another archbishop and two bishops, or else four bishops, within the king's dominions. If the prior and convent or dean and chapter do not elect the person nominated within twelve days of receipt of the *congé d'élire* and letter missive, the king may appoint his nominee by letters patent. Furthermore, anyone failing to do within 20 days what the act requires of them and anyone acting against the act is subject to the pains and penalties of the statutes of *praemunire*.

As regards the procedure of *congé d'élire*, letters missive and capitular election, the 1534 act, as we have seen, merely enshrined in statute the traditional practice. Confirmation of the election by the metropolitan was simply a restoration of practice which had been made redundant by papal provisions. Furthermore, the statute required elections and confirmation of elections but did not lay down how they should be conducted. Here there was no innovation. The procedure to be followed by a chapter in electing a bishop and by an archbishop confirming an election are two examples of sections of the medieval canon law that are still in force in the Church of England, not having been touched by subsequent legislation.[34] By contrast, the provision for confirmation of the election of an archbishop was obviously new, as was that for appointment by letters patent. Most novel was the imposition of the pains and penalties of *praemunire* for contravention of the act.

Henry VIII's act was replaced in the first year of Edward VI's reign by a new statute which abolished capitular election and provincial confirmation, so that all episcopal appointments were by letters patent, but after the interlude under Queen Mary, Elizabeth I re-enacted the 1534 act in 1559. It remains in force today, with the exception that the statutes of *praemunire* and the section of the 1534 act which referred to them were repealed by the Criminal Law Act 1967.

Change was proposed in 1641, when Bishop Williams of Lincoln (later Archbishop of York) introduced a bill which would have replaced capitular election with a system whereby the dean and chapter, together with twelve clergy from the diocese (nominated four each by the king, the House of Lords and the House of Commons) would have submitted three names, of which the Crown would appoint one by letters patent. The bill was not proceeded with after its second reading.[35] Within a few years, of course, episcopacy was abolished, but when it was restored in 1660, the 1534 act was enforced once again.

The choice of candidates, 1660–1837

Since 1660 the formal system of royal nomination, capitular election and provincial confirmation has not altered. What has changed very considerably is the way in which the candidate nominated by the Crown is chosen.

At first, appointments were made personally by the sovereign, having consulted his or her chief ministers. Elizabeth I, for example, was advised by Cecil on the basis of names sent by the Archbishop of Canterbury, Charles I by Laud. At the restoration, it was Gilbert Sheldon, Bishop of London (Archbishop of Canterbury from 1663), from whom Charles II sought advice on episcopal appointments. In 1681 a commission consisting of the Archbishop of Canterbury, the Bishop of London and four laymen was appointed to be consulted by the secretaries of state. Nevertheless, it was open to the king to make appointments purely of his own volition, as he did in appointing Thomas Ken to Bath and Wells in 1684.[36] After Mary II died, a commission was again appointed, in 1695, to advise William III, who had little knowledge of the Church of England. This commission consisted of the Archbishops of Canterbury and York and four other bishops.

Unlike her predecessor, Queen Anne took an active interest in episcopal appointments. She generally acted on the advice of her ministers, but in 1707 offered the Sees of Exeter and Chester on her own initiative without even consulting them.

Under the Hanoverians, the initiative passed to the chief minister. Under George II, Walpole generally agreed episcopal appointments with Queen Caroline (until her death in 1737). From 1723 until 1735 Walpole was guided almost entirely by Edmund Gibson, the Bishop of London. On one occasion - in 1733 - when an appointment was announced with which Gibson did not agree (because he believed the candidate, Thomas Rundle, to be an Arian), Walpole had to reverse the decision in the face of an absolute refusal by Gibson (who would have been the chief consecrator because of Archbishop Wake's incapacity) to consecrate Rundle. There are isolated incidents of both George II and George III rejecting ministerial nominations and appointing their own candidates. The most notable was in 1805, when Pitt informed George III that when Archbishop Moore died he would recommend the Bishop of Lincoln, George Pretyman Tomline, as his successor. On receiving news of Moore's death, the king rode over to Windsor and offered the archbishopric to the dean, Charles Manners-Sutton, before Pitt had the opportunity to offer formal advice. Although Pitt's audience with the king the following day was so acrimonious that Lord Sidmouth 'believed such strong language had rarely ever passed between a sovereign and his minister', Manners-Sutton duly succeeded. In 1821, however, it was established that a prime minister could insist on having the final say in ecclesiastical appointments. Under threat of resignation, Lord Liverpool required George IV to withdraw his nomination of Charles Sumner to a canonry at Windsor. However, the king retained very considerable influence, and Sumner's appointments as Bishop of Llandaff (1826) and Bishop of Winchester (1827) were both made by Lord Liverpool at the king's request.

The reign of Queen Victoria, 1837–1901

Bernard Palmer, in his study of episcopal appointments from 1837 to 1977, describes Queen Victoria's reign as 'the prime ministerial heyday', since prime ministers could ignore the wishes of Archbishops of Canterbury on the one hand and insist on having the final say against the queen's preference on the other.[37] Ironically, however, in her later years Queen Victoria not infrequently had her way over episcopal appointments.

In the first half of Victoria's reign the complexion of the bench depended very much on the preferences of her prime ministers. Viscount Melbourne (1835–41) generally appointed Whig sympathizers of moderate views. Sir Robert Peel

(1841–6) preferred moderate churchmen – mostly, in the words of Owen Chadwick, 'safe, solid, dull'.[38] Unlike his predecessor, he did not demand from potential bishops an undertaking to support him politically. Peel consulted the Archbishop of Canterbury as a matter of course, but neither his predecessor nor his successor, Lord John Russell (1846–52), felt obliged to do so. Peel also consulted Bishop Blomfield of London, but Russell did not take advice from anyone on a systematic basis; his closest confidant in these matters was Prince Albert. Viscount Palmerston (1855–8 and 1859–65) relied, especially during his first ministry, on the advice of his stepdaughter's husband, the seventh Earl of Shaftesbury, and his appointments showed a clear evangelical bias as a result. Shaftesbury did not favour academics, and in 1860 the queen felt moved to ask Palmerston not to confine his selection to 'respectable parish priests'. The bench, in her view, 'should not be left devoid of some University men of acknowledged standing and theological learning'; at a time of doctrinal controversy it would be a serious weakness if 'no value were attached to the opinions of at least some of those who are to govern' the church. Palmerston agreed that 'men of very moderate capacity have too often been chosen for the office of Bishop', but at the same time opined that the 'most able' bishops, Wilberforce and Phillpotts, 'would be better if their abilities were less'.[39]

The nine months of Benjamin Disraeli's first ministry (1868) saw a shift in the balance of power in episcopal appointments in favour of the queen, who disputed three of Disraeli's five nominations for English bishoprics and got her way on each occasion. In Disraeli, Queen Victoria, with the experience and standing of a monarch who had reigned for over 30 years, was confronted with a prime minister who had little knowledge of, or interest in, the church, and who was motivated entirely by political considerations (one of which was the usefulness of retaining the queen's favour). Having rejected a canon of St Paul's whom Disraeli proposed for Peterborough as an insignificant low churchman, and a second-choice candidate, the queen suggested William Magee. He was recommended independently by the high-church cabinet minister Lord John Manners, and Disraeli acquiesced. Emboldened by her success, Victoria wrote to Disraeli on the day of Archbishop Longley's death, suggesting the broad-church Bishop of London, A. C. Tait, to succeed him. The letter crossed with one from Disraeli nominating Bishop Ellicott of Gloucester and Bristol, a Conservative supporter, but Disraeli eventually gave in. The queen then rejected Christopher Wordsworth, the Archdeacon of Westminster, for Bishop of London, on the grounds that he lacked experience. At her suggestion, Bishop Jackson of Lincoln went to London, but she accepted Wordsworth to replace him at Lincoln. After this, the queen was able occasionally to reject prime-ministerial nominations or secure appointment of candidates of her choice. On other occasions, however, she was obliged to acquiesce in appointments which went against her preferences. Her hand was strengthened by the information about potential candidates that she received from two Deans of Windsor, Gerald Wellesley (1854–82) and Randall Davidson (1883–91).

For all but 6 of the final 32 years of Victoria's reign the prime minister was a devout Tractarian – William Ewart Gladstone (1868–74, 1880–85, 1886, 1892–4) or the third Marquess of Salisbury (1885–6, 1886–92, 1895–1902). Not surprisingly, more Tractarians were appointed as bishops. However, Gladstone generally favoured moderates of every church party and sought to divide appointments between them. Salisbury, too, never allowed his personal religious preferences to dictate his general policy. Gladstone, Salisbury and Davidson all agreed, however, that it was difficult to find evangelicals of sufficient eminence. Gladstone pointed out that bishops were appointed 'not by a single force but by many': 'If I am one of them, so the particular diocese is another, the Queen a third, the Liberal Party a fourth.'[40]

Two Victorian appointments provoked particular controversy. In 1847 a majority of the bishops (13 out of 25) signed a public protest against the (then only rumoured) appointment as Bishop of Hereford of Renn Dickson Hampden, 'in the soundness of whose doctrines the University of Oxford has affirmed, by a solemn decree, its want of confidence'. The Dean of Hereford and one of the canons voted against his election, and while three canons and eleven prebendaries voted in favour, the other twelve prebendaries did not attend. Objectors failed to secure a writ of mandamus requiring the vicar-general to hear objections before the election was confirmed (because the court was evenly divided, 2–2). This was, nonetheless, notable as the first stirring of rebellion against the system of nomination by the Crown.[41] Controversy was similarly aroused in 1869 by the appointment as Bishop of Exeter of Frederick Temple, the author of an introductory article to *Essays and Reviews* – a volume which had been condemned by the Convocation of Canterbury as 'containing teaching contrary to the doctrine received by the United Church of England and Ireland in common with the whole Catholic Church of Christ'. Temple was elected by 13 members of the Exeter chapter, but with 6 votes against and 4 abstentions. Of the 17 bishops of the Province of Canterbury, a majority (9) objected to participating in his consecration, 4 of them formally. Some of the dissidents pointed out that the fourth canon of the Council of Nicaea required the unanimous consent of the bishops of the province, but Temple was nevertheless consecrated.[42]

The archiepiscopates of Davidson and Lang, 1903–42

At the beginning of the twentieth century, changes in personnel brought about significant shift in the balance of power over episcopal appointments. In 1901 Queen Victoria was succeeded by Edward VII, who, while not uninterested in episcopal appointments, was not disposed to argue about them with his prime ministers to the extent that his mother had. He nonetheless successfully resisted the appointment of a non-graduate (to whom Archbishop Davidson also objected) as Bishop of Chichester in 1907, and secured the appointment (against the prime minister's inclination) of his own nominee as Bishop of Norwich (the diocese in which Sandringham is situated) in 1909. In 1911 his son, George V, similarly prevented the appointment as Bishop of Ripon of someone who had criticized Edward VII in a sermon on the death of Queen Victoria.[43] It is noteworthy that in one of these cases the king was in fact acting in alliance with the Archbishop of Canterbury, while in the other two personal interests were involved.

At the same time as royal influence on appointments was declining, that of the Archbishop of Canterbury grew immensely. This was due in large measure to the appointment in 1903 of Randall Davidson as Archbishop of Canterbury, and the fact that he remained in office for 25 years (until 1928). Davidson had been Queen Victoria's private adviser on ecclesiastical appointments, submitting advice both before and after she received recommendations from her prime ministers, from the time of his appointment as Dean of Windsor in 1883 until her death 18 years later, by which time he was Bishop of Winchester and Clerk of the Closet.[44] In 1901 Davidson asked Edward VII whether he should continue to offer confidential advice, and was assured that the king would like the correspondence to continue. Thus in 1903 there was, for the first time, an Archbishop of Canterbury who for 20 years had already been intimately involved in discussions about episcopal appointments. Furthermore, Davidson had the ear of the prime minister, Arthur Balfour, who was a close personal friend.[45] Davidson shaped practice with regard to episcopal appointments in two ways. First, by generally offering the prime minister a list of three or more people to be considered for each vacancy, he effectively created the field from which bishops were appointed; increasingly, the names from which the prime minister selected bishops came from the church, in the person of the archbishop of the province concerned. Secondly, he acquired for the Archbishop of Canterbury an effective veto over admission to the episcopate, in that, while men might be appointed to sees for which Davidson thought them unsuitable, in the words of his chaplain and biographer George Bell, 'if the Archbishop insisted that a particular person was wholly unsuitable for the office of Bishop, no Prime Minister ever during these twenty-five years persevered with his name'. Bell's assessment was that Davidson 'exercised a predominating influence upon the character' of the Bench of Bishops.[46]

Davidson was succeeded at Canterbury in 1928 by Cosmo Gordon Lang, who had been closely involved in episcopal appointments as Archbishop of York since 1908 and was a trusted confidant of Davidson. The customary pattern of the archbishop submitting two or more names to the prime minister continued. Prime ministers' views occasionally differed from those of the archbishops, but a bishop was never appointed against outright archiepiscopal opposition. Lang had his greatest difficulties with Winston Churchill, who knew 'almost nothing of the Church and its personalities'. There were disputes about whether the archbishop should always be given the opportunity of a personal consultation with the prime minister when a see became vacant, and whether he should be given the opportunity to register an objection when someone not recommended by the archbishop was to be appointed. It was Churchill's friend and confidant Brendan Bracken to whom Churchill was most ready to listen over episcopal appointments.[47]

Controversies and reports, 1901–40

In the early years of the century there were two further controversial episcopal appointments. The first was that of Charles Gore as Bishop of Worcester. Gore was suspect in protestant quarters both because of his editorship of *Lux Mundi* (1889) and as the founder and superior of the Community of the Resurrection at Mirfield. As in 1847, an application for a writ of mandamus requiring the vicar-general to hear objections before confirming the election was rejected and Gore was duly consecrated.[48] The second controversial appointment was that of Herbert Hensley Henson as Bishop of Hereford in 1917. Henson's appointment was the first to be made by David Lloyd George, whose status as a lapsed Welsh Baptist cannot have aided its acceptance. As with Hampden 70 years earlier, the objection to Henson was of alleged unorthodoxy. At the election, 15 members of the Hereford chapter voted for Henson, but 4 voted against and another 10 absented themselves. Bishop Gore, who initially urged his fellow bishops to make a formal protest against Henson's consecration, withdrew his objections following the publication of an exchange of letters between Davidson and Henson, but a number of bishops declined to participate in the consecration.[49] The controversy over Henson's appointment was particularly important, because it led to the first of a series of reports on the appointment of bishops which were prepared during the twentieth century. There had, in fact, been earlier reports. A joint committee of the Convocation of Canterbury had reported on the ceremony of confirmation in 1870, but no action was taken. A committee of the Lower House on church–state relations reported in 1879, and resolutions on the election and confirmation of bishops were passed as a result. Finally, a further committee of the Lower House on church–state relations issued two reports in 1901 and 1902. The second of these, following the confirmation of Bishop Gore's election, expressed satisfaction in changes in the ceremony that had recently been made.[50]

The 1919 *Report of the Joint Committee on Crown Nominations to Ecclesiastical Offices* expressed support for capitular election. The committee believed that if a manifestly unsuitable person were to be appointed, the cathedral chapter would refuse to elect and the archbishop of the province would refuse to consecrate, notwithstanding the penalties of *praemunire*, and that 'in the end it would be found impossible for the civil power to force its nominee into office'. Thus, as Gladstone had pointed out in 1880, 'the existence of the ceremony constituted a moral check on improper appointments'. The committee expressed dissatisfaction with the ceremony of confirmation, but did not believe that it was advisable to attempt to change it substantially, as this would require legislation. The report's main recommendation was that a standing committee on episcopal appointments should be constituted. This would consist of six elected bishops (four from the Province of Canterbury and two from York), three elected priests and three elected laymen – in each case two from the southern and one from the northern province – and two laymen nominated by the archbishops. This standing committee would submit the names of people suitable for appointment to the prime minister, and would be consulted by him before nominations were made to the Crown. It also recommended that for each vacancy the archdeacons should lay before the standing committee 'a statement in writing on the special circumstances and conditions of the diocese'.[51] In 1920 these recommendations were rejected by the Lower House, which instead passed a motion requesting 'that the two Archbishops should be officially consulted by the Prime Minister before the submission of any names by him to the Crown for nomination to any diocesan bishopric'. At Davidson's request, the word 'officially' was removed before the motion was finally passed by both houses. Lloyd George replied that this was already his 'invariable practice', and there the matter rested.[52]

In 1923 the new Church Assembly appointed a committee to consider the appointment of bishops. Its work proceeded very slowly, and the *Interim Report of the Appointment of Bishops Committee* was not published until 1929. The committee recommended that the law should be changed (1) to give cathedral chapters the right to refuse to elect the person proposed (but not the right to elect someone else), and (2) so that archbishops should not be liable to penalties for refusing to confirm or to consecrate. Its third recommendation was that the prime minister should be required to consult an advisory committee consisting of the archbishops and five members of the Church Assembly chosen by himself, before submitting a recommendation to the sovereign.[53] The report was received by the Church Assembly on the day that it appointed a commission on church–state relations, so the report was simply referred to the new commission.[54]

The commission's report, *Church and State*, was published in 1935. It endorsed the 1929 report's first two recommendations but rejected the third, arguing that 'to set up a Standing Advisory Committee could only result in diminishing [the Prime Minister's] personal responsibility for the choice'.[55] The Church Assembly commended the report to the attention of the Convocations, and a joint committee was set up to consider its proposals. This reported in 1938.[56] It recommended (1) that the custom of a chapter petitioning the Crown for a *congé d'élire* should be revived, and that the chapter should inform the archbishop of the province that it had done so and that it intended to consult a representative body of diocesan laity; (2) that the dean, in consultation with a standing committee of twelve laymen, should inform the archbishop of the needs of the diocese; (3) that the archbishop of the province should appoint a standing advisory committee of three bishops, three clergy and three laymen which would be available for discussion with him should he desire, and would bring names of potential bishops to his attention; (4) that a measure to allow objections on grounds of faith and morals to be considered before an election was confirmed was desirable. However, the Upper House of the Convocation of Canterbury approved only the first two of these recommendations. Against this background, the Lower House narrowly carried the following amendment: 'That pending the State conceding to the Church a decisive though not exclusive voice in the appointment of bishops, the present unsatisfactory system be left unchanged'.[57]

Meanwhile, the system of capitular election, which had hitherto applied only to cathedrals with a dean and chapter, had been extended to all English cathedrals. This prompted the Church Assembly in 1938 (in response to the report of a committee) to pass a measure repealing section 6 of the Act in Restraint of Annates, thus abolishing the penalties of *Praemunire*.[58] The Ecclesiastical Committee of Parliament ruled that the measure was not expedient, and the Legislative Committee of the Church Assembly thereupon recommended that it be dropped. In 1940 the Church Assembly adjourned consideration of the Legislative Committee's report *sine die*.

Thus in the 20 years from 1919 to 1939 five reports addressed aspects of the appointment of bishops, but no change in the system resulted.

The Archiepiscopate of Geoffrey Fisher, 1945–61

Geoffrey Fisher succeeded William Temple as Archbishop of Canterbury in 1945. The first half of his archiepiscopate fell in the reign of George VI, who, as far as is known, never attempted to overrule any of his prime ministers over a particular name.[59] However, Archbishop Cyril Garbett of York, writing in 1950, commented of the prime minister's nomination to the Crown: 'It may be assumed that this . . . is no mere formality, that the Crown is fully consulted, and is aware of all the reasons for the nomination, before the offer is actually made.'[60]

A very important development occurred in 1947, when Anthony Bevir, who had joined the Downing Street staff in 1940 and increasingly concentrated on ecclesiastical work, became secretary for appointments, advising on all prime ministerial appointments. This was, potentially at least, a powerful position, and Gerald Ellison, who was Cyril Garbett's chaplain, reported that Garbett 'expressed some fear lest he should become a kingmaker'.[61]

The 16 years of Fisher's archiepiscopate saw further strengthening of the archbishops' role in the appointment of bishops. There was now less and less pretence that consultations with them were a matter of courtesy rather than of right. During his second ministry (1951–5) Churchill simply accepted the names that Fisher put forward after discussion with Bevir. In 1956 Fisher wrote: 'I do not remember any occasion when the first name was not taken.' This may have been an exaggeration, but it indicates that by the mid-1950s at least, Fisher's wishes in the appointment of bishops largely prevailed. Envying the intelligence system that Bevir built up, Fisher circulated English diocesans and constructed a list of possible candidates for bishoprics, which was updated from time to time. He also had a small group of senior diocesans whom he consulted when he and Garbett were unable to make up their minds, or when a number of sees were vacant at the same time. He also resolved to consult the dean and chapter of a vacant diocese before suggesting names.[62]

Bevir was succeeded as Appointments Secretary in 1956 by David Stephens, who served until 1961. After an initial clash, when Stephens proposed to the prime minister a candidate of his own choice for Ely, having ascertained that he would be preferred to Fisher's nominee by the dean, people in Cambridge and the Archbishop of York, Fisher insisted that he should never advise the prime minister on a particular appointment until after he had consulted the archbishop, and should not discuss any preferences of his own with anyone he consulted. Fisher objected that 'this is really in fact appointing without reference to the Archbishop of Canterbury, and, even worse, appointment not by the P.M. but by Stephens'. As the candidate had already twice been Fisher's first name but had been passed over by the prime minister, Anthony Eden, Fisher felt obliged to acquiesce in the appointment. Stephens accepted Fisher's admonitions, but both Fisher and his new colleague at York, Michael Ramsey, soon again felt that he was getting too personally involved. Ramsey complained that his activities in the dioceses were becoming too open, and Fisher agreed, arguing that Stephens should not, for example, meet the dean and chapter as a corporate body.[63]

Fisher's archiepiscopate saw only one report that touched on episcopal appointments. *Church and State*, the report of a commission appointed by the Church Assembly in 1949, was published in 1952. With regard to the appointment of bishops, the commission endorsed, with modifications, three of the 1938 recommendations. These were (1) that a consultative body be established (by the archbishops, in consultation with the Standing Committee of the Church Assembly) to advise the archbishops on the advice which they would in turn offer to the prime minister, and that representatives of the diocese, one of whom should be a representative of the cathedral chapter, should be invited to confer with it; (2) that deans and chapters should once again petition the Crown for a *congé d'élire*; and (3) that they should, when doing so, make representations concerning the general needs of the diocese and the type of bishop required, copying these to the archbishop. However, it rejected the fourth 1938 recommendation, arguing that the ceremony of confirmation should remain 'simply a method of establishing the identity of the individual nominated and the completion of the correct formalities'. Finally, the commission made a further call for the abolition of the penalties of *praemunire*.[64] In response, the Church Assembly recommended the revival of the custom of petitioning for a *congé d'élire*. A motion calling for a committee to consider the abolition of the penalties of *praemunire* was debated but not proceeded with, and no other action was taken. In 1954 a member of the Church Assembly moved a motion that the ecclesiastical members of the Privy Council (the archbishops and the Bishop of London) rather than the prime minister should advise the sovereign on ecclesiastical appointments. An amendment, moved by Archbishop Garbett, expressing the opinion that 'the present procedure for submitting advice to the Sovereign is open to objection and should be modified' (in some unspecified way), was carried, but again no action was taken.[65] Fisher's archiepiscopate thus brought small improvements in the way the system was operated, without making any change to it.

Reports and debates, 1961–74

Geoffrey Fisher announced his retirement on 17 January 1961, and two or three days later it was announced that Harold Macmillan had appointed Michael Ramsey to succeed him.[66] The unseemly haste of this announcement was followed by Macmillan's refusal to nominate Walter Boulton, who had been Provost of Guildford since 1952, as the first Dean of Guildford. This was enough to stir the Church Assembly into action. The previous November, its House of Clergy had reaffirmed the 1954 resolution and called for discussions about how it might be implemented. Now, in November 1961, the Church Assembly requested the archbishops to establish a commission 'to examine the whole method of Crown Appointments to Ecclesiastical Offices and to make recommendations'. The Howick Report of 1964, *Crown Appointments and the Church*, was the result.[67] This proposed the appointment of an archbishops' secretary for appointments to maintain a list of potential candidates for appointment, it being open to anyone (not only diocesan bishops) to make suggestions, and the establishment by diocesan conferences of a body to produce a statement of the needs of the diocese. It recommended that election and confirmation of election should be replaced by a public ceremony of record at which the bishop-designate would take the oaths and make the declarations. If translated, the bishop would become bishop of the diocese on the date of the ceremony of record, but otherwise, on the date of consecration. Homage could be done after the enthronement if the sovereign were absent or indisposed. The penalties of *praemunire* would be abolished.[68]

An archbishops' secretary for appointments was duly appointed, and in November 1965 the Church Assembly called for the establishment of what came to be called a vacancy-in-see committee in each diocese. These could submit names for consideration, but would do so in a confidential document separate from the statement of needs. In fact, in the first seven years following the establishment of vacancy-in-see committees, names were submitted in only six out of 27 cases.[69]

The commission's other main proposal, that for a ceremony of record, had been referred to a continuation committee, which in 1965 made a new proposal, whereby appointment would be by letters patent, but there would be a ceremony of acceptance by the greater chapter and a ceremony of confirmation and investiture by the archbishop or his vicar-general, where possible on the eve of consecration. The penalties of *praemunire* should be abolished.[70] These proposals fared no better than those of the Howick Commission itself, and the Church Assembly resolved that capitular election should be retained. It would seem that many Church Assembly members wanted much more radical changes, and were unhappy with making minor amendments to the existing system. The Standing Committee therefore proposed the establishment of a new commission 'to make recommendations as to the modifications in the constitutional relationship between Church and State which are desirable and practicable and in so doing to take account of current and future steps to promote greater unity between the Churches', and that consideration of legislation on Crown appointments be postponed.[71] Resolutions to that effect were passed, and a commission was established under the chairmanship of Professor Owen Chadwick. While the commission was sitting, Parliament passed the Criminal Law Act 1967, which included among its provisions the abolition of the penalties of *praemunire*. Cathedral chapters and archbishops could now contravene the Appointment of Bishops Act 1534 with impunity.

The Chadwick Commission reported in 1970. With regard to the appointment of bishops, the commission was divided. Eight members (including the chairman) supported Proposal A – that two or more names should be submitted to the prime minister by a committee consisting of the archbishop of the province, the other archbishop or his nominee, six members appointed by the General Synod (at least one a diocesan bishop and at least three lay), two clergy and two lay members appointed by (but not necessarily from) the vacancy-in-see committee, and the dean or provost of the cathedral. The person nominated would then be elected by an electing body of representatives of the diocese, which would be not unlike the vacancy-in-see committee. Five members (including the vice-chairman, the Earl of March) argued that the involvement of the prime minister should cease, and supported Proposal B – that a committee composed as outlined above (but with the dean or provost as an assessor) should actually elect the bishop. The three members who were unable to sign the report and instead appended a Memorandum of Dissent and additional Notes (Miss Valerie Pitt, the Revd Peter Cornwell and Denis Coe, MP) would have preferred the second option.[72] Of the commission's recommendations, the General Synod proceeded first with what became the Worship and Doctrine Measure 1974. Its first substantive debate on Crown appointments came in February 1973.[73] In July 1974 it then resolved 'that the decisive voice in the appointment of diocesan bishops should be that of the Church' and that 'it would be desirable that a small body, representative of the vacant diocese and of the wider Church, should choose a suitable person for appointment to that diocese and for the name to be submitted to the Sovereign'. Amendments which would have substituted the Chadwick Commission's Proposal A, or otherwise softened the motion, were defeated on a show of hands, and the motion was then passed unamended by 270 votes to 70. At this point Michael Ramsey retired; the negotiations with the state would fall to his successor, Donald Coggan.

The Archiepiscopate of Michael Ramsey, 1961–74

Owen Chadwick's biography of Michael Ramsey offers some indications as to how the system of episcopal appointments worked in the period immediately before the establishment of the Crown Appointments Commission.

By 1974 Elizabeth II had been on the throne for 22 years. It is now generally agreed that in making episcopal appointments, the sovereign is bound by a constitutional convention to follow the advice tendered by the prime minister, even though this is personal advice rather than advice on behalf of the government or the cabinet, about which he or she cannot be questioned in Parliament.[74] This convention in fact says no more than was established by Lord

Liverpool in 1821 – that a prime minister can insist on having the last word over any ecclesiastical appointment to be made by the Crown. However, the convention applies solely to what has now become a formal nomination by the prime minister to the sovereign, made after the candidate has been asked whether he would accept appointment. It does not debar the sovereign from involvement in the discussions that lead to such an offer being made, or prevent her from seeking to influence the prime minister's decision. Kenneth Rose reports that a Dean of St Paul's once asked Elizabeth II what she could do if a prime minister submitted a name for an ecclesiastical appointment with which she was not happy. 'Nothing constitutionally,' she replied, 'but I can always say that I should like more information. That is an indication that the Prime Minister will not miss.'[75] Back in the late 1950s Harold Macmillan had found the queen even better informed than he was on the choice of new bishops.[76] Owen Chadwick reports that in Ramsey's time the queen 'was not in the habit of referring matters back', but 'where the see was important she inevitably took a larger part in the discussion'. She was fully involved in the appointment of a Bishop of Norwich (the diocese in which Sandringham is situated) and of a Dean of Windsor (her main home, Windsor Castle, being a royal peculiar and thus outside the diocesan system). Chadwick describes as 'decisive' her part in the discussions which led to the appointment of Donald Coggan to succeed Ramsey as Archbishop of Canterbury, rather than John Howe (whom Ramsey had recommended).[77]

Ramsey had little disagreement with his four prime ministers over episcopal appointments. Macmillan followed his advice in all but one case – the proposal that the ejected Bishop of Johannesburg, Ambrose Reeves, be appointed to an English diocese, which Macmillan feared would adversely affect Britain's relations with South Africa. Ramsey considered this the only politically motivated prime ministerial decision on episcopal appointments in his time. Ramsey cooperated well with both Douglas-Home and Wilson. Ironically it was Edward Heath, towards the end of his archiepiscopate, who was the one prime minister likely to take someone from Ramsey's list who was not his first choice – perhaps because, as a former news editor of the Church Times, he had more insight into church affairs than the others. On one occasion he appointed someone who was not on Ramsey's original list but who was acceptable to him (the translation of George Reindorp from Guildford to Salisbury); on another occasion he asked (not for political reasons) that one of the names on Ramsey's list be withdrawn.[78] Overall, however, Ramsey's prime ministers almost always did what he asked over episcopal appointments (especially those within the Province of Canterbury).

None the less, in an essay entitled 'Church and State in England', which Ramsey wrote specially for the volume *Canterbury Pilgrim* in 1974, he said: 'It seems . . . that the Archbishop's influence was probably at its greatest in the primacy of

Cosmo Lang and the earlier years of Fisher . . . The new phenomenon was the highly competent and officially designated [Prime Minister's] Appointments Secretary known as such to the Church at large as the man concerned.' After praising the work of the prime minister's appointments secretary, he added:

> It is also certain that there will be strange 'non-appointments' and chances missed – for the knowledge is filtered through the mind of one man, and no man is without his prejudices and blind spots. I do not doubt that divine providence can use the procedure, and that the bishops who are consecrated receive the gifts of the Holy Spirit for their office. But when all this has been said the system leaves me sharing the view that this is not the right way for any Church's chief pastors to be chosen.[79]

As we have seen, both Ramsey and Fisher had felt that David Stephens, the prime minister's appointments secretary from 1956 to 1961, had exceeded his proper role. John Hewitt, the appointments secretary from 1961 to 1973 (almost the whole of Ramsey's time at Canterbury), developed the role even further.[80] Ramsey found, for example, that he could not get Eric Kemp, whose expertise in canon law and synodical government he needed on the bench of bishops, appointed to a diocesan see. He attributed this to the conservative John Hewitt's hostility to Eric Kemp's radical views on church–state relations. Dr Kemp finally became Bishop of Chichester a few months after Hewitt's retirement. Hewitt similarly blocked the appointment of Hugh Montefiore because of a single utterance in which he associated Jesus with homosexuals. Ramsey concluded that there were certain individuals whom it would be pointless to include in a shortlist because of the appointments secretary's hostility to them. Thus although the prime ministers generally accepted his proposals, his influence over appointments was limited in an unprecedented way, in that the proposals were conditioned to some extent by the personal views of the prime minister's appointments secretary.[81]

Bernard Palmer has suggested that the result of the liaison between the prime ministers' appointments secretary and the new archbishops' appointments secretary was 'to gather more power into the hands of the two officials', and that this was 'especially so in the case of the prime minister's secretary for appointments'. A leading opponent of the system, the Revd Christopher Wansey, sent an open letter to Hewitt's successor, Colin Peterson, in 1974, in which he claimed that

> The apostolic succession goes through a filing-cabinet presided over by the Secretary for Appointments, for no one who is not filed there has the remotest chance of becoming a bishop. So, in this episcopal garden, it is not the royal gardener who does the

planting and transplanting, nor even the gardener's boy – the Prime Minister. No, it is the gardener's boy's boy – your own good self. You are the one and only bishop-maker in the Church of England today. I respectfully ask: 'Who are you to choose the successor of St Augustine?'[82]

After 1965, Ramsey's selection of names for inclusion in his list on each occasion was constrained (and his influence thereby reduced) in another way – by the views expressed by vacancy-in-see committees. Chadwick records that Ramsey valued the committees and had no desire to do without them, but by 1973–4 he was wondering whether the diocesan influence on appointments, formerly too weak, was not now too weighty. The system now put the needs of the diocese first, but what about the need of the national church as a whole for intellectual and political leadership?[83] The existence of vacancy-in-see committees and their right to suggest names gave rise to an expectation in some quarters at least that the bishop appointed would be one of those whose names were suggested by the diocese. In 1973 eight prebendaries made a formal protest at the chapter meeting to elect Gerald Ellison (who, unlike Graham Leonard, was not one of the three candidates recommended by the vacancy-in-see committee).[84]

Establishment of the Crown Appointments Commission, 1976–7

In July 1974 the General Synod had, as we have seen, resolved (by 270 votes to 70) that 'the decisive voice in the appointment of bishops should be that of the Church' and that 'it would be desirable that a small body, representative of the vacant diocese and the wider Church, should choose a suitable person for appointment to that diocese and for the name to be submitted to the Sovereign'. It fell to Archbishop Coggan and Sir Norman Anderson, the chairman of the House of Laity, who had moved the motion, to negotiate the implementation of the Synod's wishes with the prime minister – first Harold Wilson and then James Callaghan – and the leaders of the main opposition parties. The response was given by Prime Minister Callaghan in a written answer on Tuesday 8 June 1976. In this he rejected the main point of the Synod's resolution – that the church should have 'the decisive voice', a single name going direct from a church body to the sovereign, on the grounds that 'The Sovereign must be able to look for advice on a matter of this kind and that must mean, for a constitutional Sovereign, advice from Ministers', and that as the archbishops and some bishops sit by right in the House of Lords 'their nomination must therefore remain a matter for the Prime Minister's concern'. He did, however, concede that 'the Church should have, and be seen to have, a greater say in the process of choosing its leaders'. His proposal, supported by the leaders of the main opposition parties, was that the church should set up a small committee, of which both appointments secretaries would be members. It would draw up a shortlist of names, which might be given in order of preference. 'The Prime Minister would retain the right to recommend the second name, or to ask the committee for a further name or names.' For the appointment of an Archbishop of Canterbury, 'the Committee might then be chaired by a layman chosen by the Prime Minister'.[85]

While the Synod had in effect asked for the Chadwick Commission's Proposal B, it had in fact essentially been offered something close to Proposal A. The Standing Committee nevertheless recommended acceptance of the agreement, and the Synod endorsed it in July 1976 by 390 votes to 29.[86] The Standing Committee's proposals for implementation were endorsed, with minor amendment, in November, and the standing orders constituting the Crown Appointments Commission and the Vacancy in See Committees Regulation putting these bodies on a uniform constitutional footing were approved in February 1977.[87] In June 1977 the appointments of Peter Walker as Bishop of Ely and David Young as Bishop of Ripon, the last to be made under the old system, were announced. The first appointment to be made under the new system was announced in October 1977: Hugh Montefiore, whose appointment to the bench John Hewitt had opposed, was to be Bishop of Birmingham.[88] A new era in the history of the choosing of bishops had begun.

The 'Perry Report', 1999–2003

Beginning in 1999, the whole process was reviewed by a group chaired by Baroness Perry of Southwark. Its report, *Working with the Spirit: Choosing Diocesan Bishops*,[89] made 60 recommendations, which were debated by the General Synod in July 2001. A steering group was established to follow up the recommendations; its report, *Choosing Diocesan Bishops*,[90] was in turn debated in November 2002. The fruits of this process included amendments to the Vacancy in See Committees Regulation and amendments to the Crown Appointments Commission Standing Order (all of which came into force on 1 December 2003), and other changes which did not require legislation.

The commission was renamed the Crown Nominations Commission and its diocesan membership increased from four to six (a change recommended neither by the Review Group nor by the Steering Group). In the case of a vacancy in the See of Canterbury, the prime minister would be obliged to consult before appointing a layperson to preside at the commission's meetings, and the primate or presiding bishop of one of the other churches of the Anglican Communion would be a voting member. The rules governing voting at commission meetings were changed, so as to require a two-thirds majority only for the decision that a name should be submitted to the prime minister.

It was agreed that the commission would in future meet twice (rather than just once) to consider each vacancy, and that an advertisement would announce the dates of these meetings and invite members of the public to send in names and comments. Both the Review Group and the Steering Group rejected the idea that candidates should be interviewed by the commission. However, it was agreed that the information circulated to the commission about each candidate should include factual information agreed by the candidate, with a recent photograph; a statement by the candidate; and references by two referees named by him. In response to a recommendation by the Review Group, the language and proceedings for the confirmation of elections were updated.

These changes, which were aimed at bringing about greater openness, transparency and fairness, represented a further example of development of the system in response to changed circumstances and emphases. Once again, the system had been adapted rather than replaced; the formal changes were few and not particularly significant, but the way in which the system operated would, it was hoped, differ significantly from the practice of a quarter-century earlier.

Afterword

If the Church is truly the Body of Christ (and thus, as Charles Gore said, 'the extension of the Incarnation'[1]), then its parts and the way they relate to each other are of fundamental theological importance. Such belief in the importance of ecclesiology has led Anglicans to urge (against the instinct of some Protestant ecumenical partners) the importance of keeping faith and order together. Indeed, the use in the English language of the theological term 'order' in the phrase 'faith and order', rather than a more administrative or political term like *Kirchenverfassung* or *constitution* (as in the German and French names for the Faith and Order Movement), itself testifies to the fact that for Anglicans (who played a significant part in the founding of that movement) the structures of the Church have theological significance. Archbishop Robert Runcie highlighted this Anglican emphasis on the inseparability of 'faith' and 'order' thus:

> Was it not, after all, Anglicans like Bishop Charles Brent who tirelessly insisted in the beginnings of the Ecumenical Movement that faith and order go together. They are not of equal importance, but apostolic order is the means of maintaining the unity in diversity of the church's life.[2]

The value of studying and discussing the structures of the Church has nevertheless sometimes been questioned by those who believe such activity to be a distraction from the things of the Spirit. But the supposed dichotomy between church order and Spirit is a false one: the Spirit does not just represent principles of freedom. The Holy Spirit is not only like the wind, which 'blows where it wills' (John 3.8); he is also the Spirit of order. In the beginning God, whose Spirit 'was moving over the face of the waters' (Genesis 1.2), brought order out of chaos. Wisdom may be seen as another manifestation of the Holy Spirit: the Book of Wisdom says that Wisdom 'is a breath of the power of God, and a pure emanation of the glory of the Almighty' (Wisdom 7.25). Here, too, the Spirit is the Spirit of order: Wisdom 'reaches mightily from one end of the earth to the other, and she orders all things well' (Wisdom 8.1). In the Nicene Creed, belief in the one holy, catholic and apostolic Church is confessed as part of confession of belief in the Holy Spirit, and the primary occasion when the Holy Spirit, the *Creator Spiritus*, is invoked to bestow his sevenfold gifts is at ordinations, when holy order is bestowed on the Church.[3]

Ecclesiology tends to be written by theologians, ecumenists and canon lawyers. When written by exponents of one of these disciplines without regard to the others, it can be unsatisfactory. In particular, some theologians appear to have a remarkably untheological view of ecclesiastical law, rejecting it as dry legalism. Rightly understood, ecclesiastical law (embracing not only canon law but also, in the Church of England, statute law – now formulated by the General Synod) is nothing less than the expression of the mind of the Church; it realizes ecclesiology in practical, concrete form. It cannot and should not be a barrier to the promptings of the Spirit or to change, for if the mind of the Church changes, its law must be changed to reflect that. (What it is, however, is a brake on change that has not been thought and argued through and cannot be said to represent the Church's settled mind.) If the Church is the Body of Christ, then its canons are the sinews that hold the body together and prevent individual parts from flying off on their own; much the same could be said of church structures more generally. Canon law is one of the ways in which the Spirit orders the Church. Attention to ecclesiastical law is especially important when studying Anglican ecclesiology: the practical and pragmatic English approach means that much is implicit in the canons, structures and practices of the Church of England that is not explicitly spelled out in any authoritative statement.

The fact that much is reflected in practice that is not necessarily reduced to a theoretical formulation also makes the consulting of history essential when writing ecclesiology. Indeed, the Church of England's ecclesiology can only be understood in the context of its history. Hence the emphasis on history in this particular book, written not by a theologian nor by a canon lawyer, but by a church historian and practitioner.

✠

Despite the disparate origins of this book's chapters, there are several themes that have run through the book as a whole. Chief among these are catholicity, continuity and the nature of change.

By *catholicity* I mean here the understanding (expressed in Chapter 3) that the Church of England is not complete in itself, but fundamentally (not just incidentally) part of something greater and wider; in the words of the Declaration of Assent (examined in Chapter 4), 'The Church of England is *part* of the one, holy, catholic and apostolic Church'.[4]

As we saw in Chapter 2, the Oxford Movement, which in the 1830s highlighted the Church of England's identity as part of the catholic Church in continuity with the Church of the apostles – and hence its essential independence of the state – began as a response to a revolution in the relations between church and state. In subsequent generations the catholic movement in the Church of England has grown and branched out; being a catholic Anglican came also to involve a sacramentally rooted catholic spirituality and discipline of life, a catholic style of worship and a catholic theology focusing especially on the doctrine of the Incarnation. Fundamentally, however, the Catholic Movement rooted in the Oxford Movement is about ecclesiology – about the Church of England's identity as part of the one, holy, catholic and apostolic Church.

More particularly, the Church of England comprises two provinces of the Western Catholic Church, and, as one would expect, there is still a strong resemblance to other members of that family. In some respects, the resemblance is actually more to the rest of the Western Church as it used to be than to the continental Roman Catholic Church as it now is. When remote communities become cut off from the main body (and viewed from Rome, the Church of England is surely just such a community), practices often survive in them that have been abandoned elsewhere. For example, surplices continue to be worn in some Central European Lutheran churches more than 200 years after they were abandoned by most of German Protestantism in the Age of Enlightenment. The office of archdeacon is just one instance of the survival in England of institutions that were once much more widespread. What may now seem to be Anglican peculiarities are in fact reminders of a shared history with the Church across the Channel.

This points to a second recurring theme of this book – *continuity.* Recent studies of the English Reformation have rightly stressed the radical discontinuities in doctrine and worship, spirituality and life that characterized the history of the church in mid-sixteenth-century England.[5] That is a salutary reminder, though to understand the Church of England today one has to bear in mind – metaphorically as well as literally – not only the 'stripping of the altars'[6] but also their restoration, both in the 1630s under Archbishop Laud[7] and again from 1660 after the hiatus of the Interregnum,[8] and their further embellishment in the nineteenth and twentieth centuries. The story is not just one of loss and recovery, however. Discontinuity in doctrine and worship, spirituality and life occurred within a framework of continuity. That continuity was not merely the fragile continuity of the succession in the laying on of hands at episcopal ordinations[9] – important as that was and is. Rather, it was a complete continuity of structure. The ordering of the two English provinces – dioceses, archdeaconries and deaneries – was unaffected by the Reformation as such (though, as might be expected in a period of reform, some new dioceses were created). Much of the canon law of the medieval Church remained in force, and it was administered by church courts which continued unaltered. As Eamon Duffy has said, the Church of England 'retained totally unchanged the full medieval framework of episcopal church government'.[10] Ecclesiologically, the continuity of the body is of more fundamental significance than the shifting patterns of its liturgy, devotion and thought, important as these unquestionably are.

Diarmaid MacCulloch has pointed to a further important element of continuity with the medieval Church: the cathedral foundations. Not only did the non-monastic cathedrals survive the Reformation, but Henry VIII refounded the monastic cathedrals as secular 'new foundations', adding several other former monasteries as cathedrals for his new dioceses. The fact that the cathedral foundations were retained and renewed in this way made the Church of England unique in the European Reformation. Furthermore, with their choral foundations, pipe organs and large staff of clergy they were to develop an Anglican tradition of elaborate choral services and become, in MacCulloch's words, 'an ideological subversion of the Church of England re-established in 1559', which was otherwise Reformed Protestant in sympathy.[11]

Such an emphasis on continuity might seem to betoken a desire for static changelessness, but to suppose that continuity implies this would be to misunderstand not only the history of the Church of England – and indeed of England itself – but also the nature of tradition, of which continuity is the expression. In 1963 the Fourth World Conference on Faith and Order defined Tradition as follows: 'By the Tradition is meant the Gospel itself, transmitted from generation to generation in and by the Church, Christ Himself present in the life of the Church.'[12] *Traditio* (the process of handing over or handing on the Tradition) is an action, not a state; it involves movement. Thus tradition is a dynamic concept, not a static one. The Anglican–Roman Catholic International Commission's report *The Gift of Authority* commented:

> The Church must continue faithful so that the Christ who comes
> in glory will recognise in the Church the community he founded;
> it must continue to be free to receive the apostolic Tradition in
> new ways according to the situations by which it is confronted
> ... There may be a rediscovery of elements that were neglected
> ... There may also be a sifting of the formulations of what has
> been received because some of the formulations of the Tradition
> are seen to be inadequate or even misleading in a new context.
> This whole process may be termed re-reception.[13]

In the words of the Declaration of Assent, the Church is called upon to proclaim the faith 'afresh in each generation'.[14] It is the same faith, but it may need to be expressed in new ways. Bishop John Hind has written:

> Development must occur. It happens every time the gospel is
> preached, announced and expressed. Every time a preacher
> opens his or her mouth, he or she clothes the Word in new
> words. Most of these new formulations are ephemeral. But some
> become established, because they serve the needs of the Church

in changing circumstances . . . New formulations are constantly being made, of which some will prove necessary and be accepted as true.[15]

Living tradition also involves growth and fresh discovery. We are promised that the Spirit will guide us into all truth (John 16.13), and that leading and guiding by the Spirit continues. *The Gift of Authority* speaks of theologians in particular 'exploring whether and how new insights should be integrated into the ongoing stream of Tradition'.[16] That which ceases to change and develop ceases to be alive; as Cardinal Newman famously wrote, 'Here below, to live is to change, and to be perfect is to have changed often.'[17] At the same time, change must be development rather than degeneration; it must be such that the essential nature remains the same, rather than being destroyed; to quote Newman again, a great idea 'changes . . . in order to remain the same'.[18] The fact that change is necessary and desirable does not mean that all change is good.

Hence a third theme of this book is *the nature of change* in the Church of England. The accounts of the history of synodical government (Chapter 7) and the history of the choosing of diocesan bishops (Chapter 9) exemplify the Anglican, indeed English, way of development and change, which is generally a conservative one, proceeding mostly by evolution, not revolution. Time-honoured structures and procedures are often filled with new life, instead of being overthrown. Thus, synodical government in the Church of England is both new and old; the General Synod has no precise medieval antecedent, but retains as its chief component parts the Convocations of Canterbury and York, and thus stands in structural continuity with the synods of the medieval English Church. In the choosing of bishops one sees how first the role of the cathedral chapter, then the role of the sovereign and now, increasingly, that of the prime minister have become largely formal. However, the fact that they retain their roles in the process not only symbolizes important things about the Church of England, but is also arguably not entirely without influence on the choices that are made.

Change – in the sense of development – is a necessary sign of life, but the classically Anglican way of changing is one which maintains catholicity and continuity. Central to the debates that divide Anglicans is the question of whether the changes under consideration are such as will maintain and foster catholicity and continuity, and hence the Church of England's faithfulness to its identity, expressed in the Declaration of Assent, as 'part of the One, Holy, Catholic and Apostolic Church'.

Notes

Foreword

1. See *The Ordination of Women to the Priesthood: The Synod Debate, 11 November 1992: The Verbatim Record*, London, Church House Publishing, 1993.
2. Statement by the Archbishop of Canterbury: *Church Times*, 11 July 2003, p. 2.
3. Cf. 'The Virginia Report: The Report of the Inter-Anglican Theological and Doctrinal Commission' in *The Official Report of the Lambeth Conference 1998*, Harrisburg, PA: Morehouse Publishing,1999, pp. 15–68, at p. 57: the bishop is 'one who represents the part to the whole and the whole to the part, the particularity of each diocese to the whole Communion and the Communion to each diocese'.

1   The origins and development of the Church of England

1. The essay on which this chapter is based was first published in *Anglican–Moravian Conversations: The Fetter Lane Common Statement with Essays in Moravian and Anglican History*, Council for Christian Unity Occasional Paper No. 5, London, GS 1202, 1996, pp. 37–43. For a survey of the history of episcopacy in the Church of England, see C. Hill, 'Episcopacy in our churches: England', in *Together in Mission and Ministry: The Porvoo Common Statement with Essays on Church and Ministry in Northern Europe*, GS 1083, London: Church House Publishing, 1993, pp. 125–46.
2. P. Wormald, 'The Venerable Bede and the "Church of the English"', in D. G. Rowell (ed.), *The English Religious Tradition and the Genius of Anglicanism*, Wantage: Ikon, 1992, pp. 13–32, at p.17.
3. Quoted by D. McClean, 'The changing legal framework of establishment', *Ecclesiastical Law Journal*, 7, 2004, pp. 292–302, at p. 293.
4. See E. Duffy, 'Primitive Christianity revived: religious renewal in Augustan England', in D. Baker (ed.), *Renaissance and Renewal in Christian History*, Studies in Church History, 14, Oxford: Basil Blackwell, 1977, pp. 287–300.

2   High churchmen, church and state, 1801–38

1. I am grateful to the Rt Revd Dr Geoffrey Rowell for his comments on an earlier draft of this chapter.
2. J. D. Walsh and S. J. C. Taylor, 'The church and Anglicanism in the long eighteenth century', in J. Walsh, C. Haydon and S. Taylor (eds), *The Church of England, c.1689–c.1833: From Toleration to Tractarianism*, Cambridge: Cambridge University Press,1993, p. 49.
3. G. O. Trevelyan, *Life and Letters of Lord Macaulay*, new edn, Oxford, 1932, vol. 1, p. 64n.

4. E. Elbourne, 'The foundation of the Church Missionary Society: the Anglican missionary impulse', in Walsh, Haydon and Taylor (eds), *The Church of England c.1689–c.1833*, p. 249.

5. S. J. Brown, *The National Churches of England, Ireland and Scotland, 1801–46*, Oxford: Oxford University Press, 2001, p. 58.

6. G. F. A. Best, *Temporal Pillars: Queen Anne's Bounty, the Ecclesiastical Commissioners, and the Church of England*, Cambridge: Cambridge University Press, 1964, p. 242.

7. P. B. Nockles, *The Oxford Movement in Context: Anglican High Churchmanship, 1760–1857*, Cambridge: Cambridge University Press, 1994, pp. 25f.

8. J. J. Sack, *From Jacobite to Conservative: Reaction and Orthodoxy in Britain, c. 1760–1832*, Cambridge: Cambridge University Press, 1993, p. 192.

9. F. C. Mather, 'Church, Parliament and penal laws: some Anglo-Scottish interactions in the eighteenth century', *English Historical Review*, 92, 1977, pp. 540–72, at p. 557.

10. Mather, 'Church, Parliament and penal laws', p. 570.

11. See Chapter 3, pp. 29–30.

12. Sack, *From Jacobite to Conservative*, p. 192.

13. Sack, *From Jacobite to Conservative*, pp. 13, 69, 192f.

14. D. G. Rowell, *The Club of Nobody's Friends: A Memoir on its Two-Hundredth Anniversary*, Edinburgh: The Pentland Press, 2000.

15. F. C. Mather, *High Church Prophet: Bishop Samuel Horsley (1733–1806) and the Caroline Tradition in the Later Georgian Church*, Oxford: Oxford University Press, 1992, p. 218.

16. Mather, *High Church Prophet*, p. 217.

17. A. Webster, *Joshua Watson: The Story of a Layman, 1771–1855*, London: SPCK, 1954, p. 24; Nockles, *The Oxford Movement in Context*, p. 14.

18. P. B. Nockles, 'Watson, Joshua (1771–1855)', *Oxford Dictionary of National Biography*, Oxford: Oxford University Press, 2004.

19. E. A. Varley, *The Last of the Prince Bishops: William Van Mildert and the High Church Movement of the Early Nineteenth Century*, Cambridge: Cambridge University Press, 1992, p. 31.

20. Rowell, *The Club of Nobody's Friends*, p. 2.

21. See Nockles, *The Oxford Movement in Context*, pp. 15–17.

22. Rowell, *The Club of Nobody's Friends*, p. 32.

23. Varley, *The Last of the Prince Bishops*, p. 46; Webster, *Joshua Watson*, p. 26.

24. Nockles, *The Oxford Movement in Context*, p. 16.

25. Webster, *Joshua Watson*, p. 25; Nockles, *The Oxford Movement in Context*, p. 272.

26. A. Burns, *The Diocesan Revival in the Church of England, c.1800–1870*, Oxford: Oxford University Press, 1999, p. 20.

27. Burns, *The Diocesan Revival in the Church of England*, p. 71.

28. P. B. Nockles, '"Lost causes and . . . impossible loyalties": the Oxford Movement and the university', in M. G. Brock and M. C. Curthoys (eds), *The History of the University of Oxford, vi: Nineteenth Century Oxford*, part I, Oxford, 1997, p. 209.

29. J. R. Garrard, 'William Howley (1766–1848): Bishop of London, 1813–28; Archbishop of Canterbury, 1828–48', unpublished DPhil. thesis, University of Oxford, 1992, pp. 9, 136, 7.

30. Varley, *The Last of the Prince Bishops*, p. 57; C. Dewey, *The Passing of Barchester*, London and Rio Grande, OH: The Hambledon Press, 1991, p. 157.
31. See Dewey, *The Passing of Barchester*.
32. Brown, *The National Churches of England, Ireland and Scotland*, p. 50.
33. *A Letter to the Society for Promoting Christian Knowledge*, quoted in Varley, *The Last of the Prince Bishops*, p. 66.
34. Brown, *The National Churches of England, Ireland and Scotland*, p. 59.
35. Varley, *The Last of the Prince Bishops*, p. 68.
36. H. Cnattingius, *Bishops and Societies: A Study of Anglican Colonial and Missionary Expansion, 1698–1850*, London: SPCK, 1952, pp. 69f.
37. Varley, *The Last of the Prince Bishops*, pp. 68, 75, 79; Webster, *Joshua Watson*, pp. 16f., 115.
38. W. F. Hook, *An Attempt to Demonstrate the Catholicism of the Church of England and the other Branches of the Episcopal Church: In a sermon preached in the Episcopal Chapel at Stirling, on Sunday, March XX, MDCCCXXV, at the Consecration of the Right Rev. Matthew Luscombe*, London, 1825, p. 43.
39. Webster, *Joshua Watson*, p. 115.
40. Cnattingius, *Bishops and Societies*, pp. 82–5, 106, 137; Webster, *Joshua Watson*, p. 119.
41. Varley, *The Last of the Prince Bishops*, p. 48; Nockles, *The Oxford Movement in Context*, p. 19.
42. Webster, *Joshua Watson*, pp. 35f.
43. Webster, *Joshua Watson*, pp. 49–57.
44. Varley, *The Last of the Prince Bishops*, p. 83.
45. Webster, *Joshua Watson*, pp. 58–69; Varley, *The Last of the Prince Bishops*, pp. 81–8; Brown, *The National Churches of England, Ireland and Scotland*, pp. 68–71.
46. Webster, *Joshua Watson*, pp. 44–5.
47. Varley, *The Last of the Prince Bishops*, pp. 149–68.
48. Webster, *Joshua Watson*, pp. 74–5.
49. Burns, *The Diocesan Revival in the Church of England*, p. 1.
50. Burns, *The Diocesan Revival in the Church of England*, pp. 260f.
51. Burns, *The Diocesan Revival in the Church of England*, pp. 14f., 19, 20–22, 261f.
52. Nockles, *The Oxford Movement in Context*, p. 48.
53. Brown, *The National Churches of England, Ireland and Scotland*, pp. 64f.
54. Brown, *The National Churches of England, Ireland and Scotland*, pp. 73, 91.
55. P. B. Nockles, 'Pusey and the question of church and state', in P. Butler (ed.), *Pusey Rediscovered*, London: SPCK, 1983, pp. 255–97, at pp. 259–60.
56. Brown, *The National Churches of England, Ireland and Scotland*, pp. 138f.
57. Lord Holland to Henry Fox, 10 April 1828, quoted in J. C. D. Clark, *English Society, 1660–1832: Religion, Ideology and Politics during the Ancien Régime*, 2nd edn, Cambridge: Cambridge University Press, 2000, p. 532.
58. Brown, *The National Churches of England, Ireland and Scotland*, p. 144.
59. Nockles, '"Lost causes and . . . impossible loyalties"', p. 202.
60. Clark, *English Society*, pp. 534f.
61. Clark, *English Society*, pp. 542ff.
62. W. O. Chadwick, *The Victorian Church*, part I, 3rd edn, London: A. & C. Black, 1971, pp. 26–35.

63. Clark, *English Society*, p. 545.
64. Brown, *The National Churches of England, Ireland and Scotland*, pp. 150–54, 160–65.
65. C. Daubeny, *An Appendix to the 'Guide to the Church'*, London, 1799, vol. 1, pp. 114f., quoted in Nockles, *The Oxford Movement in Context*, pp. 65f.
66. Pusey House, Oxford, Liddon Bound Volume (LBV) 11, fols 154f.: Keble to A. P. Perceval, 25 March 1829. Curiously, George Herring interprets this quotation as indicating that Keble saw 'positive advantages in a separation' – G. Herring, *What was the Oxford Movement?*, London: Continuum, 2002, pp. 18f.
67. MS letter, 31 March 1831, quoted by J. R. Griffin, 'John Keble: radical', *Anglican Theological Review*, 53, 1971, pp. 167–73, at p. 172.
68. MS letter, 8 May 1832, quoted by Griffin, 'John Keble', p. 172.
69. [J. Keble], 'Church reform, No. IV', *British Magazine*, 3, March 1833, pp. 366, 377.
70. Pusey House, Oxford, LBV 11, fols 263–4: Keble to A. P. Perceval, 1 March 1833.
71. Keble's view reported by R. H. Froude in a letter to A. P. Perceval, 18 August 1833, quoted by Griffin, 'John Keble', p. 171.
72. J. H. Newman, *Apologia pro Vita Sua, being a History of his Religious Opinions*, ed. M. J. Svaglic, Oxford: Clarendon Press, 1967, p. 43.
73. Tract 1: R. W. Church, *The Oxford Movement: Twelve Years, 1833–1845*, ed. G. Best, Chicago/London: University of Chicago Press, 1970, pp. 81f.
74. *The Letters and Diaries of John Henry Newman*, ed. I. Ker and T. Gornall, vol. 4, Oxford, 1980, p. 40: Newman to A. P. Perceval, 6 Sept. 1833 (Pusey House, Oxford, LBV 11, fol. 346).
75. *Letters and Diaries*, vol. 4, p. 22: Newman to Keble, 5 Aug. 1833.
76. *Letters and Diaries*, vol. 4, p. 23: Keble to Newman, 8 Aug. 1833.
77. See S. A. Skinner, '"The duty of the state": Keble, the Tractarians and establishment' in K. Blair (ed.), *John Keble in Context*, London: Anthem Press, 2004, pp. 33–46.
78. *Letters and Diaries*, vol. 4, p. 35: Newman to F. Rogers, 31 Aug. 1833.
79. J. H. L. Rowlands, *Church, State and Society: The Attitudes of John Keble, Richard Hurrell Froude and John Henry Newman, 1827–1845*, Worthing: Churchman Publishing, 1989, p. 87 (see also p. 120).
80. [R. H. Froude], 'Conservative principles', *British Magazine*, 4, 1833, p. 51.
81. [R. H. Froude], 'Hooker's views of state interference in matters spiritual', *British Magazine*, 4, 1833, p. 496.
82. From the introduction to the complete paper, 'Remarks on state interference in matters spiritual', in *The Remains of the Late Richard Hurrell Froude*, part 2, vol. 1, Derby, 1839, p. 185.
83. [Froude], 'Hooker's views of state interference in matters spiritual', p. 494.
84. [Froude], 'Conservative principles', p. 54.
85. *Remains*, p. 274.
86. J. R. Griffin, 'The radical phase of the Oxford Movement', *Journal of Ecclesiastical History*, 27, 1976, pp. 47–56, at pp. 49f.; cf. J. R. Griffin, 'The Anglican politics of Cardinal Newman', *Anglican Theological Review*, 55, 1973, pp. 434–43, at pp. 437f.
87. Griffin, 'The radical phase of the Oxford Movement', pp. 55f.; cf. Griffin, 'John Keble', p. 173.

88. Griffin, 'John Keble', p. 169. This places a question mark against J. H. L. Rowlands's conclusion that 'for all his radical utterances between 1833 and 1839, Keble never seriously contemplated disestablishment': 'He was only too well aware of the spiritual advantages of the Establishment. Instead, he advocated supreme perseverance in all adversity' (Rowlands, *Church, State and Society*, p. 215).
89. Newman, *Apologia pro Vita Sua*, p. 46.
90. Newman, *Apologia pro Vita Sua*, p. 47.
91. O. J. Brose, *Church and Parliament: The Reshaping of the Church of England, 1828–1860*, Stanford, CA: Stanford University Press; London: Oxford University Press, 1959, pp. 121f., 217.
92. Varley, *The Last of the Prince Bishops*, p. 180.
93. Webster, *Joshua Watson*, p. 86.
94. Varley, *The Last of the Prince Bishops*, p. 189.
95. Varley, *The Last of the Prince Bishops*, pp. 190ff.
96. Brose, *Church and Parliament*, pp. 125–30.
97. Nockles, *The Oxford Movement in Context*, pp. 83, 88, 274.
98. Nockles, *The Oxford Movement in Context*, pp. 20, 287ff.
99. W. F. Hook to A. Perceval, 25 May 1831, in W. R. W. Stephens, *The Life and Letters of Walter Farquhar Hook*, 2 vols, 3rd edn, London, 1879, vol. 1, pp. 221f.
100. Nockles, *The Oxford Movement in Context*, pp. 287f.
101. Varley, *The Last of the Prince Bishops*, pp. 102f.
102. Nockles, *The Oxford Movement in Context*, pp. 325f.
103. Nockles, *The Oxford Movement in Context*, p. 282.
104. P. Butler, *Gladstone: Church, State and Tractarianism. A Study of his Religious Ideals and Attitudes, 1809–1859*, Oxford: Clarendon Press, 1982, pp. 23, 38, 51f., 157.
105. D. Newsome, *The Parting of Friends: The Wilberforces and Henry Manning*, new edn, Grand Rapids, MI: Eerdmans and Leominster: Gracewing, 1993, pp. 199f.
106. Newsome, *The Parting of Friends*, p. 366.
107. Nockles, *The Oxford Movement in Context*, pp. 87f.
108. Clark, *English Society*, pp. 562ff.

3   The Anglican Communion: idea, name and identity

1. This chapter was first published in the *International Journal for the Study of the Christian Church*, 4, 2004, pp. 34–9. The research on which it is based was undertaken during a period of study leave in the autumn of 2001, for which I thank my employers, the Archbishops' Council of the Church of England. I am indebted to the then principal and librarians of Pusey House, Oxford, for their congenial and convivial hospitality and for allowing me to make full use of the remarkable riches of Dr Pusey's Library. I am also indebted to the Ven. Dr W. M. Jacob and Dr Mary Tanner, and especially to Prebendary Dr Paul Avis, for their comments on earlier drafts of the article.
2. The Lambeth Commission on Communion, *The Windsor Report 2004*, London: Anglican Communion Office, 2004, p. 75, para. 157.
3. An excellent recent study is W. M. Jacob, *The Making of the Anglican Church Worldwide*, London: SPCK, 1997.

4. M. Lochhead, *Episcopal Scotland in the Nineteenth Century*, London: John Murray, 1966, p. 36.
5. 26 Geo. 3 c. 84.
6. For one example of differences obscured by the use of common terminology, see Chapter 5, p.70.
7. 40 Geo. 3 c. 67.
8. 26 Geo. 3 c. 84, s. III.
9. 32 Geo. 3 c. 63, quoted by L. E. Luscombe, 'Matthew Luscombe – 1776–1846: missionary bishop in Europe of the Scottish Episcopal Church', MPhil. thesis, Dundee, 1991, p. 224.
10. 3&4 Vict. c. 33.
11. 6&7 Vict. Private Acts c. 32.
12. 27&28 Vict. c. 94.
13. 37&38 Vict. c. 77.
14. George Gaskin to Bishop John Skinner, 26 March 1790, explaining the views of Bishop Samuel Horsley of St Davids, in J. Skinner, *Annals of Scottish Episcopacy, from the Year 1788 to the Year 1816*, Edinburgh, 1818, p. 158.
15. F. C. Mather, 'Church, Parliament and penal laws: some Anglo-Scottish interactions in the eighteenth century', *English Historical Review*, 92, 1977, pp. 540–72, at pp. 555–7, 569–70.
16. British Library, Add. MS 39312, fol. 3v: J. Skinner to G. Gleig, 14 Oct. 1784 (copy).
17. Mather, 'Church, Parliament and penal laws', p. 547.
18. D. G. Rowell, *The Club of Nobody's Friends: A Memoir on its Two-Hundredth Anniversary*, Edinburgh: The Pentland Press, 2000.
19. Mather, 'Church, Parliament and penal laws', pp. 570–72; F. C. Mather, *High Church Prophet: Bishop Samuel Horsley (1733–1806) and the Caroline Tradition in the Later Georgian Church*, Oxford: Oxford University Press, 1992, pp. 137–8.
20. P. B. Nockles, 'Bowdler, John (1746–1823)', *Oxford Dictionary of National Biography*, Oxford: Oxford University Press, 2004.
21. Mather, *High Church Prophet*, pp. 122–3; E. A. Varley, *The Last of the Prince Bishops: William Van Mildert and the High Church Movement of the Early Nineteenth Century*, Cambridge: Cambridge University Press, 1992, p. 20.
22. R. Bosher, *The American Church and the Formation of the Anglican Communion, 1823–1853*, Evanston, IL: Seabury-Western Theological Seminary, 1962, p. 5.
23. For further details of the visit, see G. F. A. Best, 'Church parties and charities: the experiences of three American visitors to England, 1823–1824', *English Historical Review*, 78, 1963, pp. 243–67.
24. W. R. W. Stephens, *The Life and Letters of Walter Farquhar Hook*, 2 vols, 3rd edn, London, 1879, vol. 1, pp. 101–4.
25. W. F. Hook, *An Attempt to Demonstrate the Catholicism of the Church of England and the other Branches of the Episcopal Church: In a sermon preached in the Episcopal Chapel at Stirling, on Sunday, March XX, MDCCCXXV, at the Consecration of the Right Rev. Matthew Luscombe*, London, 1825, pp. 24–5 (the quotation is from 1 Corinthians 12.26.)
26. M. H. Luscombe to D. Low, 10 Oct. 1825, quoted in W. Blatch (ed.), *A Memoir of the Right Rev. David Low*, London, 1855, pp. 129–31.
27. Stephens, *Life and Letters of Walter Farquhar Hook*, vol. 2, pp. 89–90.

28. Bosher, *The American Church and the Formation of the Anglican Communion*, p. 19.
29. H. Caswall, *The Last Week of the Jubilee; or, What I Saw and Heard in London, on the 15th, 16th and 18th of June, 1852*, 3rd edn, London, 1852, pp. 6f.
30. T. E. Yates, *Venn and Victorian Bishops Abroad: The Missionary Policies of Henry Venn and their Repercussions upon the Anglican Episcopate of the Colonial Period, 1841–1872*, London: SPCK, 1978, p. 84.
31. Yates, *Venn and Victorian Bishops Abroad*, p. 89.
32. Yates, *Venn and Victorian Bishops Abroad*, p. 90.
33. Cf. P. B. Nockles, *The Oxford Movement in Context: Anglican High Churchmanship, 1760–1857*, Cambridge: Cambridge University Press, 1994, pp. 60ff.
34. Lambeth Palace Library, Fulham Papers, Blomfield, vol. 65, fol. 7r (copy): Blomfield to Luscombe, 19 March 1829.
35. *Proceedings at a Meeting of the Clergy and Laity . . . for the purpose of raising a fund towards the endowment of Additional Colonial Bishoprics*, London, 1841, p. 3.
36. H. H. Norris to R. Churton, 30 Sept. 1812, quoted in Nockles, *The Oxford Movement in Context*, p. 154.
37. *The Colonial Church Chronicle and Missionary Journal*, 1, 1847–8, pp. 3–5.
38. See pp. 36–7 below.
39. *Thirty Years' Correspondence between John Jebb . . . and Alexander Knox*, ed. C. Forster, 2nd edn, London, 1836, vol. 2, p. 125.
40. Mather, *High Church Prophet*, p. 73.
41. C. J. Blomfield, *A Letter to His Grace the Lord Archbishop of Canterbury, upon the Formation of a Fund for Endowing Additional Bishoprics in the Colonies*, London, 1840, p. 16.
42. Pusey House, Oxford, Liddon Bound Volume 72, fol. 32: J. M. Kaye to [J. Beaven?], 27 Oct. 1841 (copy).
43. 26 Hen. 8 c. 1: for the text, see G. R. Elton (ed.), *The Tudor Constitution: Documents and Commentary*, Cambridge: Cambridge University Press, 1972, p. 355.
44. Elton, *Tudor Constitution*, p. 366.
45. P. Avis, 'What is "Anglicanism"?', in S. Sykes, J. Booty and J. Knight (eds), *The Study of Anglicanism*, rev. edn, London: SPCK, 1998, p. 460.
46. *Oxford English Dictionary*, 2nd edn.
47. E.g. Lambeth Palace Library, Fulham Papers, Howley, vol. 4, p. 1013: E. Law to E. C. Disbrowe, 20 Aug. 1825 – 'the other Anglican churches in the Empire of Russia'; Guildhall Library, MS 9532 A-3: Diocese of London Act Book, 1828–42, p. 12 (13 March 1829) – 'the Anglican community at Trieste'.
48. J. H. Newman, *Lectures on the Prophetical Office of the Church viewed relatively to Romanism and Popular Protestantism*, London, 1837, p. 21: 'what is called Anglicanism, the religion of Andrewes, Laud, Hammond, Butler, and Wilson'. In the second edition (1838) Newman substituted 'Anglo-Catholicism' for 'Anglicanism'. The term 'Anglicanism' occurs in French – initially in a non-ecclesiastical sense – from 1801 (J. R. Wright, 'Anglicanism, *Ecclesia Anglicana*, and Anglican: an essay on terminology', in Sykes, Booty and Knight (eds), *The Study of Anglicanism*, p. 481 n. 2).

49. Nockles, *The Oxford Movement in Context*, p. 40.
50. Strictly speaking, it would perhaps need to be 'English and Welsh', though at the time Wales was legally, administratively and ecclesiastically part of England.
51. *Colonial Church Chronicle*, 1, 1847–8, p. 396.
52. Bosher, *The American Church and the Formation of the Anglican Communion*, pp. 21 and 28 n. 66.
53. *Colonial Church Chronicle*, 8, 1854–5, p. 64.
54. Lambeth Palace Library, Longley Papers, vol. 6, fols 251v–252r: W. J. Trower to C. T. Longley, 25 March 1867.
55. C. H. Lyttkens, *The Growth of Swedish–Anglican Intercommunion between 1833 and 1922*, Lund: Gleerup, 1970, pp. 61–3.
56. A. M. G. Stephenson, *Anglicanism and the Lambeth Conferences*, London: SPCK, 1978, p. 7.
57. G. F. Fisher, speech at a meeting marking his return from a tour of Australia and New Zealand, Westminster Central Hall, 30 Jan. 1951, quoted in *Church Times*, 2 Feb. 1951, p. 1.
58. S. Neill, *Anglicanism*, 3rd edn, Harmondsworth: Penguin, 1965, p. 417.
59. J. W. C. Wand, *Anglicanism in History and Today*, London: Weidenfeld & Nicolson, 1961, p. 227: 'We have no special and peculiar doctrines of our own . . . We claim to believe what is in the Creeds and in the Bible, that is to say, what is common to all Christendom'; J. Macquarrie, 'What still separates us from the Catholic Church? An Anglican reply', *Concilium*, 4/6, April 1970, pp. 45–53, at p. 45: 'It is often claimed that Anglicanism has no special doctrines of its own and simply follows the universal teaching of the Church. When one considers the nature of the English Reformation, one sees that there is strong support for the claim.'
60. A. M. Ramsey, 'What is Anglican theology?', *Theology*, 48, 1945, pp. 2–6, at p. 6.
61. Ramsey, 'What is Anglican theology?', p. 2.
62. H. R. McAdoo, *The Spirit of Anglicanism: A Survey of Anglican Theological Method in the Seventeenth Century*, London: A. & C. Black, 1965, p. 1. Cf. p. v: 'Anglicanism is not a theological system and there is no writer whose work is an essential part of it . . . Richard Hooker has some claim to be the greatest Anglican writer, but his work was to state a method in theology rather than to outline a system.'
63. S. W. Sykes, 'Anglicanism and the doctrine of the church', in S. W. Sykes, *Unashamed Anglicanism*, London: Darton, Longman & Todd, 1995, pp. 101–21 (the article was first published in 1988).
64. P. Avis, 'The distinctiveness of Anglicanism', in C. J. Podmore (ed.), *Community – Unity – Communion: Essays in Honour of Mary Tanner*, London: Church House Publishing, 1998, pp. 141–55.
65. P. Avis, 'The churches of the Anglican Communion', in P. Avis (ed.), *The Christian Church: An Introduction to the Major Traditions*, London: SPCK, 2002, pp. 132–3.
66. Avis, 'The churches of the Anglican Communion', p. 134.
67. See pp. 27–8 above.
68. See Chapter 8, p. 125.
69. S. F. Bayne, 'Anglicanism – the contemporary situation: this nettle, Anglicanism', *Pan-Anglican: A Review of the World-wide Episcopal Church*, 5/1, Epiphany 1954, pp. 39–45, at pp. 43–4.

70. D. M. Paton, *Anglicans and Unity*, London: A. R. Mowbray & Co., 1962, p. 20. I am indebted to Dr Mary Tanner for drawing my attention to this quotation.
71. *The Truth Shall Make You Free: The Lambeth Conference 1988*, London: Church House Publishing, 1988, p. 13. Again, I am indebted to Dr Mary Tanner for drawing my attention to this quotation.
72. A. M. Ramsey, *The Gospel and the Catholic Church*, London: Longmans Green & Co., 1936, p. 220.

4   The Church of England's Declaration of Assent

1. This chapter was first published in the *Ecclesiastical Law Journal* at (1999) 5 Ecc LJ 241. It is reproduced here in a revised form with the permission of the editor.
2. *May They All Be One: Response of the House of Bishops of the Church of England to Ut Unum Sint*, GS Misc 495, London: Church House Publishing, 1997, paras 58, 28, 17.
3. For what follows, see *Subscription and Assent to the Thirty-nine Articles*, London: SPCK, 1968, paras 1–7.
4. E. J. Bicknell, *A Theological Introduction to the Thirty-nine Articles of the Church of England*, London, 1947, p. 26.
5. *Subscription and Assent*, para. 8.
6. *Subscription and Assent*, paras 51–7.
7. *Subscription and Assent*, para. 89.
8. *Subscription and Assent*, para. 94.
9. Lambeth Palace Library, Archbishop's Commission on Christian Doctrine, vol. 1, Minutes, 23–24 Feb. 1968: fol. 68v, nos 38(iv) and 39.
10. Archbishop's Commission on Christian Doctrine, vol. 1, Paper 26: suggested emendations, fol. 105r; Minutes, 29–30 May 1968: fols. 115–116, no. 47.
11. Archbishop's Commission on Christian Doctrine, vol. 1, Minutes, 29–30 May 1968: fol. 116, no. 47.
12. Archbishop's Commission on Christian Doctrine, vol. 1, Minutes, 19 July 1968: fol. 118, no. 55.
13. Archbishop's Commission on Christian Doctrine, vol. 1, Minutes, 23–24 Sept. 1968, fol. 136, no. 81(c); note appended to *Subscription and Assent*.
14. *Subscription and Assent*, para. 99.
15. *Report of Proceedings*, vol. 3, 1972, pp. 789–804.
16. *Report of Proceedings*, vol. 3, p. 791: the Revd P. J. M. Bryan (Peterborough).
17. *Report of Proceedings*, vol. 3, p. 797.
18. *Report of Proceedings*, vol. 3, pp. 802–3: Mr K. Haye (Lincoln).
19. Church of England Record Centre, GSA/CNS/C15/1: Proposals from Members of the Synod (DA(73)1), Letter from Lady Alethea Eliot (DA(73)2), Further Correspondence (DA(73)3); *Declaration of Assent: Report of the Revision Committee*, GS 116A, 1973.
20. Church of England Record Centre, GSA/CNS/C15/1, DA(73)1, p. 2.
21. Church of England Record Centre, GSA/CNS/C15/1: untitled document.
22. Church of England Record Centre, GSA/CNS/C15/1, DA(73)1, p. 6.
23. *Report of Proceedings*, vol. 3, 1972, p. 797.
24. Church of England Record Centre, GSA/CNS/C15/1: E. A. Eadie to M. F. Elliott-Binns, 31 Jan. 1973, enclosing draft amendments.

25. Church of England Record Centre, GSA/CNS/C15/1, DA(73)1, p. 3, DA(73)3, p. 5.
26. *Declaration of Assent. Draft Canon . . . as amended by the Revision Committee*, GS 116A,1973, p. 1.
27. GS 116A, 1973: Report of the Revision Committee, p. 7, para. 10.
28. Church of England Record Centre, GSA/CNS/C15/1: Elliott-Binns to Lewis, 6 Feb.
29. Church of England Record Centre, GSA/CNS/C15/3: Elliott-Binns to Lewis, 15 Feb.
30. Church of England Record Centre, GSA/CNS/C15/3: Elliott-Binns to Lewis, 19 March.
31. Church of England Record Centre, GSA/CNS/C15/1.
32. Church of England Record Centre, GSA/CNS/C15/3: Lewis to R. J. Byrom, 5 April.
33. Church of England Record Centre, GSA/CNS/C15/1: Further Communication from the Chairman (DA(73)7).
34. Church of England Record Centre, GSA/CNS/C15/3: C. R. Campling to Elliott-Binns, 4 May 1973.
35. GS 116A, 1973, p. 6, paras 8–9.
36. *Report of Proceedings*, vol. 4, 1973, pp. 475–80.
37. *Report of Proceedings*, vol. 4, 1973, pp. 475–80.
38. *Draft Amending Canon No. 4: Report by the House of Bishops*, GS 116C, 1975.
39. *Subscription and Assent*, para. 95.
40. Canon C 15, para. 4.
41. *Clergy Discipline (Doctrine)*, GS 1554, 2004, para. 107.
42. *Ordination Services. Report of the Revision Committee*, GS 1520Y, 2005, p. 17, para. 61.
43. See Chapter 3, p. 35.

5 Primacy in the Anglican tradition

1. This chapter first appeared in C. J. Podmore (ed.), *Community – Unity – Communion: Essays in Honour of Mary Tanner*, London: Church House Publishing,1998, pp. 277–93. I am grateful to the Rt Revd Dr Geoffrey Rowell, the Ven. Dr W. M. Jacob, Mr John Clark, Dr Gillian Evans, the Rt Revd David Hamid and Dr Mary Tanner for their comments on an earlier draft. A new final section, dealing with developments in 1998 and subsequently, has been added.
2. Pope John Paul II, Encyclical *Ut Unum Sint*, para. 96.
3. *Episcopal Ministry: The Report of the Archbishops' Group on the Episcopate*, GS 944, London: Church House Publishing, 1990, p. 181, para. 403.
4. Bede, *Historia Gentis Anglorum Ecclesiastica*, 1.29.
5. F. L. Cross and E. A. Livingstone (eds), *Oxford Dictionary of the Christian Church*, 3rd edn, Oxford: Oxford University Press, 1997, s.v. 'Primacy'.
6. J. C. Dickinson, *The Later Middle Ages: From the Norman Conquest to the Eve of the Reformation*, London: A. & C. Black, 1979, p. 68.
7. See C. Wordsworth, *The Precedence of English Bishops and the Provincial Chapter*, Cambridge, 1906, esp. pp. 74–6, and E. W. Kemp, 'The Canterbury provincial chapter and the collegiality of bishops in the middle ages' in *Etudes d'Histoire du Droit Canonique dédiées à Gabriel Le Bras*, Paris, 1965, vol. 1, pp. 185–94.
8. Cf. 'The form of proceeding in the business of confirming the election of the Right Reverend Father in God George Leonard, by Divine Permission Lord Bishop of Bath

and Wells, to the archiepiscopal See of Canterbury, in the church of St Mary-le-Bow, Cheapside, in the City of London on Wednesday 27 March 1991 at 12 noon'; and St Paul's Cathedral: service booklet for Confirmation of the Election of the Most Reverend Doctor Rowan Williams as Lord Archbishop of Canterbury, Primate of All England and Metropolitan, Monday 2 December 2002, 1200.

9. Kemp, 'The Canterbury provincial chapter', pp. 185–6.
10. See, for example, the Church of England (Miscellaneous Provisions) Measure 1983, section 7.
11. 'Due obedience' is technically distinct from 'canonical obedience': see *Episcopal Ministry*, p. 227, para. 519.
12. *The Canon Law of the Church of England: Being the Report of the Archbishops' Commission on Canon Law . . .*, London: SPCK, 1947, pp. 163f., 199f. (Canons LXXI, CXVI).
13. Michael Smith, Letter to the Editor, *Ecclesiastical Law Journal*, 3, 1993–5, p. 264.
14. Report of the Working Party on Ecclesiastical Visitations, *Ecclesiastical Law Journal*, 2, 1990–92, p. 350.
15. Standing Order 40 (c).
16. See Chapter 7, pp. 114–5 and 121–2.
17. See E. W. Kemp, *Counsel and Consent*, London: SPCK, 1961, pp. 110–12.
18. General Synod constitution, Article 7 (1).
19. Quoted in *Government by Synod: Synodical Government in the Church of England*, CA 1600, London: Church Information Office, 1966, p. 98.
20. Quoted in *Government by Synod*, p. 15.
21. *Report of Proceedings*, vol. 28, 1998, pp. 672, 674.
22. H. Lowther Clarke, *Constitutional Church Government in the Dominions Beyond the Seas and in other parts of the Anglican Communion*, London: SPCK, 1924, p. 35.
23. *The Six Lambeth Conferences, 1867–1920*, ed. R. Davidson, 2nd edn, London: SPCK, 1929, p. 70; cf. p. 84 (1878), p. 187 (1897).
24. *The Six Lambeth Conferences*, p. 150.
25. Lowther Clarke, *Constitutional Church Government*, pp. 240, 29.
26. *The Six Lambeth Conferences*, p. 200.
27. R. A. Giles, *The Constitutional History of the Australian Church*, London: Oxford University Press, 1929, p. 210.
28. Lowther Clarke, *Constitutional Church Government*, p. 41.
29. Lowther Clarke, *Constitutional Church Government*, p. 231.
30. Lowther Clarke, *Constitutional Church Government*, p. 240; *The Six Lambeth Conferences*, p. 200.
31. Lowther Clarke, *Constitutional Church Government*, pp. 227, 241.
32. J. W. C. Wand (ed.), *The Anglican Communion: A Survey*, London: Oxford University Press, 1948, pp. 82, 120.
33. *The Six Lambeth Conferences*, p. 418.
34. *The Six Lambeth Conferences*, p. 419.
35. Lowther Clarke, *Constitutional Church Government*, p. xvi.
36. *The Lambeth Conference 1948*, London: SPCK, 1948, p. 84.
37. *The Lambeth Conference 1968: Resolutions and Reports*, London: SPCK and New York: Seabury Press, 1968, p. 137.

38. *Resolutions and Reports*, p. 141.
39. *The Report of the Lambeth Conference 1978*, London: Church Information Office, 1978, p. 98.
40. 'The Virginia Report: The Report of the Inter-Anglican Theological and Doctrinal Commission', in *The Official Report of the Lambeth Conference 1998*, Harrisburg, PA: Morehouse Publishing, 1999, pp. 15–68, at p. 57.
41. The Porvoo Common Statement in *Together in Mission and Ministry: The Porvoo Common Statement with Essays on Church and Ministry in Northern Europe*, GS 1083, London: Church House Publishing,1993, paras 34, 49, 56.
42. The Porvoo Common Statement, para. 49.
43. *The Lambeth Conference 1930*, London: SPCK, n.d., p. 52.
44. *The Report of the Lambeth Conference 1978*, pp. 102 ff.
45. J. Howe, *Highways and Hedges: Anglicanism and the Universal Church*, London: Church Information Office, 1985, p. 15.
46. *The Lambeth Conference 1930*, p. 57, res. 54.
47. *The Lambeth Conference 1968*, p. 47.
48. *The Report of the Lambeth Conference 1978*, p. 103.
49. *The Report of the Lambeth Conference 1978*, p. 41, res. 11.
50. *May They All Be One: A Response of the House of Bishops of the Church of England to Ut Unum Sint*, GS Misc 495, London: Church House Publishing, 1997, p. 18, para. 47.
51. J. Rosenthal and N. Currie (eds), *Being Anglican in the Third Millennium: The Official Report of the 10th Meeting of the Anglican Consultative Council*, Harrisburg, PA: Morehouse Publishing, 1997, p. 185: resolution 15 On Rwanda.
52. *The Official Report of the Lambeth Conference 1998*, pp. 410f: res. IV.13.
53. See p. 68 above.
54. *The Official Report of the Lambeth Conference 1998*, pp. 398ff: res. III.8. The quotation is from 'The Virginia Report', p. 54.
55. *The Official Report of the Lambeth Conference 1998*, pp. 396f.: res. III.6.
56. *The Official Report of the Lambeth Conference 1998*, pp. 200f.
57. www. forwardinfaith.com: G. Carey to J. Broadhurst, 27 Aug. 2002.
58. www. forwardinfaith.com: R. Williams to G. Kirk, 4 Sept. 2002.
59. 'A Statement by the Primates of the Anglican Communion meeting in Lambeth Palace, 16 October 2003' in The Lambeth Commission on Communion, *The Windsor Report 2004*, London: Anglican Communion Office, 2004, pp. 98–101.
60. *The Windsor Report 2004*, p. 13.
61. *The Windsor Report 2004*, p. 59, para. 109.
62. www.anglicancommunion.org: The Anglican Primates' Meeting Communiqué, February 2005, para. 10.

6 *Territoriality, communion and parallel episcopates*

1. I am indebted to the Revd Canon Dr Herman Browne, William Fittall, Dr Mary Tanner and David Williams for their comments on earlier drafts of this chapter.
2. *Ecclesiastical Law, being a reprint from Halsbury's Laws of England*, 3rd edn, Church Assembly Edition, London: Butterworth & Co., 1957, p. 33.
3. 24 Hen. 8 c. 12 (G. R. Elton (ed.), *The Tudor Constitution: Documents and Commentary*, Cambridge: Cambridge University Press, 1960, p. 344). For the

background to the concept of the English realm as an 'empire', see W. Ullmann, 'This realm of England is an empire', *Journal of Ecclesiastical History*, 30, 1979, pp. 175–203.

4. 26 Hen. 8 c. 1 (Elton, *Tudor Constitution*, p. 355).
5. 1 Eliz. 1 c. 1 (Elton, *Tudor Constitution*, p. 366).
6. See J. R. Wright, 'Anglicanism, *Ecclesia Anglicana*, and Anglican: an essay in terminology', in S. Sykes, J. Booty and J. Knight (eds), *The Study of Anglicanism*, rev. edn, London: SPCK, 1998, p. 480. See also Chapter 3, p. 35 above.
7. Cheslyn Jones, quoted in R. Greenacre, *The Catholic Church in France*, CCU Occasional Paper No. 4, 1996, p. 45.
8. Y. Brilioth, *The Anglican Revival: Studies in the Oxford Movement*, 2nd edn, London: Longmans Green & Co.,1933, p. 1.
9. The English Reformation was, of course, exported to Ireland (or at least, to those areas of Ireland that were under English control), and developments in England were not without influence (positive and negative) on the complicated history of the Reformation in Scotland.
10. D. MacCulloch, 'The Church of England, 1533–1603', in S. Platten (ed.), *Anglicanism and the Western Christian Tradition: Continuity, Change and the Search for Communion*, Norwich: Canterbury Press, 2003, pp. 18–41, at p. 18. See also Chapter 3, pp. 38–41 above.
11. C. S. L. Davies, 'The Reformation in the Crown's French dominions – Calais, Boulogne and the Channel Islands', unpublished lecture, April 2002.
12. C. C. A. Pearce, 'The offshore establishment of religion: church and nation in the Isle of Man', *Ecclesiastical Law Journal*, 7, 2003, pp. 62–74.
13. C. S. L. Davies, 'International politics and the establishment of Presbyterianism in the Channel Islands: the Coutances connection', *Journal of Ecclesiastical History*, 50, 1999, pp. 517–21.
14. Davies, 'International politics', p. 508. Though technically in the Diocese of Thérouanne, Calais had been under the jurisdiction of the Archbishop of Canterbury since 1379 (p. 499 n. 4).
15. See Chapter 3, p. 28.
16. See Chapter 5, p. 65.
17. The Diocese in Europe Constitution 1995, s. 2. Sections 5 and 6 of the Diocese in Europe Measure 1980 provided that certain measures 'shall have effect as if the Diocese were in the province of Canterbury'.
18. The Canons of the Church of England, Canon C 18 (italics added).
19. The Diocese in Europe Constitution 1995, s. 1.
20. H. J. C. Knight, *The Diocese of Gibraltar: A Sketch of its History, Work and Tasks*, London: SPCK, 1917, p. v.
21. Knight, *The Diocese of Gibraltar*, p. 117.
22. This story is often told but may well be apocryphal. Mrs Margaret Pawley suggests that if the comment was actually made, it would have been by Pope John XXIII to Stanley Eley, who was Bishop of Gibraltar from 1960 to 1970.
23. Cf. P. Barber, 'What is a peculiar?', *Ecclesiastical Law Journal*, 3, 1993–5, pp. 299–312.
24. Barber, 'What is a peculiar?', p. 301. In the ancient division of the country into parishes, certain areas were left extra-parochial (*Halsbury's Laws of England*, 4th

edn, vol. 14, London, 1975, p. 266, para. 563). Extra-parochial places may be created by pastoral scheme under the Pastoral Measure 1983, s. 17.

25. Barber, 'What is a peculiar?', p. 302.
26. Barber, 'What is a peculiar?', p. 304.
27. *Being in Communion*, GS Misc 418, 1993.
28. *Bishops in Communion: Collegiality in the Service of the Koinonia of the Church*, GS Misc 580, London: Church House Publishing, 2000.
29. 'The Virginia Report: The Report of the Inter-Anglican Theological and Doctrinal Commission', in *The Official Report of the Lambeth Conference 1998*, Harrisburg, PA: Morehouse Publishing, 1999, pp. 15–68, at p. 36.
30. *The Truth Shall Make You Free: The Lambeth Conference 1988*, London: Church House Publishing, 1988, p. 16.
31. 'A Statement by the Primates of the Anglican Communion meeting in Lambeth Palace, 16 October 2003' in The Lambeth Commission on Communion, *The Windsor Report 2004*, London: Anglican Communion Office, 204, pp. 98–101.
32. *The Lambeth Conference 1958: The Encyclical Letter from the Bishops together with the Resolutions and Reports*, London: SPCK, 1958, 2.23.
33. Cf. *The Porvoo Agreement: A Report by the House of Bishops*, GS 1156, 1995, para. 24.
34. Cf. presidential statement by Archbishop Runcie to the General Synod, 8 Nov. 1988, in *Report of Proceedings*, vol. 19, 1988, pp. 699–705.
35. Overseas and Other Clergy (Ministry and Ordination) Measure 1967, s. 6(2).
36. Church Representation Rules, Rule 54(5).
37. *Acts of the Convocations of Canterbury and York, 1921–1970*, ed. H. Riley and R. J. Graham, London: SPCK, 1971, p. 176.
38. *Acts of the Convocations*, pp. 175f.
39. *Report of Proceedings*, vol. 3, 1972, p. 255.
40. *Report of Proceedings*, vol. 5, 1974, p. 762.
41. *Report of Proceedings*, vol. 26, 1995, p. 210.
42. Cf. *The Porvoo Agreement: A Report by the House of Bishops*, para. 37.
43. *Acts of the Convocations*, pp. 189–91.
44. *Acts of the Convocations*, pp. 192f.
45. *Report of Proceedings*, vol. 3, 1972, pp. 578f.
46. *Report of Proceedings*, vol. 3, 1972, pp. 494–6.
47. *Report of Proceedings*, vol. 15, 1984, pp. 1197–201.
48. This section is based on material which first in appeared in C. J. Podmore, '"The Moravian episcopate and the Episcopal Church": a personal response', *Anglican and Episcopal History*, 72, 2003, pp. 351–84.
49. *Report of Proceedings*, vol. 35, 2004, p. 469.
50. *The Truth Shall Make You Free*, pp. 215–16: res. 17; *The Official Report of the Lambeth Conference 1998*, pp. 404–5: res. IV.1–IV.3.
51. *The Official Report of the Lambeth Conference 1998*, res. IV.1: 'Commitment to Full, Visible Unity'.
52. *The Porvoo Agreement: A Report by the House of Bishops*, p. 14, para. 30.
53. Total membership, of whom 2,204 communicants (2001 figures: 1,865, of whom 1,762 communicants).

54. Easter communicants: 1,265,000 (2001 figures: electoral roll 1,337,000, Easter communicants 1,134,900).
55. The Porvoo Common Statement, para. 23, in *Together in Mission and Ministry: The Porvoo Common Statement with Essays on Church and Ministry in Northern Europe*, GS 1083, London: Church House Publishing, 1993, p. 13. The quotation is from a statement of the Roman Catholic/Lutheran Joint Commission.
56. The Fetter Lane Common Statement, para. 53, in *Anglican–Moravian Conversations: The Fetter Lane Common Statement with Essays in Moravian and Anglican History*, Council for Christian Unity Occasional Paper No. 5, London, GS 1202, 1995, p. 29.
57. The Porvoo Common Statement, para. 58b(iv), in *Together in Mission and Ministry*, p. 31.
58. *Communion with the Nordic and Baltic Lutheran Churches: A Report by the Council for Christian Unity*, GS Misc 427, 1993, p. 6, para. 13.
59. See pp. 82–3 above.
60. M. Root, '"Reconciled diversity" and the visible unity of the Church', in C. J. Podmore (ed.), *Community – Unity – Communion: Essays in Honour of Mary Tanner*, London: Church House Publishing, 1998, pp. 237–51.
61. Root, '"Reconciled diversity"', p. 242.
62. Root, '"Reconciled diversity"', pp. 246–7.
63. Root, '"Reconciled diversity"', p. 245.
64. M. Root, 'Once more on the unity we seek: testing ecumenical models', in J. Morris and N. Sagovsky (eds), *The Unity We Have and the Unity We Seek: Ecumenical Prospects for the Third Millennium*, London: T&T Clark, 2003, pp. 167–77.
65. Root, 'Once more on the unity we seek', p. 175.
66. Root, 'Once more on the unity we seek', p. 174.
67. Episcopal Ministry Act of Synod 1993, section 5(3).
68. I. Jones, *Women and Priesthood in the Church of England: Ten Years On*, London: Church House Publishing, 2004, p. 195.
69. D. Hope, 'The truth in love' (sermon at the celebration of the tenth anniversary of episcopal consecrations and the Act of Synod, St Bartholomew's, Armley, Leeds, 3 March 2004), *New Directions*, April 2004, pp. 5–6.
70. *Church Times*, 29 Nov. 2002.
71. *Women Bishops in the Church of England? A Report of the House of Bishops Working Party on Women in the Episcopate*, GS 1557, London: Church House Publishing, 2004, pp. 218–23.
72. Romans 12.2.

7   Synodical government in the Church of England

1. The paper on which this chapter is based was given at an international colloquium on 'Synod and Synodality in the Churches', organized by the Fondazione per le scienze religiose 'Giovanni XXIII' (Bologna), which was held at the English Convent, Bruges, in September 2003. Another version appears in A. Melloni and S. Scatena (eds), *Synod and Synodality*, Münster, 2005, pp. 213–36.
2. Act for the Submission of the Clergy 1534 (25 Henry VIII, c. 19), section 7, quoted

in G. Bray (ed.), *Tudor Church Reform: The Henrician Canons of 1535 and the Reformatio Legum Ecclesiasticarum*, Woodbridge, Suffolk: The Boydell Press, Church of England Record Society, vol. 8, 2000, p. xix.

3. Bishop of Exeter v. Marshall (1868), quoted in *Ecclesiastical Law, being a Reprint from Halsbury's Laws of England*, 3rd edn, Church Assembly Edition, London: Butterworth & Co.,1957, p. 9.

4. See Bray (ed.), *Tudor Church Reform.*

5. The Provinces of Canterbury and York were commonly referred to as *Ecclesia Anglicana* from the mid-twelfth century – most famously in Magna Carta; from the later fourteenth century, *Ecclesia Anglicana* was normally translated 'Church of England' (see Chapter 3, p. 35 and Chapter 6, p. 80).

6. Y. Brilioth, *The Anglican Revival: Studies in the Oxford Movement*, 2nd edn, London: Longmans Green & Co., 1933, p. 1.

7. E. W. Kemp, 'The spirit of the canon law and its application in England', *Ecclesiastical Law Journal*, 1/1, 1987, p. 9.

8. E. W. Kemp, *Counsel and Consent: Aspects of Government of the Church as Exemplified in the History of the English Provincial Synods*, London: SPCK, 1961.

9. E. Gibson, *Synodus Anglicana; or, The Constitution and Proceedings of an English Convocation, Shown from the Acts and Registers Thereof to be Agreeable to the Principles of an Episcopal Church* (London, 1702), ed. E. Cardwell, Oxford, 1854.

10. Gibson, *Synodus Anglicana*, p. liii.

11. Gibson, *Synodus Anglicana*, p. 3.

12. Gibson, *Synodus Anglicana*, p. 1.

13. Gibson, *Synodus Anglicana*, pp. 140f.

14. Gibson, *Synodus Anglicana*, p. 130.

15. Act for the Submission of the Clergy 1534 (25 Henry VIII, c. 19), sections 1 and 3, quoted in Bray (ed.), *Tudor Church Reform*, pp. xviii–xix.

16. A 1966 Act of Parliament had ended the automatic dissolution of the Convocations – requiring fresh elections – when Parliament was dissolved. The proposals which resulted in the Synodical Government Measure were set out in *Government by Synod: Synodical Government in the Church of England*, CA 1600, London: Church Information Office, 1966.

17. An Act of Synod is defined as 'the embodiment of the mind or will of the Church of England as expressed by the whole body of the Synod' (*Standing Orders of the General Synod*, S.O. 40).

18. See Chapter 4.

19. Church of England (Worship and Doctrine) Measure 1974, section 4(1). In the measure, references to the doctrine of the Church of England have to be construed in accordance with the following statement (identical with the text of Canon A 5): 'The doctrine of the Church of England is grounded in the holy Scriptures, and in such teachings of the Fathers and Councils of the Church as are agreeable to the said Scriptures. In particular such doctrine is to be found in the Thirty-nine Articles of Religion, *The Book of Common Prayer* and the Ordinal' (section 5(1)).

20. Church of England (Worship and Doctrine) Measure 1974, section 4(2).

21. Until 2005, there were nine elected suffragan and assistant bishops.

22. Until 2005 the House of Clergy had 260 members, including one archdeacon from

each diocese, 15 cathedral deans, the Dean of Jersey or Guernsey, six proctors of the university clergy, two representatives of the religious communities (all elected by their constituencies), the archdeacons of the Army, Royal Navy and Royal Air Force and the Chaplain General of Prisons.

23. Until 2005 the House of Laity also had about 260 members. Apart from three elected representatives of the religious communities and the first and second Church Estates Commissioners, all the members were representatives of the laity in each diocese, elected by the lay members of deanery synods, with room for five co-options.

24. R. A. Burns, *The Diocesan Revival in the Church of England, c. 1800–1870,* Oxford: Oxford University Press, 1999, p. 218.

25. Burns, *Diocesan Revival,* pp. 218–33.

26. Burns, *Diocesan Revival,* pp. 250–57.

27. *Chronicle of Convocation,* vol. 7, pp. 857–8 (4 June 1867), p. 997 (7 June 1867), p. 1291 (21 Feb. 1868). The report's recommendation 'That the Clergy and Laity should have an equal voice' was amended by the Upper House to read 'That in case the Bishop should think fit to put any matter to the vote, the Clergy and Laity should have an equal voice'.

28. Burns, *Diocesan Revival,* p. 257.

29. Burns, *Diocesan Revival,* pp. 95f.

30. Church Representation Rules 2001 (hereinafter CRR), rules 24 (1), 28 (1) (a), 25 (6).

31. Synodical Government Measure 1960, section 5 (3).

32. CRR, rule 30 (1), (2).

33. CRR, rule 30 (3); *Model Standing Orders for Diocesan Synods* (4th edn, reprinted 1995), S. O. 5, S. O. 7.

34. CRR, rule 31 (8).

35. CRR, rule 34 (1) (c). If the diocese is divided into episcopal areas and these have area synods, the diocesan synod may meet just once a year.

36. Synodical Government Measure 1960, section 4 (2), as amended by the Synodical Government (Amendment) Measure 2003.

37. Synodical Government Measure 1960, section 4 (3).

38. Synodical Government Measure 1960, section 4 (4).

39. CRR, rule 34 (1) (g).

40. CRR, rule 34 (1) (e).

41. These provisions do not apply to references under Article 8 of the General Synod's constitution, since the diocesan bishop will have the right to vote on the same matter as a member of the House of Bishops of the General Synod at final approval stage. A matter referred under Article 8 is deemed to have been approved by the diocesan synod if the House of Clergy and House of Laity (voting separately) have both approved it (CRR, rule 34 (1) (e), (h)).

42. Canons of the Church of England, Canon C 18, para. 5.

43. Synodical Government Measure 1960, section 4 (5).

44. This is true of governance but not of jurisdiction: metropolitical jurisdiction over each province rests with its archbishop and not with the bishops collectively. ('The archbishop has throughout his province at all times metropolitical jurisdiction . . . and, during the time of his metropolitical visitation, jurisdiction as Ordinary' (Canons of the Church of England, Canon C 17, para. 2).) For this,

see Chapter 5, pages 60–62. It is also important to note that the archbishops are not accountable to the General Synod for the exercise of their metropolitical jurisdiction.

8   Synodical government in the Church of England: Ordination of women

1. An earlier version of this chapter appeared as 'Le gouvernement synodal dans l'Eglise d'Angleterre et son illustration dans le cas de l'ordination des femmes à la prêtrise', *Unité Chrétienne*, 121, Feb. 1996, pp. 38–47.
2. For an illuminating journalistic account of the entire process leading to the ordination of women to the priesthood, see J. Petre, *By Sex Divided: The Church of England and Women Priests*, London: HarperCollins, Fount, 1994.
3. A summary (GS 104A) was published in 1973 and a supplementary report (GS 104B) in 1975.
4. *The Ordination of Women: Report of the Standing Committee on the Reference to the Dioceses*, GS 252, 1975.
5. *Report of Proceedings*, vol. 6, 1975, pp. 542–614.
6. *Report of Proceedings*, vol. 9, 1978, pp. 996–1070.
7. *Report of Proceedings*, vol. 15, 1984, pp. 1078–142.
8. *The Ordination of Women to the Priesthood: The Scope of the Legislation*, GS 738, 1986.
9. *The Ordination of Women to the Priesthood: The Scope of the Legislation (GS 738): Memorandum by the House of Bishops*, GS Misc 246, 1986.
10. *Report of Proceedings*, vol. 17, 1986, pp. 632–82.
11. *The Ordination of Women to the Priesthood: First Report by the House of Bishops*, GS 764, 1987.
12. *Report of Proceedings*, vol. 18, 1987, pp. 294–367.
13. GS 830–34.
14. Church of England Assembly (Powers) Act 1919.
15. *The Ordination of Women to the Priesthood: A Second Report by the House of Bishops of the General Synod of the Church of England*, GS 829, 1988; *Report of Proceedings*, vol. 19, 1988, pp. 421–77.
16. *Report of Proceedings*, vol. 19, 1988, pp. 514–618.
17. *Report of Proceedings*, vol. 20, 1989, pp. 947–1063, 1181–298.
18. *Report of Proceedings*, vol. 20, 1989, pp. 1235–42.
19. GS Misc 336, 337, 1990.
20. *AAMBIT: The Newsletter of the Association for the Apostolic Ministry*, 9, Feb. 1992; *Church Times*, 6 Dec. 1991.
21. *Ordination of Women to the Priesthood – Reference of the Legislation to the Dioceses: Voting Figures*, GS 996, 1992; *Report of Proceedings*, vol. 23, 1992, pp. 44–64, 70–85.
22. *Government by Synod: Synodical Government in the Church of England*, CA 1600, London: Church Information Office, 1966, pp. 15, 97f.
23. See *The Ordination of Women to the Priesthood: The Synod Debate, 11 November 1992: The Verbatim Record*, London: Church House Publishing, 1993.
24. Church of England Assembly (Powers) Act 1919.

25. *Reports by the Ecclesiastical Committee upon the Priests (Ordination of Women) Measure and the Ordination of Women (Financial Provisions) Measure,* Ecclesiastical Committee 203rd and 204th reports: HL Paper 116, HC 895, 1993.

26. For an account of the genesis of the Act of Synod and of the theological thinking on which it was based, see M. Tanner, 'The Episcopal Ministry Act of Synod in context', in P. Avis (ed.), *Seeking the Truth of Change in the Church: Reception, Communion and the Ordination of Women,* London: T&T Clark, 2004, pp. 58–74.

27. *Ordination of Women to the Priesthood: Pastoral Arrangements. Report by the House of Bishops,* GS 1074, 1993.

28. GS Misc 418, 1993.

29. *Report of Proceedings,* vol. 24, 1993, pp. 672–703.

30. *Report of Proceedings,* vol. 24, 1993, pp. 982–96.

31. *Report of Proceedings,* vol. 25, 1994, pp. 7–9.

32. Cf. GS Misc 246 and Archbishop Habgood's speech, in which he commented: 'There was some horror in the House of Bishops when we found ourselves faced with a selection of recommendations, all of which, either directly or indirectly, affected our own ministry as bishops. We felt that it was highly important to assert as a principle that the Synod really cannot come in and pre-empt some things which very specially belong to us' (*Report of Proceedings,* vol. 17, 1986, pp. 669–70).

33. See Archbishop Runcie's comments, quoted on p. 132 above.

34. Cf. D. G. Rowell, 'Learning to live with difference', in P. Avis (ed.), *Seeking the Truth of Change in the Church,* pp. 139–51 at p. 139.

9   The choosing of bishops

1. This chapter first appeared in *Working with the Spirit: A Review of the Operation of the Crown Appointments Commission and Related Matters,* GS 1405, London: Church House Publishing, 2001. A concluding section has been added to bring the story up to date.

2. This chapter is solely concerned with diocesan bishops; in it, 'bishop' accordingly means 'diocesan bishop' unless otherwise stated.

3. H. Chadwick, *The Early Church,* Pelican History of the Church, Harmondsworth: Penguin, 1967, pp. 50, 165–6; for the canons of Nicaea, see J. Stevenson (ed.), *A New Eusebius,* London: SPCK, 1968, pp. 358–64.

4. G. Dix, 'Ministry in the early Church', in K. E. Kirk (ed.), *The Apostolic Ministry: Essays on the History and the Doctrine of Episcopacy,* London: Hodder & Stoughton, 1946, p. 278.

5. H. Chadwick, 'Church leadership in history and theology' (1989), in *Senior Church Appointments,* GS 1089, London: Church House Publishing, 1992, pp. 78–80, and F. E. Brightman, Memorandum (1927), in *Interim Report of the Appointment of Bishops Committee,* CA 282, 1929, pp. 28–30.

6. Brightman, Memorandum; R. L. Benson, *The Bishop-Elect: A Study in Medieval Ecclesiastical Office,* Princeton, NJ: Princeton University Press, 1968, p. 26.

7. W. Ullmann, 'Episcopal elections and political manipulation', in G. Alberigo and A. Weiler (eds), *Election – Consensus – Reception: Concilium,* vol. 7 no. 8, 1972, pp. 80–84.

8. J. Gaudemet, 'From election to nomination', in P. Huizing and K. Walf (eds), *Electing our own Bishops: Concilium*, Sept. 1980, pp. 11–12. See also Benson, *The Bishop-Elect*, pp. 27–31.

9. See J. Godfrey, *The Church in Anglo-Saxon England*, Cambridge: Cambridge University Press, 1962, pp. 384-6, and H. R. Loyn, *The English Church, 940–1154*, Harlow: Longman, 2000, p. 4.

10. For this and what follows, see F. Barlow, *The English Church, 1000–1066: A Constitutional History*, London: Longman, 1963, pp. 99–115.

11. Barlow, *The English Church*, p. 101.

12. J. Gaudemet, *Les Elections dans L'Eglise Latine des origines au XVIe siècle*, Paris: Editions Fernand Lanore,1979, pp. 8f.

13. 'Ernennung und Wahl bilden keinen Gegensatz' (quoted by Barlow, *The English Church*, p. 101).

14. C. Garbett, *Church and State in England*, London: Hodder & Stoughton,1950, p. 33.

15. V. Ortenberg, 'The Anglo-Saxon church and the papacy', in C. H. Lawrence (ed.), *The English Church and the Papacy in the Middle Ages*, rev. edn, Stroud: Sutton Publishing, 1999, p. 49.

16. R. W. Southern, *Western Society and the Church in the Middle Ages*, Pelican History of the Church, Harmondsworth: Penguin,1970, pp. 156-7.

17. F. Barlow, *The English Church, 1066–1154*, London: Longman, 1979, pp. 118–20.

18. Loyn, *The English Church, 940–1154*, p. 103.

19. C. R. Cheney, *From Becket to Langton: English Church Government, 1170–1213*, Manchester: Manchester University Press, 1956, pp. 20–21, 93–5.

20. Brightman, Memorandum, p. 32; A. H. Thompson, Memorandum (1927), in *Interim Report of the Appointment of Bishops Committee*, pp. 33–4.

21. See A. Parsons, *Canonical Elections: An Historical Synopsis and Commentary*, Catholic University of America Law Studies No. 118, Washington, DC, 1939, pp. 52–68. See also J. W. Legg, 'On the three ways of canonical election', in J. W. Legg, *Ecclesiological Essays*, London, 1905, pp. 59–88.

22. Gregory the Great did decide in 1274 that a numerical majority of two-thirds might be supposed to have reason on its side: G. Barraclough, 'The making of a bishop in the later Middle Ages: the part of the pope in law and fact', *Catholic Historical Review*, 19, 1933, pp. 275–319, at p. 277.

23. Gaudemet, *Les Elections*, p. 9.

24. B. Schimmelpfennig, 'The principle of the *Sanior Pars* in the election of bishops during the Middle Ages', in Huizing and Walf (eds), *Electing our own Bishops*, pp. 16–23. Canon 24 of the council said 'maior vel sanior pars', whereas the decretal of Innocent III in which it was embodied (X, i.6.42) said 'maior et sanior pars' (ibid., p. 21). Gradually, the idea of majority voting began to win through. Gregory IX reduced the scope for argument about whether one party was the *maior pars* by declaring that *maior pars* meant an absolute majority; and in the Council of Lyons (1274) Gregory X declared that a two-thirds majority should be assumed to have greater reasons and discernment on its side and hence should always prevail. By requiring a strictly secret vote in monastic elections, the Council of Trent prevented any claim in such elections that the minority was *sanior* (Parsons, *Canonical Elections*, pp. 60f.).

25. F. M. Powicke, *King Henry III and the Lord Edward*, vol. 1, Oxford: Clarendon Press, 1947, p. 274.

26. E. F. Jacob (ed.), *The Register of Henry Chichele, Archbishop of Canterbury 1414–43*, vol. 1, Oxford: Clarendon Press, 1943, p. lxxxix; Southern, *Western Society and the Church in the Middle Ages*, p. 158.

27. C. H. Lawrence, 'The thirteenth century', in Lawrence (ed.), *The English Church and the Papacy in the Middle Ages*, p. 146.

28. For this and what follows, see W. A. Pantin, *The English Church in the Fourteenth Century*, Cambridge: Cambridge University Press, 1955, pp. 54–7.

29. Thompson, Memorandum, pp. 13–14.

30. The statute is named after the writ of *praemunire* (a corruption of *praemoneri*), so called from the words with which its operative part begins: 'Praemunire facies *A.B.* – 'cause *A.B.* to be forewarned that he appear before us to answer the contempt with which he stands charged' (*Report of the Committee Appointed to Consider the Penalties of Praemunire in Relation to the Appointment of Bishops*, CA 566, 1937, pp. 3, 10).

31. A. H. Thompson, *The English Clergy and their Organization in the Later Middle Ages*, Oxford: Clarendon Press, 1947, pp. 16, 23–4.

32. Jacob (ed.), *The Register of Henry Chichele*, vol. 1, pp. lxxxix–xci.

33. The text of the relevant sections is printed as an appendix to GS 517, which was in turn reprinted as an annex to *The Election of Bishops: Motion by Canon Yates (Derby): Note by the Standing Committee*, GS Misc 522, 1998.

34. *The Canon Law of the Church of England*, London: SPCK, 1947, p. 67. The procedure to be followed in the election of a bishop is governed by the constitution *Quia propter* (see p. 139 above), and that for the confirmation of an election by a constitution of Boniface VIII (VI, i.6.47). Of the three methods prescribed in the constitution *Quia propter*, J. Wickham Legg reported in 1905 that *quasi per inspirationem* was then the usual method of electing English bishops, although *per compromissum* was used in London (Legg, 'On the three ways of canonical election', pp. 66, 76, 79).

35. S. F. Ollard, Memorandum (1929), in *Interim Report of the Appointment of Bishops Committee*, CA 282, 1929, p. 25.

36. For this and what follows, see *Report of the Joint Committee on Crown Nominations to Ecclesiastical Offices*, Convocation of Canterbury, No. 516, 1919, pp. 13–18.

37. B. Palmer, *High and Mitred: Prime Ministers as Bishop-Makers, 1837–1977*, London: SPCK, 1992, p. 7. This book forms the basis for this section of the chapter.

38. W. O. Chadwick, *The Victorian Church*, vol. 1, 3rd edn, London: A. & C. Black, 1971, p. 228.

39. Palmer, *High and Mitred*, pp. 49–50.

40. Quoted by Palmer, *High and Mitred*, p. 89.

41. Palmer, *High and Mitred*, pp. 30–35; S. M. Waddams, *Law, Politics and the Church of England: The Career of Stephen Lushington, 1782–1873*, Cambridge: Cambridge University Press, 1992, pp. 304–7.

42. Palmer, *High and Mitred*, pp. 92–5.

43. Palmer, *High and Mitred*, pp. 138–40, 153–5, 160–61, 164–5.

44. An account of Davidson's involvement in episcopal appointments during this period is given in G. K. A. Bell, *Randall Davidson*, 3rd edn, London: Oxford University Press, 1952, pp. 162–81.
45. Palmer, *High and Mitred*, pp. 139, 142.
46. Bell, *Randall Davidson*, pp. 1237–8. For Davidson's role in episcopal appointments during his archiepiscopate, see pp. 1236–53.
47. Palmer, *High and Mitred*, pp. 214–20.
48. Palmer, *High and Mitred*, pp. 126–8.
49. Palmer, *High and Mitred*, pp. 169–74.
50. *Report of the Joint Committee on Crown Nominations to Ecclesiastical Offices*, Canterbury Convocation, No. 516, 1919, p. 2.
51. *Report of the Joint Committee*, pp. 8–11.
52. *Crown Appointments and the Church* [The Howick Report], London: Church Information Office, 1964, pp. 12–13.
53. *Interim Report of the Appointment of Bishops Committee*, CA 282, 1929, pp. 11–12.
54. *Crown Appointments and the Church*, p. 14.
55. *Church and State: Report of the Archbishops' Commission on the Relations between Church and State*, 2 vols, London, 1935, vol. 2, pp. 90–92.
56. Canterbury Convocation, No. 622, 1938.
57. *Crown Appointments and the Church*, p. 15.
58. *Report of the Committee Appointed to Consider the Penalties of Praemunire in Relation to the Appointment of Bishops*; [draft] Praemunire (Appointment of Bishops) Abolition Measure, CA 580A, 1938.
59. Palmer, *High and Mitred*, p. 208.
60. Garbett, *Church and State in England*, p. 193.
61. Palmer, *High and Mitred*, p. 236.
62. Palmer, *High and Mitred*, p. 230.
63. Palmer, *High and Mitred*, pp. 248–50, 255.
64. *Church and State, being the Report of a Commission appointed by the Church Assembly in June, 1949*, London, 1952, pp. 34–48, 64.
65. *Crown Appointments and the Church*, p. 18.
66. Palmer, *High and Mitred*, p. 260.
67. *Crown Appointments and the Church*, pp. 18–19.
68. *Crown Appointments and the Church*, pp. 46–53.
69. *Crown Appointments: Further Report by the Standing Committee*, GS 313, 1976, p. 17.
70. *Report of the Crown Appointments Continuation Committee*, CA 1545, 1965, pp. 4–6.
71. *Crown Appointments: A Report by the Standing Committee*, CA 1550, 1965, pp. 2–4.
72. *Church and State: Report of the Archbishops' Commission*, London: Church Information Office, 1970, pp. 32–43. Among the five who supported Proposal B was the future secretary-general of the General Synod W. D. (later the Revd Sir Derek) Pattinson.
73. *Crown Appointments: A Report by the Standing Committee*, GS 210, 1974, p. 1.

74. V. Bogdanor, *The Monarchy and the Constitution*, Oxford: Oxford University Press, 1995, p. 227. Norman Doe points out that the duty to follow ministerial advice classically applies to the exercise of prerogative power, that the monarch's power to appoint is derived from statute, and thus technically not a prerogative power but a statutory one, and that a convention fettering the use of a statutory power would arguably be illegal (N. Doe, *The Legal Framework of the Church of England*, Oxford: Clarendon Press, 1996, p. 166 n. 35).

75. K. Rose, *Kings, Queens and Courtiers* (1992), p. 92, quoted in Bogdanor, *The Monarchy and the Constitution*, p. 72.

76. Palmer, *High and Mitred*, p. 253.

77. W. O. Chadwick, *Michael Ramsey: A Life*, Oxford: Oxford University Press, 1991, p. 142, cf. pp. 380f.

78. Chadwick, *Michael Ramsey*, pp. 135–8.

79. A. M. Ramsey, *Canterbury Pilgrim*, London: SPCK, 1974, pp. 182–3.

80. Palmer, *High and Mitred*, p. 256.

81. Chadwick, *Michael Ramsey*, pp. 139–41.

82. Palmer, *High and Mitred*, p. 266.

83. Chadwick, *Michael Ramsey*, p. 141.

84. Palmer, *High and Mitred*, p. 273; Chadwick, *Michael Ramsey*, p. 133.

85. *Crown Appointments: Report by the Standing Committee*, GS 304, 1976.

86. *Report of Proceedings*, vol. 7, 1976, p. 761.

87. *Report of Proceedings*, vol. 7, 1976, pp. 1452–99, cf. *Crown Appointments: Further Report by the Standing Committee*, GS 313, 1976; *Report of Proceedings*, vol. 8, 1977, pp. 18–64, cf. *Twelfth Report of the Standing Orders Committee*, GS 321, 321A, 321B, 1977, and *Vacancy in See Committees Regulation 1977*, GS 323, 1977.

88. Palmer, *High and Mitred*, pp. 275–6.

89. *Working with the Spirit: A Review of the Operation of the Crown Appointments Commission and Related Matters*, GS 1405, London: Church House Publishing, 2001.

90. *Choosing Diocesan Bishops: The Report of the Steering Group Appointed to Follow up the Recommendations of Working with the Spirit*, GS 1465, 2002.

Afterword

1. Cf. J. Carpenter, *Gore: A Study in Liberal Catholic Thought*, London: Faith Press, 1960, pp. 221f., 226.

2. Cf. R. Runcie, *Authority in Crisis? An Anglican Response*, London: SCM Press, 1988, p. 45.

3. I owe these insights to Bishop Geoffrey Rowell's unpublished sermon 'The Spirit who orders all things', given at the Glastonbury Pilgrimage on 25 June 1994.

4. Canon C 15 (italics supplied).

5. Cf. D. MacCulloch, 'The Church of England, 1533–1603', in S. Platten (ed.), *Anglicanism and the Western Christian Tradition: Continuity, Change and the Search for Communion*, Norwich: Canterbury Press, 2004, pp. 18–41, and E. Duffy, 'The shock of change: continuity and discontinuity in the Elizabethan Church of England', in Platten (ed.), *Anglicanism*, pp. 42–64.

6. Cf. E. Duffy, *The Stripping of the Altars: Traditional Religion in England, c.1400–c.1580*, New Haven, CT/London: Yale University Press, 1992.
7. K. Fincham, 'The restoration of altars in the 1630s', *Historical Journal*, 44, 2001, pp. 919–40.
8. K. Fincham, '"According to ancient custom": the return of altars in the Restoration Church of England', *Transactions of the Royal Historical Society*, 6th ser., 13, 2003, pp. 29–54.
9. The succession came perilously close to extinction during the Interregnum (see Chapter 1, p. 4.
10. Duffy, 'The shock of change', p. 43.
11. MacCulloch, 'The Church of England, 1533–1603', pp. 30–31.
12. P. C. Rodger and L. Vischer (eds), *The Fourth World Conference on Faith and Order, Montreal 1963*, Faith and Order Paper No. 42, London: SCM Press, 1964, p. 50, para. 39. I am indebted to Dr Mary Tanner for this quotation.
13. *The Gift of Authority: Authority in the Church III. An Agreed Statement by the Anglican–Roman Catholic International Commission*, London: Catholic Truth Society; Toronto: Anglican Book Centre; New York: Church Publishing Incorporated, 1999, pp. 15–16, paras 24–25.
14. See Chapter 4, p. 51.
15. J. Hind, 'Reception and communion', in P. Avis (ed.), *Seeking the Truth of Change in the Church: Reception, Communion and the Ordination of Women*, London: T&T Clark, 2004, pp. 40–57 at p. 47.
16. *The Gift of Authority*, p. 17, para. 28.
17. J. H. Newman, *An Essay on the Development of Christian Doctrine*, London, 1845, p. 39.
18. *An Essay on the Development of Christian Doctrine*, p. 39.

Index